Menace of Our Time

Menace of Our Time

The Long War Against American Communism

AARON J. LEONARD

Rutgers University Press
New Brunswick, Camden, and Newark, New Jersey
London and Oxford

Rutgers University Press is a department of Rutgers, The State University of New Jersey, one of the leading public research universities in the nation. By publishing worldwide, it furthers the University's mission of dedication to excellence in teaching, scholarship, research, and clinical care.

978-1-9788-4180-2 (cloth)
978-1-9788-4182-6 (epub)
978-1-9788-4183-3 (pdf)

Cataloging-in-publication data is available from the Library of Congress.

LCCN 2024058520

A British Cataloging-in-Publication record for this book is available from the British Library.

rutgersuniversitypress.org

For Aydan, Achilles, and those who come next

Contents

Preface

This book was going to be about the U.S. communist underground—the secret protocols, couriers, and spy craft the Communist Party USA (CPUSA or CP) employed as it traversed the intricacies of doing political work as part of an international movement in a hostile landscape. As I began the research and writing, however, I kept getting pulled in another direction. Examining the party's "secret apparatus" continually brought me square up against the overall repression leveled at the group in the twentieth century. Despite repeated attempts to avoid a study of that repression—the overall effort seemed daunting—I finally gave in. That was the book I needed to write.

Deciding on that path, I quickly discovered there was no single volume on that repression. While there are many good books on its components—the first Red Scare of the early twentieth century, the Second Red Scare (or McCarthy Era, the misnomer for the period)—and a fair amount of writing about anticommunist laws, hearings, and repressive pushes that took place betwixt and between, there is no book that presents the drive against U.S. communism as one extended repressive campaign.

On one level, that seems a mystery. Enough time has passed that the raw material is out there—the memoirs, the secondary sources, the congressional transcripts, the hundreds of thousands of pages of FBI files. Why, then, is there no overall account? I can't help but think it is bound up with the peculiar legacy of anticommunism in the United States. Put simply, the story of the repression aimed at the CP is not a worthy one because by and large, that repression was legitimate and necessary. While there is a consensus among historians and the larger population that Joe McCarthy went too far—and damaged the credibility of the political system he was supposed to have served—McCarthy's sin, according to the predominating view, is that he overstated the threat, not that it wasn't real. The operating assumption being that the communists needed repressing.

Readers familiar with my writing are aware that I spent a considerable amount of my adult life as a dedicated Maoist, ascribing to its dictates and outlook, albeit in a world that was seeing the diminution of that trend along with the broader Marxist-Leninist current. As such, my view on the CPUSA was firm. It was an antirevolutionary, "revisionist" organization whose history was shot through with their denigration and sullying of true Leninism. For their part, they saw my comrades and my outlook as infantile, sectarian, and ultraleftist. Having moved past all that, it is clear to me that . . . we were both right. I mention this because, during this writing, I have gained a deeper appreciation of how similar the commitment of my close comrades and me was to that of those in the CP, especially during the latter's more radical—if often problematic—period of 1917 to 1956.

All of which is to say that writing this has been a bittersweet experience. The bravery, principled stands, and resolve of the comrades of the CP, at their best, jump out. However, the party's dogmatism, subservience to a dictatorial hierarchy, arrogance, worship of U.S. patriotic tropes, and, paradoxically, fealty to the Soviet Union also stand out. The CP, like so many would-be revolutionaries and radical reformers to emerge in the last century, were as freighted with problems as they were with inspiration. One would hope to unearth a story of unrecognized visionaries, but alas.

Saying that, this book's aim is neither to extol nor to offer corrective advice for a group and model that has largely faded into the past. Rather, the objective is to highlight the depths and extent to which the U.S. power structure went in trying to suppress and destroy an entity that was anathema to their entire socioeconomic system. For those looking for a more focused critique of U.S. communism, there is no shortage of other works to turn to—my attention lay elsewhere.

***

What follows is a survey of the measures brought to bear against the communists. While it draws on the rich and ample literature, I also spent a fair amount of time scouring the records of the FBI, which experience has taught me often reveal hidden insights and firsthand accounting—with all the necessary caveats of assessing such material with appropriate skepticism.

One thing the reader will notice, as I examine the period from 1956 on, are the abundant references to the bureau's Counterintelligence Program (COINTELPRO). The term COINTELPRO is too often used as shorthand for all FBI activity in the period of the Long Sixties (1956–1973) rather than what it was. COINTELPRO was an initiative begun in 1956 to disrupt the internal operations of the CPUSA, which it viewed as an agent of a foreign power: through poison-pen letters, schemes to label loyal comrades as informants, circulation of provocative material, planting problematic stories in the press, and other underhanded means. It was a dirty and cheap method of disruption. Though the cost to the bureau's legitimacy when the program was exposed would be considerable.

While most people today associate COINTELPRO with measures leveled at the Black Panther Party, Martin Luther King, and the antiwar Left, it was a program whose overriding focus was the CPUSA. Between 1956 and 1971, approximately 60 percent of all COINTELPRO efforts were aimed at one entity, the CP. Notably, in setting out to write this book, it was only after extensive searching that I luckily found the corpus of the bureau's COINTELPRO-CPUSA on Gales Archives Unbound—courtesy of the Los Angeles County Library. This is, as near as I have found, the first time those records have ever been examined in a popular account, in any systematic way.

That said, the aim of this work is not to simply highlight the FBI's measures but to give an overall picture of the repressive efforts aimed at a group that occupied such an important historical space.

Abbreviations

ACLU American Civil Liberties Union

AFL American Federation of Labor

AHC Ad Hoc Committee (for a Marxist-Leninist Party)

CIO Congress of Industrial Organizations

CISPES Committee in Solidarity with the People of El Salvador

COINTELPRO Counterintelligence Program

Comintern Communist International

CPA Communist Political Association

CPSU Communist Party of the Soviet Union

CPUSA/CP Communist Party USA

FISA Foreign Intelligence Surveillance Act

FISC Foreign Intelligence Surveillance Court

HUAC House Committee on Un-American Activities

ILD International Labor Defense

INS Immigration and Naturalization Service

IWW Industrial Workers of the World (or Wobblies)

NMU National Miners' Union

NYO New York office (of the FBI)

PLM Progressive Labor Movement

PLP/PL Progressive Labor Party

SA FBI Special Agent

SAC FBI Special Agent in Charge

SOLO Code used for informants Morris and Jack Childs

SWP Socialist Workers Party

TOPLEV Top Level (FBI program to recruit informants)

UCP United Communist Party

UMWA United Mine Workers of America

YCL Young Communist League

Note on the Text

The term *communist* in the text refers to members and supporters of the Communist Party USA. While CPUSA members were not the only ones to lay claim to the term—Trotskyists, for example, also considered themselves communists—for simplicity, I reserve it for members of the CPUSA. Also, while the acronym for the House Committee on Un-American Activities correctly is HCUA, I use the more popular HUAC.

Menace of Our Time

Introduction

Communism is the major menace of our time.

J. EDGAR HOOVER

They had come in early September for a late summer concert. The weather was obliging, the afternoon high hit eighty-five degrees, and rain did not interrupt the event. The concert took place at the Hollow Brook Golf Course in Peekskill, New York, nestled in the state's Hudson Valley. The star of the show was the baritone and international star Paul Robeson. For those attending—most of whom had traveled from New York City ninety miles away—it was the performance they had hoped for. Then it was time to go home.

What happened next was a nightmare, as the reactionary fury of several thousand men, women, and children—organized by the local American Legion and other right-wing forces—set loose upon those headed home. The mob, who lined the road or positioned themselves in the trees along the exit route, unleashed a fusillade of stones from stores they had piled up in advance, assaulting the buses and cars trying to leave the area.

When the hours-long attack ended, at least forty-eight people required hospital treatment, mainly for injuries due to shattered glass. Four of those hurt, however, had more serious head trauma. One woman lost a finger. Irving Potash, one of those injured, who was attending the concert while his trial for violating the anticommunist Smith Act would soon send him to prison for five years, was treated for shattered glass that had struck his eye. The car in front of him, carrying the communist New York City councilman from Harlem Ben Davis, also a Smith Act defendant, almost flipped over when hit by a strategically aimed rock.

During the attack, rioters unleashed a steady stream of shouts and screams, making clear their near-pathological hatred for communism and the mix of people who embraced and supported it: "Get the dirty Jews." "Kill the k-kes." "Hang the Robeson n-----s with a rope." "Lynch 'em.'" "Send 'em back to Russia." "We're going to kill all of you."[1]

The riot in Peekskill, coinciding with the prosecution of the Communist Party's leaders, marked a high point of anticommunist fervor in the United States. High point or not, it in no way signaled that such measures were anywhere near an end.

***

Beginning at the turn of the century and ending only with the Soviet Union's collapse in 1991, the U.S. government and powerful elements in the wider society undertook an unrelenting effort to suppress and criminalize domestic communism. In contrast to huge swaths of Europe, where the trajectory of communist parties went from marginalization and repression—especially in the late nineteenth to mid-twentieth century—to one where the communists, if they did not come to power outright, as in Soviet-aligned countries such as Poland, Romania, and Bulgaria, were legitimated to the point that they contended openly (if in less-than-radical ways), such as in France and Italy, and even held elected offices. In the United States, matters were starkly different.

The U.S. anticommunist repression began at the dawn of the twentieth century. Starting with the assassination of William McKinley in 1901, the U.S. government undertook measures to legally proscribe radical socialism, with drives against anarchists and the emerging communists. Laws were passed at the federal and state level making all manner of perceived subversive speech illegal. The radicals themselves were rounded up en masse in 1919 and 1920, with hundreds deported and the nascent American communist leaders charged and imprisoned under newly minted state laws against criminal anarchy and criminal syndicalism. These laws made it a felony to advocate—not plan for, let alone undertake—revolutionary change.

As the twenties gave way to the thirties, the process continued. Along with an incessant leveling of charges under state anti-advocacy laws were the systemic harassment, arrests, and beatings of communists—not for undertaking violent actions, but for efforts at the forefront of the fight for unions, racial equality, and the unemployed. Added to this were the congressional investigations, from the Fish Committee of the early thirties to the inauguration of the House Committee on Un-American Activities—an entity that would develop fierce power in the ensuing decades.

In the late thirties, as the United States prepared to enter the Second World War—and the communists stood in alliance with the Union of Soviet Socialist Republics (USSR)—hearings gave way to repressive legislation. There was the Voorhis Act, mandating registration of groups with foreign loyalties; the Hatch Act, barring employment of communists in the federal government; and the Smith Act, which made it a federal crime to teach and advocate the principles of revolutionary Marxism.

As communism encountered crisis after crisis, from Khrushchev's denunciation of Stalin in 1956 and the Sino-Soviet split of the early 1960s to the disintegration of the Soviet Union in the late 1980s, the attacks on U.S. communism diminished but did not stop. Here, the FBI, who had been in the vanguard of pursuing the party since the beginning of the century, carried on, conducting more secretive and underhanded operations.

The efforts against American communism constituted the longest-lasting domestic repressive campaign ever undertaken in the United States against a political entity. Communists were, as a matter of routine, arrested, imprisoned, assaulted, and prohibited from working in their chosen field; had their reputations shattered; and were cast as dangerous pariahs in the society they inhabited. At the same time, the country's intellectual currency was corralled into a framework of one that dared not impugn capitalism, let alone whisper the desirability of a system—such as socialism or communism—that transcended it.

While this undertaking did not involve the torture, mass murder, and purges that took place in the Soviet Union and other countries, its hallmarks were nonetheless a direct rebuke to the stated freedoms enshrined in the United States' founding documents. And it was all officially sanctioned—from the lowest of authorities to those occupying the highest seats of government.

Why was this the case? While there are various reasons offered and continuing debate, the main reason seems clear. Much in the way Christianity and Islam came to predominate in earlier millennia, the twentieth century was the era of communism. One need only trace its trajectory, beginning with the shock of the Bolshevik seizure of power in 1917 to its exponential expansion in the aftermath of World War II. The world went from having zero countries adopting radical socialism to being one in which nominal communist governments occupied 26 percent of the world's geography, encompassing nearly 35 percent of its population.[2] Seen from the geopolitical perspective of the United States, communism was a wildfire burning out of control. It was only when that fire began to burn itself out that the repression abated.

That this is no longer the stepping-off point in analyzing such matters reflects how shaken Western capitalism was by communism's proliferation in the twentieth century, and the capitalists and their advocates' aim—conscious or otherwise—to relegate it to a historic anomaly never to be repeated. Whether such is true or otherwise is beyond this work. The reality of it, however, is foundational to understanding why it was seen as the menace of its time.

What follows is an overview of the repression leveled at the Communist Party USA: its leaders, members, and supporters, throughout the twentieth century. While there is considerable overlap in this work with the extensive literature on the first and second Red Scares, this book's focus is aimed at the arc of repression on the communist organization over seven decades.[3] Methodologically, rather than a comprehensive accounting that would catalog every repressive measure—a book that would likely run thousands of pages—the aim here is to present a concise and readable volume.

Regardless, in examining this history, it is hoped we can gain further insight into the past and a clearer picture of the mechanics of social and political repression that abound in the society we still inhabit.

1

Opening Salvos (1901–1920)

> We believe the time has come for a thorough, vigorous campaign for the protection of our institutions.
>
> **SENATOR CLAYTON L. LUSK**, November 1919

The fireworks display at the Pan-American Exposition in Buffalo on September 5, 1901, was a sight to behold. A highlight of the pyrotechnics was a display that spelled out the message "Welcome President McKinley, Chief of Our Nation and Our Empire," an homage to the commander in chief of the United States, who had arrived to speak at the event—and the recent colonial acquisition of the Philippines, Puerto Rico, Cuba, Hawaii, and Guam, during the Spanish-American War.[1]

The following day, the president greeted a crowd of exhibition attendees who had gathered to meet him. One of those waiting was a man who appeared to be extending his hand but in fact had a gun wrapped in a handkerchief. To the astonishment of those around him, the man, Leon Czolgosz, a twenty-eight-year-old former steelworker, proceeded to fire two shots directly into McKinley's chest. While Czolgosz was quickly wrestled to the ground, it was too late for McKinley. He was mortally wounded. While at first it seemed he would survive, he would succumb to his wounds eight days later.

The shock at the assassination was met with a call for the blood of the assassin. Within a week of the president's passing, Czolgosz was put on trial, convicted, and sentenced to death. On October 29, less than two months after the shooting, he was executed in the electric chair.[2]

McKinley's killing was an act of neither madness nor personal animosity. Czolgosz was an unaffiliated anarchist, though it was learned he had recently attended a speech by the prominent anarchist Emma Goldman. As such, this gave the murder a dangerous political cast.

Despite Czolgosz making clear he acted on his own initiative, a wave of paranoia coursed through the country.[3] In Camden, New Jersey, a man named Ethelbert Stone was arrested, this while McKinley still clung to life, on the charge of "aiding and abetting the attempted assassination." His crime? He had remarked that he "would not be surprised if McKinley was killed." He was only released after it was established he was not an anarchist. Another man, Pella Condomenico, was arrested after stabbing a man named John Alphonso in the throat. The two men had fought after accusing each other of being anarchists—neither was—who supported the shooting.[4] Beyond such serious, if absurd, incidents were larger roundups. One raid took place after a furniture manufacturer reported being threatened after he had fired thirteen of his employees, who had "danced and shouted with delight" when they heard of the McKinley shooting.

Along with police actions were demands from various corners of society for laws targeting anarchism. One such call came from what media reports described as a "Prominent Secret Order" called the National Concatenation of the Hoo-Hoo. The Hoo-Hoo—whose uniforms were a combination of circus clown and darkly clad Klansmen—was ostensibly a society of lumbermen but more accurately consisted of businessmen in the lumber industry. The group passed a resolution calling on the government to "Stamp Out Anarchy."[5]

While the federal government did not respond immediately to such calls, the New York State government did. The following April, the state legislature enacted a statute known as the criminal anarchy law, which made advocating the overthrow of the government a felony. The law criminalized not only the making of revolutionary speeches but also anyone who "prints, publishes, edits, issues or knowingly circulates, sells, distributes or publicly displays any book, paper, document, or written or printed matter in any form, containing or advocating" insurrection.[6] The law would soon be put to use against the country's burgeoning communist movement.

The New York law was followed by repressive federal legislation passed in response to the United States' entry into the First World War. This was a situation where significant elements of the domestic population—especially radical socialists—were opposed to enlisting in that fight. The government passed two laws to force compliance with their war mobilization. In June 1917, soon after the United States entered the war, they adopted the Espionage Act, a statute that, among other things, made it a crime to "cause or attempt to cause insubordination, disloyalty, mutiny, refusal of duty." That legislation was followed in 1918 by the Sedition Act—passed in the wake of the Bolshevik Revolution—which made it a crime to "utter, print, write, or publish any disloyal, profane, scurrilous, or abusive language about the form of government of the United States."[7] These laws were not only enacted to support the United States' ability to field an army in a European conflict but were a response to the insurrectionary fervor that had gripped the former Russian Empire, one that would soon spread to Germany, Hungary, and other countries in Europe and Asia.

The Sedition Act was not limited to antiwar anarchists, socialists, and communists, but it impacted anyone who interfered with the United States' participation in the war. As such, it was also used against followers of Pastor Charles Taze Russell, founder of the Millenarian Bible Student Movement—which would later spawn the breakaway Jehovah's Witnesses. Seven of Russell's followers—Russell died in 1916—were arrested in March 1918 and tried for "conspiracy to cause insubordination, disloyalty, and refusal of duty in the military." Their crime was distributing a book written by Russell, *The Finished Mystery*. Among the offending passages in the book was one stating that "under the guise of Patriotism, the civil governments of earth demand of peace-loving men the sacrifice of themselves and their loved ones." It also proclaimed war as an "utter violation of Christianity."[8] Because of the promotion of this staunch pacificism, seven men—including Joseph F. Rutherford, president of the International Bible Students Association—were convicted of violating the Sedition Act. On June 21, 1918, they were sentenced to twenty years in prison.[9]

On June 30, little more than a week after the "Russellites" were convicted, Eugene V. Debs, a four-time presidential candidate and prominent socialist, was arrested as he entered a Socialist picnic in Cleveland.[10] Debs was charged under the federal Espionage Act for giving a speech two weeks earlier in Canton, Ohio, where he had called out the war as one the capitalists were waging to enrich themselves. As he told the crowd, "You need at this time especially to know that you are fit for something better than slavery and cannon fodder."[11] Like the Russellites, Debs would be put on trial and convicted. On September 18, 1918, he was sentenced to ten years in federal prison.[12]

While the legislation to support the U.S. war effort appeared extraordinary in its repressive reach, it would turn out to be a Draconian prelude rather than a culmination.

A Bomb Goes Off in Washington

On June 2, 1919, A. Mitchell Palmer, the U.S. attorney general, had just turned off the lights in his library and was headed up to bed when he heard a crashing sound against his front door. Then there was an explosion. The blast was forceful enough to blow out the windows in buildings across the street. It also annihilated the hapless bomber, later identified as Carlo Valdinoci, part of a group of anarchists associated with political violence—"the propaganda of the deed"—advocated by Luigi Galleani and the anarchist paper *Cronaca Sovversiva*.[13] According to Franklin Roosevelt, who lived across the street from Palmer, the man must have been poorly dressed because of "the kind of socks he wore."[14] Roosevelt's appraisal aside, the Washington bomb was not unique. It was one of seven planted that day, the others in Boston, New York, Paterson (New Jersey), Philadelphia, Pittsburgh, and Cleveland. While no one was killed in those incidents, the impact—and the fact that most of the attacks occurred at the homes of officials—was shocking.[15]

The attack on the Palmer residence took place less than two months after a wave of bomb mailings, intended to ignite on May 1, which targeted thirty different governmental officials. Those mailings, like the attack on Palmer, were largely unsuccessful, with one exception. A Black maid, who worked for the former Senator Thomas Hardwick, had her hands blown off by the device.[16]

These bombings came at a point when the United States was navigating multiple crises. It had been just seven months since the end of the First World War, only four months had passed since the five-day general strike that paralyzed the city of Seattle, and the country was still in the throes of the influenza epidemic. Capping all this off was the October 1917 Bolshevik seizure of power by Lenin and communists in Russia, followed in March 1919 by the formation of the Communist International—a global organization of revolutionary communist parties. Those events, more than anything else, informed the government's response.

Anarchists and Communists

Throughout the early years of the twentieth century, domestic socialists and communists had been planting radical roots in the growing industrial economy. With the seizure of power by the communists in Russia, who had gained control over what had been the Russian Empire, they now had a model to point to in their aims for a worker's state. While a good deal of ink in the media and governmental circles was given over to anarchists—and their political violence was a challenge that could not go unanswered—the simple fact was that their doctrine and strategy had limited popular appeal. While they were disruptive, at times extremely so, they did not constitute the threat to the standing political order that organized socialism did.

All its disruptive activity considered, anarchism did serve as a useful instrument for the authorities in maligning radicalism more broadly. As such, they were routinely grouped with the communists. This was on display in the aftermath of the Palmer bombing. Pointedly, *The New York Times*—despite their own coverage that showed otherwise—leveled a finger at the communists: "That the attempt [on Palmer] was made by anarchists or Bolsheviki was evident from the fact that anarchist literature and leaflets, were scattered around the street in front of the wrecked home of the Attorney General."[17] Amid such conflating of distinctions, the authorities set about rounding up anarchists *and* communists, the latter having had nothing to do with the bombing.

The Lusk and Palmer Raids

In March 1919, a few months before the bombing in Washington, New York State established a committee, headed by Republican State Senator

Clayton R. Lusk, to investigate and pursue communists. After the Palmer bombing, the committee snapped into action.

On June 12, acting on instructions from the committee, state police raided the Soviet Mission in New York, seizing material and issuing subpoenas to the staff.[18] Nine days later, the same authorities raided New York's Rand School of Social Science, headquarters of the Left Wing Socialists—where author John Reed had his office—and where the IWW (Industrial Workers of the World, or Wobblies) offices were located. There they issued subpoenas and carted away stacks of literature.

Within days of that raid, federal authorities also got into the act, announcing a plan to deport "2,000 radicals of various kinds."[19] The "various kinds," disproportionately targeted Russian immigrants—many of whom were gravitating to the communism of Lenin. This was on clear display in New York where feds raided the Russian People's House, taking two hundred people into custody.[20] The timing was symbolic, coming on November 8, the second anniversary of the Bolshevik Revolution.

The roundups were aided in no small measure by the administrative work of a Department of Justice up-and-comer, J. Edgar Hoover. At the time, Hoover was head of the Bureau of Investigation's Radical Division (or General Intelligence Division). One of the first projects he developed while there was an "Editorial Filing System"—a database of records—which drew on his previous experience working at the Library of Congress. The new system, which grew to contain one hundred thousand records within its first two years, was a leap in efficiency. It was touted to allow bureau agents to locate any given file within two minutes.[21] With that information ready in hand, it was a relatively simple task to compile a corresponding list of radicals to be seized. Going forward, the compilation of such lists would be at the core of the work of Hoover and the later renamed Federal Bureau of Investigation.

In the meantime, the Lusk Committee continued its actions. On December 29, as members of the Central Executive of Buffalo's Communist Party prepared to meet at their headquarters, thirty police officers raided the gathering and proceeded to confiscate party records and literature. They would also arrest twenty-two people. They would eventually charge those arrested, and sixteen others, with criminal anarchy.[22]

The November raids served as phase one of an extensive clampdown on radicals. Things culminated on January 2, 1920, when federal law enforcement agents, working from Hoover's lists, dispatched G-men (government

FIG. 1.1 J. Edgar Hoover
Underwood and Underwood, photographer, John Edgar Hoover, 1895–1972, half-length portrait, seated at desk, facing left, May 16, 1932, http://hdl.loc.gov/loc.pnp/cph.3b10753

men) throughout the country to arrest members of the Communist Party of America and the Communist Labor Party. The results were astonishing. Seven hundred people were arrested in New York, 400 in Detroit, 200 in Philadelphia, and 135 in Buffalo. They were joined by scores of others taken into custody in smaller cities.

As would become a pattern in suppressing communists, no actual criminal activity was charged; rather, it was their *ideas* that led to their arrests. According to a statement issued by the Department of Justice, they were detained "on the charge that these organizations advocate and teach the overthrow of the United States Government by force and violence."[23]

In total, the January raids apprehended 2,600 people, with another three thousand taken into custody in the ensuing weeks. According to the soon-to-be communist leader William Z. Foster, the numbers were higher; he estimated that ten thousand in total were arrested. While that was likely an exaggeration, more accurately he pointed out that "Most of the two Communist parties' leaders were in jail."[24]

For his part, J. Edgar Hoover could not have been happier. Following the January raids, he bragged about their efficiency. As he told the press afterward, of the 3,600 detained, 3,000 were "perfect" cases for deportation.[25]

Trials

While many of the immigrants arrested would, after some pushback, be allowed to stay in the United States, the nascent communist leadership confronted a different situation. Among the more prominent of them in that regard was Benjamin Gitlow, a leader of the Communist Labor Party. Gitlow, who had been arrested in the raids, would be charged under New York's post–McKinley assassination legislation, the criminal anarchy law.

Gitlow's crime, such as it was, was distributing something called the "Left Wing Manifesto," a document that emerged out of contention within the then-dominant Socialist Party. According to that manifesto, "The old order is in decay. Civilization is in collapse. The proletarian revolution and the Communist reconstruction of society—the struggle for these—is now indispensable. This is the message of the Communist International to the workers of the world."[26] For the New York criminal justice system, such writing was a clear example of flagrant violation of their legislation.

At his trial in January 1920, Gitlow was convicted and sentenced to five to ten years in prison. After appealing all the way to the Supreme Court, the conviction was upheld. The opinion delivered in 1925 by Justice Edward Sanford was ominous: "A State may punish utterances endangering the foundations of organized government and threatening its overthrow by unlawful means. These imperil its own existence as a constitutional State. Freedom of speech and press . . . does not protect disturbances to the public peace or the attempt to subvert the government."[27] It was a ruling that boldly upheld the repressive New York law.

Two of the justices, Louis Brandeis and Oliver Wendell Holmes, dissented. In their view, the manifesto presented no imminent threat: "The question in every case is whether the words used are used in such circumstances and are of such a nature as to create a clear and present danger."[28] It was an eloquent dissent, but it did nothing to stop the law, which mandated that simply advocating revolution was a crime. That precedent would remain in place until 1969—itself a tumultuous period but one where the threat of domestic communism was a whisper of what it had been.[29]

That, however, was in the future, it did nothing for Gitlow at the time. In February 1920, he was sentenced to five years in prison, of which he served thirty-five months before being granted bail pending an appeal, which he would lose. In June 1925, he returned to prison, before finally being pardoned that December by New York Governor Al Smith.[30]

Gitlow was not alone in being pursued by the criminal anarchy statute. Harry Winitsky, an editor of the daily newspaper *Freiheit*, would also be convicted and sentenced to incarceration. He would spend two years in prison—as a cellmate of Gitlow—in New York's Dannemora Prison. Conditions in prison were harsh. According to the Communist press, while there Winitsky "was beaten repeatedly and brutally, [and] threatened with confinement in an insane asylum."[31]

Another man convicted under the law was James Larkin, an Irish national. Larkin spent two years in prison before being pardoned by New York Governor Al Smith. The pardon, however, was only a brief respite. On his release, he was immediately deported.[32]

Finally, there were Communist Party members Isaac E. Ferguson and Charles Ruthenberg. Both would spend nineteen months in prison. They would gain release on bail pending appeal. In their case, however, their conviction would be overturned.[33] There too it was only temporary relief, especially as we will see for Ruthenberg.

Beyond the prosecutions of people such as Ruthenberg and Gitlow, the New York law served as a catalyst for other states adopting similar legislation. In the ensuing years, more than thirty would come to pass some version of an antisedition law.[34] In a 1924 study undertaken by the American Civil Liberties Union, those laws had been used in twenty of the thirty-four states—as well as the four territories and dependencies—that had adopted them. The net result, in human terms, was that 114 men went to prison in seven different states. In the West, it was mainly members of the IWW; in the East, Communists.[35] The thing they held in common is that they had violated laws against advocacy.

***

In December 1919, 249 of those who had been apprehended in the first wave of Red Scare raids, including the anarchists Andrew Berkman and Emma Goldman, were deported to the Soviet Union.[36] The press had a day of it, dubbing the ship they sailed on, the U.S. Army transport ship *The*

Buford, as "the Soviet Ark."[37] That, however, would be the high-water mark for the Department of Justice in carrying out its Draconian effort.

The outrageousness of the raids—thousands scooped up despite having committed no crime—led to dissension among various ruling authorities. By spring, Woodrow Wilson's assistant secretary of labor, Louis Post, would authorize the release of five thousand communists being held. As a result of his actions, the House Rules Committee called him in to explain himself. Post's attorney, Jackson H. Ralston, decried the raids, saying, "We in America have sunk to the level of the police Government of Russia under the Czarist regime."[38] While Ralston's remarks come across as a liberally inclined call for the United States to hold tight to its principles, one also hears a caution of the potential unwelcome consequences of extraordinary repression—the Czar, after all, had been violently deposed.

In the end, rather than a master stroke of preventative action, the first Red Scare did more harm than good. It scratched the democratic patina the United States wanted to project to the world as it pursued greater global authority. The tilt away from such repression—and the infighting among authorities over it—did not, however, occur before a good deal of momentum had already been built up and new suppressive methodologies developed. As a result of the raids, new laws had been inaugurated and tested, and the Bureau of Investigation had begun the later actionable process of cataloging radicals. Measures were now in place that would not readily disappear. And the emerging factions of the communist parties would face an extended period of repression in the years that soon followed.

2

Underground and Above (1921–1927)

It cannot be said that the State is acting arbitrarily or unreasonably when in the exercise of its judgment as to the measures necessary to protect the public peace and safety, it seeks to extinguish the spark without waiting until it has enkindled the flame or blazed into the conflagration.

U.S. SUPREME COURT, upholding New York's criminal anarchy law

Still reeling from the Palmer and Lusk raids, the communists, riven by internal political disputes, existed as two major formations—the Communist Party of America and the Communist Labor Party—though they were working their way to merging into a single party. The government, for its part, was not making this easy.

In 1920, the CLP held a secret convention in Bridgman, Michigan, where they were able to bring in members of a faction of the Communist

Party of America. They then renamed themselves the United Communist Party (UCP).[1] In August 1922, they sought to extend that unity by way of a second convention. That attempt was less successful—disastrous, actually—not because of programmatic issues but because of a police spy.

Francis A. Morrow was a shipfitter in Camden, New Jersey, who had established a small circle of communists that included his wife and two friends. To his political friends, he was known as Comrade Day. To the Bureau of Investigation—the predecessor of the FBI—he was Special Agent K-97.[2]

Because of his circle in Camden—all of whom were in on his work as a government informant—Morrow was able to secure a place as a delegate for the 1922 Bridgman unity convention. That convention was organized under conditions of secrecy, with delegates traveling to it moving discreetly from one location to the next. As such, it was not until he reached Grand Rapids, Michigan, that Morrow learned the proximity of the conference in St. Joseph, Michigan. Because of this, the best he could do was send a letter—this being long before the time of burner phones—alerting his handlers as to where he was headed. The feds then duly snapped into action, dispatching four agents to the area. Those agents in turn enlisted the local sheriff and a posse of twenty townspeople to prepare to raid the gathering.

Things, however, did not go smoothly for the would-be raiders. The feds, needing to firmly identify the spot where the convention was being held, first sent two agents—pretending to be summer people on a walk and asking for a drink of water—to scout the location. Unfortunately for them, they were recognized by several delegates, including William Z. Foster—leader of the 1919 Great Steel Strike and then head of the Trade Union Unity League—who alerted the gathering. As a result, most of the delegates were able to evacuate in advance of the raid, with the more vulnerable immigrants leaving first. After the immigrants were safely on their way, those with various criminal charges pending departed. This left mostly native-born members with no legal charges hanging over them remaining. As things turned out, only seventeen members—including Charles Ruthenberg, who had been slotted to leave last—were still on-site when the raiding party arrived. All of them were arrested.[3]

The government, not content with that meager haul, pursued those who had eluded them. They were successful in this when, in December, they raided a meeting in Chicago. There they arrested sixteen people, including Foster, who would later stand trial. However, in that case, the jury was unable to reach a verdict. As for the others arrested, they were never tried, though the charges hung over them for years until finally being dropped in 1933.[4]

Ruthenberg, however, was not as lucky. In May 1923, he was convicted under Michigan's criminal syndicalism law.[5] This would be his second imprisonment—the first being his two-year sentence under New York's criminal anarchy law.[6]

Outlaws

This period was onerous for American communists. An early member of the Communist Party of America, Max Bedacht, said of the group in this period, "Formally it was not outlawed. But when you did Party work you were liable to be sent to prison for having violated some 'anti'-law or other."[7] This repressive cloud was certainly true for the American-born radicals. For the foreign born, who constituted the greater base of U.S. communists in its early days, the direct threat of deportation made it even more true.

Benjamin Gitlow—who would later become an anticommunist—discussed the situation in the aftermath of the first Red Scare: "Thousands of members dropped out. The organization was very badly crippled. A simple necessity as vital to any organization as conducting correspondence with its members and local subdivisions became impossible for the time being. Organizers had to be sent out to reestablish contacts, and when they returned the reports were very disheartening because most of the former contacts had been lost completely and the new ones established to replace them were only a fraction of the old."[8] To stanch the bleeding, the communists adopted measures they hoped would allow them to, if not function openly, at least avoid imprisonment and deportation.

Working Underground

While the communists did not operate as a wholly illegal entity—there was no law on the book dictating such—they were not free to operate fully in the open.

Gitlow describes how the movement, in order to protect itself, operated in a state of semi-illegality. To that end, they did such things as adopt assumed names, often changed where they slept, and when meeting organizationally, they did so in small groups.[9] Also, when meeting, they did it in nonpublic spaces, such as private homes, which were "carefully guarded."[10]

All this was highly stressful. Gitlow, with some humor, explained how pseudonyms worked in practice: "One lost his real name and adopted a party name. Sometimes we adopted more than one name. For example, I went under two names, Tom Paine and John Pierce. Many times the legal and the illegal, as we called the underground names, became confused. At an underground meeting, we sometimes called a comrade by his right name; whereupon, he would protest most violently."[11]

In instituting such measures, the foreign language groupings appeared to have fared better. This was largely because they had social and cultural organizations they could draw on. Because of this, according to Gitlow, they were "able to re-establish a good part of their membership in the underground." By contrast, the ranks of the English-speaking members—with no similar organizational mechanisms—were greatly reduced.

While such measures offered a modicum of safety, as Bedacht points out, there were also corrosive effects. As he said, "Some party members began to like 'underground' work. As they practiced it, it was very easy. One had practically nobody to work with or to work on. One's work was confined to attending some meetings and to listening to discussions between comrades."[12] Some people, in other words, became comfortable staying out of the crosshairs—doing nothing and still laying claim to being a revolutionary. All this underscored the limits of underground work. This would be something that would reappear three decades later with similar, less-than-desirable results.

Rules on Secrecy

While pseudonyms, nonpublic meeting places, and so on come off as common sense, it was not simply a reaction to conditions. Rather, it was part of a discipline protocol put in place at the prompting of the Communist International (Comintern)—the organization Lenin formed following the Bolshevik seizure of power to unify communist parties worldwide.

The Comintern had instructed the CPA—it is unclear if the CLP was asked to submit something similar—to draw up a plan for illegality. By way of response, the group outlined a list of ten rules. That list mandated such self-protective measures as "DON'T betray Party work and Party workers under any circumstances," "DON'T let any spies follow you to appointments or meetings," and "DON'T answer any questions if arrested, either at preliminary hearings or in the court."[13] The points, meant as easily remembered rules to live by, also included key elaborations. For example, violating the point on betraying the party was considered an "unpardonable crime . . . equal to outright treason." Communists were also offered advice on how to code addresses, using a simple encryption method whereby the letters of a person's name stood in for a given number. They were also counseled that while the authorities in the United States "cannot do very much for your *reading* [emphasis added] revolutionary literature," they could "tuck you in for distributing it."

The advice, strictly applied, theoretically could go a long way toward helping the communists weather the repressive period. Unfortunately, matters were not so simple.

***

In May 1921, New York police arrested three men: John Edward Siebert (his actual name was Edward Lindgren), Israel Amter, and Abraham Jakira, whom the press called leaders of the United Communist Party. Following up on those arrests, police raided the men's homes.[14]

While reports offered no details on how the men came to police attention—Siebert/Lindgren was arrested at a movie theater, the others at an apartment on Bleeker Street—all of them had been under intensive surveillance by the Bureau of Investigation. We know this because of a report on the surveillance of Lindgren by bureau agents. In it, they describe how Lindgren (who they identify in their report as "Flynn") was surveilled, first on the train he took into New York's Pennsylvania Terminal, then as he traveled to Midtown Manhattan. That report also describes the apartment search of Jakira and Amter: "Agents found a bundle that was turned over to JAKIRA by FLYNN [Lindgren] under a dresser. This bundle contained the minutes [of an unidentified meeting] and other valuable documents belonging to the [United] Communist Party. The rooms occupied by these two men were filled with Communist Literature." For the authorities, it was quite a haul. But what they also found was even more problematic for the communists. In searching the apartment, police uncovered a trunk containing copies of the rules of secrecy, apparently to be distributed at a meeting scheduled for the following day. *The New York Times*, in a move in service to authorities, reprinted the rules in full in the next day's paper.[15]

While the men were charged with criminal anarchy, those charges would later be dropped. It was, however, a small victory compared to the discovery in their apartment. Any hope on the part of the communists that they would keep their rules on secrecy secret had vanished.

The Trials of Louis Fraina

Beyond physical surveillance and raids, an even more daunting challenge confronting the communists—as seen by Special Agent K-97—was the problem of informants.

Louis Fraina was a founding member of the Communist Party of America and author of the "Left Wing Manifesto," the document used by the government to prosecute Benjamin Gitlow and others in New York. Fraina was also the first American delegate to the Comintern.[16] In 1919 he was selected to travel to Amsterdam and then the Soviet Union to attend a conference and then a meeting of the Third International. To facilitate his travels, a New York party committee appointed a man named Jakob Nosovitsky to accompany him. Nosovitsky was a Russian émigré who had been part of the Russian federation of communists, which had emerged from the Socialist Party, in the United States. Unbeknown to Fraina and his comrades, Nosovitsky was supplying information to the U.S. Department of Justice as an informant, code-named N-100.[17]

There was, however, another issue that would further problematize things for Fraina. As he was about to embark on his journey, a man named Ferdinand Peterson—a member of the Finnish Socialists (in the United States)—denounced him as a spy. According to Peterson, he'd seen Fraina at the Department of Justice headquarters in New York, an accusation he took to Santeri Nuorteva, secretary of the Russian Soviet Bureau in the United States. What ensued was a hall of mirrors investigation culminating in an internal trial of Fraina, where *the spy* Jakob Nosovitsky testified to Fraina's good name. The conclusions of the investigation were unambiguous, "These charges have been proven to be absolutely false, contradictory and unreliable."[18] This was not especially surprising. Peterson, it turns out, was also on the payroll of the U.S. Department of Justice as Special Agent FF-22.

***

Thus cleared, Fraina traveled to Amsterdam, along with Nosovitsky, who continued to report on his subject to the FBI as well as Scotland Yard, whom he was also keeping abreast of things. However, a police raid in the Netherlands raised Fraina's suspicions, and he parted company with Nosovitsky.[19] Nonetheless, a cloud of mistrust had been kicked up. As such, Fraina was subject to *another* review when he reached the Soviet Union, where he was again cleared.

Nonetheless, the aura of suspicion and recrimination redirected the communist's attention to fraught internal, rather than expansive political, matters. More consequentially, it pointed up the shortcomings of the revolutionaries in vetting and identifying disruptive traitors in their own ranks. It was a problem that would dog them throughout their existence.

Surfacing

According to William Z. Foster, invoking the term *underground* about the communists' organization was greatly "exaggerated and distorted in the press." In his view, the government "did not succeed in stopping completely the open and public activities of the Communist movement." By way of example, he pointed to the publications of the United Communist Party (the group founded at the Michigan meeting before it was attacked).[20] Among them were *The Toiler* and *Der Kampf*, the first Jewish communist paper, as well as the operations of various language organizations that continued, including publishing newspapers. Also, the Workers' Council, which called itself "An Organization of the Third International," was able to operate openly and publish a newspaper.[21] His point is valid, to a degree, and underscores the relatively anomalous situation that existed in the United States—nominally legal but working under conditions of extreme repression.

More than that, Foster's emphasis was in line with the Comintern's view that being above ground was a far more effective means of operating organizationally. This comes through in a full-page article in the October 1921 issue of *The Workers' Council*—billed as an organ for the Third International—titled "The Open Communist Party: The Task of the Hour." The piece argued for the quickest return to an aboveground organization: "Two years have taught us the hopelessness of reaching the American workers [through] so-called 'illegal organizations.' . . . In America, the great public has no patience with secret political organizations. It still believes that the Constitution provides an opportunity for the outlet of all shades and variations of opinion."[22] The argument for constitutional liberty would become something of a hallmark of the communists in the coming decades—despite their antagonism to the larger U.S. constitutional system.

There was, however, opposition to leaving the underground. This was especially true for the foreign born, who according to Max Bedacht were "aghast at the idea of eliminating pseudonyms and stealth and thereby opening the entire communist organization to a full frontal attack from federal and state agents of law enforcement."[23] However, the limits of the underground far exceeded its benefits. As such, the communists, as the two groups pushed ahead to consolidate into a single aboveground party, sought to surface and operate as an open organization.

The culmination of unity, creating a single Communist Party, was accomplished via a secret convention in May 1921, held outside of Woodstock, New York. That event, however, did not go off flawlessly. As the article on legality in *Workers' Council* had pointedly noted, among the perils of working underground was the fact that the secrets "carefully kept from the membership" actually "become in short time, the property of the authorities, thanks to the espionage system that is its inevitable accompaniment."[24] In other words, well-placed informants—privy to information kept from regular members—could access and report on secret plans. The truth of this can be seen in a report on the founding convention in the Bureau of Investigation's internal files. That report was submitted by one of the congress's delegates, who was also a federal spy.[25]

The FBI's Watching

The negative fallout from the Palmer Raids led Mitchell Palmer's replacement, Harlan Fiske Stone, to attempt curtailment and rectification in an effort to bolster the Bureau of Investigation's legitimacy. As such, he demanded Hoover's agency keep within the limits of the law in its operations. He also had the agency shut down the work of its Radical Division (or General Intelligence Division), which rode point during the Palmer Raids.[26]

In doing this, Stone, who would be appointed to the Supreme Court as chief justice, articulated his concern. As he wrote, "There is always a possibility that a secret police may be a menace to a free government and free institution. . . . The Bureau of Investigation is not concerned with political or other opinions of individuals. It is concerned only with their conduct and then only with such conduct as is forbidden by the laws of the United States. When a police system passes beyond these limits, it is dangerous to the proper administration of justice and to human liberty, which it should be our first concern to cherish." The sentiment, lofty as it was, reflected a fanciful and unsustainable view.

While the bureau nominally eliminated its division dealing with radicals, it did not stop their pursuit. Already by the mid-twenties, the FBI had become veterans in aggressively keeping tabs on communists. Early bureau reports show how communist leadership, in particular, was a target. For example, in 1925 they reported, "Reference is made to bureau letter of March 30, 1925 . . . wherein inquiry is made as to the present whereabouts of WILLIAM Z. FOSTER and C.E. RUTHENBERG"[27] Beyond such investigatory scrutiny, informant penetration kept up. This can be seen by way of a report on William Z. Foster, "Through a confidential source it was learned that WILLIAM Z. FOSTER'S new underground name is HERBERT ZAM."[28] Along with these measures, was the entertaining of criminal pursuit. An early file also includes reports of an intensive investigation to determine whether the communist, and later Trotskyist leader, James P. Cannon made a false statement on his passport application by misidentifying his real wife. As they reported, "If the statement was fraudulent, appropriate action with a view to prosecution may then be taken."[29] While that investigation does not appear to have led to prosecution, such scrutiny of international travel would become routine.

***

Surveillance or not, the communists were moving toward operating fully above ground. As Foster argued, "In America, the great public has no patience with secret political organizations."[30] He was joined in this view by none other than V. I. Lenin, who, on learning that a pamphlet by Soviet theorist Nikolai Bukharin had been printed legally in the United States, argued there was no need for an illegal party.[31] As such, in 1923, the Communist Party of America became the Workers Party of America, which in 1925 became the Workers (Communist) Party—its name until 1929, when it became the Communist Party USA.[32] As such, according to Foster, the " 'underground' period of the Communist Party forced upon it by the barbarities of the Palmer raids, came to an end after 29 months."[33] Above ground or not, it did not end the measures against them.

3

The Third Period (1928–1933)

> There can be no compromise between a communist and a loyal American citizen. There can not be any compromise between the red flag and the American flag.
>
> **REP. HAMILTON FISH JR.** (R-NY), 1930

The communists surfaced in a situation in which they saw renewed opportunities for revolution. Their counterparts ruling over the United States saw the need to hold them in check. This contestation would culminate with the onset of a global depression that rattled the stewards of the system of capitalism throughout the globe while reinforcing the communists' prognostications of imminent success. As such, any illusions of easy legality or unfettered operation for the new CPUSA quickly confronted a different reality.

Ruthenberg's Death

The powers that be in the United States did not employ assassination as a method to neutralize the leadership of the Communist Party. They did, however, pursue a policy that targeted its top leadership for arrest and prosecution, aiming effectively to decapitate—if figuratively—the group. In this, they were often successful, starting with an early leader of the party.

From the period before the founding of the Communist Party of America in 1919, until his death from appendicitis in March 1927, Charles Ruthenberg was either under indictment, awaiting the serving of a sentence, or in prison. In 1918, he served eleven months in prison in Canton, Ohio, for organizing union members to demonstrate against the First World War. The sentence may have been short, but it was hardly light. As one account detailed, when he was brought from the Canton workhouse to court to testify in support of Eugene V. Debs, he was described as having "grown gaunt and emaciated."[1] In 1919 he was again imprisoned, this time convicted of criminal anarchy in New York. As a result, he spent two and a half years in New York's Sing Sing Prison. He was released in 1922, but in 1923 he was convicted for criminal syndicalism in Michigan. For that, he was sentenced to five years in prison—a sentence that was pending before the Supreme Court in 1927 when he died.

Ruthenberg—described in the press as the "head of the communists in America"—would have his ashes interred in Moscow's Kremlin Wall, which *The New York Times* snidely described as "the Westminster Abbey of communist Russia."[2] For Ruthenberg, the days of confronting prison and other repressive moves of the authorities were over. For his remaining comrades, things were just getting started.

The Third Period

The Workers (Communist) Party—soon to be the CPUSA—imagined the period of the late twenties into the early thirties as one in which they were on the cusp of a new wave of revolutionary upsurge. According to the Comintern, which handed down the marching orders for its associated members, "The capitalist system as a whole is approaching its final collapse. The dictatorship of finance capital is perishing to give way to the dictatorship of the proletariat."[3] It was a bold pronouncement based on a catechismal reading of Marx and a superficial understanding of the actual historical developments underway.

Regardless, in their view, the communists were now in the "Third Period"—the first being the revolutionary years surrounding World War I and the second being the relative calm surrounding the period of consolidation in pursuit of revolutionary goals (particularly in the Soviet Union) that came after. As such, the task at hand in this Third Period was to increase the level of struggle—with a particular focus on opposing liberal-democratic forces, especially social democrats who had gained governmental positions in the twenties. This was no more pointed than in Weimar, Germany, where the German Communist Party (KPD) expended a considerable amount of energy targeting the Social Democratic Party of Germany (SPD)—or, as they called them, the social fascists. While the right-wing social democrats were hostile to the communists, the Third Period strategy of singling them out would contribute to catastrophic consequences for both.

In the United States, the Third Period coincided with the seminal economic shock of the twentieth century—the stock market crash and the onset of the Great Depression. While the Depression set loose a wave of misery for people living in the United States, unemployment, homelessness, and hunger, it expanded the audience for the communists, leading to a significant increase in influence. It also posed a far greater challenge to the standing order, this in ways the Red Scare years had only alluded to.[4]

Sacco and Vanzetti

Among the struggles the CP took on in this period was one ironically antithetical to their political ideology and strategy. This was the case of Nicola Sacco and Bartolomeo Vanzetti. The pair, Italian immigrants, had been arrested in April 1920, accused of robbing the paymaster and his guard of a shoe factory in South Braintree, Massachusetts. As a result, they were put on trial for murder and robbery.

This, however, was not a routine criminal prosecution. The men were anarchists, both of whom subscribed to the politically charged publication *Cronaca Sovversiva* (Subversive chronicle). Not only had they raised money to support it, but Vanzetti had written articles for the paper. The publisher, Luigi Galleani, was a major target of the authorities—accused of being the ringleader of the wave of bombings that precipitated the Palmer Raids.[5] Further complicating matters for the pair was the fact that they were Italian immigrants, this in a period when a certain kind of immigrant was being stamped as subversive. As such, their case represented something beyond the immediate facts of their prosecution. While the two maintained their innocence, they were nonetheless convicted at their 1921 trial. Their sentence was death by the electric chair.

Throughout their prosecution and appeals, there was two-sided contention. An array of forces on the left and in the liberal mainstream supported the pair. On the other end, major elements of the superstructure—the political, media, and cultural institutions that reinforced the status quo—pushed for their conviction. Pointedly, *The New York Times* applauded the judge in the case for refusing to grant a new trial for the pair, noting he was "determined to do justice unswayed by clamor."[6] By contrast, the prominent jurist Felix Frankfurter, a soon-to-be Supreme Court justice, wrote a lengthy piece in *The Atlantic* questioning the validity of the verdict and the denial of a retrial—this as the two men's execution date approached.[7]

Among the most aggressive forces arguing for the pair was the Workers (Communist) Party. In the days before the execution, they launched an all-out effort to stop the state-sanctioned killing. Banner headlines in their paper, *The Daily Worker*, called for a strike: "All Down Tools Today: Save Sacco, Vanzetti!"[8] On the opinion page, columnist Mike Gold romantically cast the men as "two lonely immigrant workers." He also, however, broached bigger issues, "When this is over, they [the powers that be] will move on to the next step in the great chess game. They will be ready for their mass attack on the immigrant workers then—their registry bills in Congress, their deportations, the raids, and arrests."[9]

Despite a massive effort—which included protests that spanned the globe—on August 27, 1927, the men were put to death.[10] Much in the way Julius and Ethel Rosenberg would be put to death a quarter of a century later, the Sacco-Vanzetti execution was emblematic of the causes the communists would embrace and the extremes the ruling authorities would go to in protecting their order.

Gastonia

The failure to win a reprieve for Sacco and Vanzetti would not be the only defeat suffered by communists in this period. Regardless, and in keeping with the political line of the Comintern, they soldiered on, engaging in other struggles, with the view of the imminence of revolution. On the labor front, because of the perceived lateness of the hour, they abandoned working inside established unions such as the American Federation of Labor (AFL) and the United Mine Workers of America (UMWA). Instead, they set about forming their own organizations. The result was entities such as the National Miners Union (NMU), the National Textile Workers Union, and the Needle Trades Workers Industrial Union.[11] These undertakings put them at odds with established unions, companies, and local law enforcement.

This was on sharp display in April 1929 in Gastonia, North Carolina. There, the party had sent organizers to the Loray textile mill, after workers went on strike in response to the company's moves to reduce the workforce. What resulted was a contentious struggle, marked by violence.[12] On June 7, a confrontation escalated to gunfire between strikers and local police who had moved on a tent colony established for strikers. When the smoke cleared, the police chief, O. F. Aderholt, lay dead.

That killing further inflamed the situation. It was followed that September by local vigilantes who kidnapped three union men, including Ben Wells, a British communist. The captives were not only held but, in the ugly tradition of the South, flogged. A sense of the hostile terrain can be seen in the fact that at the trial of the men accused of kidnapping the union men, their attorney argued the victims had actually "kidnapped themselves" for "advertising purposes"—that is, the publicity. The jury deliberated for just forty-five minutes before acquitting all four of the men.[13]

The crisis in Gastonia culminated in early September amid the trial of the men accused of killing Police Chief Aderholt. When the proceedings ended in a mistrial—a later trial would result in convictions—vigilantes snapped into action. On September 14, they chased down a truck carrying pro-strikers and opened fire. One of the workers in the truck, Ella Mae Wiggins, was shot dead.[14] The tragedy of Wiggins's death was the final blow for the strike. Organizers would soon retreat from North Carolina.

Harlan

An even more volatile labor battle took place in the Kentucky coalfields, this in 1931. The precipitating event for the outbreak stemmed from the coal industry, reeling from the effects of the Depression, undertaking efforts in Harlan County to stanch its diminishing profitability by cutting the wages of miners. In response, miners pushed back, going on strike. What followed was a bitter conflict, which escalated to greater and greater levels of violence.

The pivotal event occurred on May 5, 1931, when a three-car caravan carrying supplies for strikebreakers was confronted by armed miners in Evarts, Kentucky. When a shot was fired—by whom is unclear—a fifteen-minute battle broke out. When the shooting stopped, Jim Daniels, a despised mine guard, along with two deputies and one miner were dead.[15] While the strike had been spearheaded by the UMWA, the communists' union, the NMU, would send organizers to Kentucky after events in Evarts.

In the subsequent trials of seventeen men charged with the violence in Evarts, accusations of communism were abundant.[16] Prosecuting attorney W. C. Hamilton, in his closing address in one of the cases, said, "In Russia, they will read the fate of this man [a defendant] . . . and if you turn him loose there will be celebrations in thousands of places and in Moscow the red flag will be raised higher."[17] *The Knoxville News-Sentinel* pointed out that a good proportion of Hamilton's speech was, in fact, devoted to denouncing radicals, despite there being no evidence introduced to indicate that W. B. Jones (accused of killing Jim Daniels) was affiliated with any radical organization.

While those events were playing out in Harlan County, in nearby Knox County, a young communist organizer named Harry Simms was shot dead by a sheriff's deputy as he attempted to speak to a miners' demonstration. While Simms was lauded in the north and ten thousand people turned out for his funeral in New York, the NMU was isolated in Kentucky. By March 1932, it was over for them. As historian Tony Bubka writes, "The N.M.U., aware of its shortcomings and mistakes, formally declared the strike a failure and retreated from the Kentucky coal fields."[18]

The Imperial Valley

Things were similarly volatile in the agricultural Imperial Valley of California. When workers in the lettuce fields there staged a walkout in 1930, the communists sent organizers to support and energize the strike. In turn, three of them, Harry Harvey, Tsuji Hiriuchi, and Eugene Dennis (then going by his birth name, Frank Waldron), would be arrested on charges of vagrancy when they worked to support the strikers.[19] Dennis, then only twenty-four, would later become leader of the Communist Party.

While Dennis was able to avoid jail on those charges, he encountered bigger problems as the result of a demonstration of the unemployed that same year—this, as we will see, being part of a national campaign. The demonstration, at Los Angeles City Hall, saw Dennis—in the thick of things and playing a leading role—targeted by police, who beat him into unconsciousness then dragged him, along with his comrades, to jail.

Dennis was not alone in being brutalized. The *Los Angeles Times* described how "a good many of the men arrested received thwacking on their heads," which, according to the paper, occurred when they resisted police. Going the extra mile to downplay the brutality, the report went on to say, "Aside from a few scratches, and bumps, none of them [demonstrators] received injuries to display to their 'comrades.'"[20] That the brazen police brutality was written off as a joke was indicative of the hostile environment protesters confronted.

Even more consequentially, in the aftermath of the demonstration, authorities put seventeen people on trial—all charged and convicted of criminal syndicalism.[21] Dennis, however, did not appear for sentencing. Instead, he skipped bail, an action that would become problematic for him two decades later when he was a key leader of the CP.[22]

Criminal Syndicalism

While the situation after the first Red Scare may have witnessed an abatement of the high-profile deportations of communist immigrants, the use of the criminal syndicalism and related laws birthed in that same period did not.

A search through the records of the time reveals no small number of prosecutions. For example, in June 1930 in Newark, New Jersey, there was the case of Dozier Graham, a sixty-three-year-old Black man convicted of inciting an assault on a police officer. Graham, who was the Communist candidate for the U.S. Senate in New Jersey, had been indicted with eight others for "advocating the destruction of the government." His trial was, to put it mildly, highly politically charged. For example, the judge in the case refused to even allow seven defense witnesses to testify because "a witness who does not believe in God might not testify in the course of New Jersey."[23]

***

In another case, this in April 1930 in Cadiz, Ohio, a jury "of nine farmers and three merchants," took all of three hours to convict two young women, Betty Gannett and Zorki Yoki, of criminal syndicalism. Their crime was that they had distributed "anti-government" literature.[24] In Georgia, six communists were arrested in July 1930 for distributing literature. They were held under anti-insurrectionary laws passed after the Civil War.[25] Syndicalism laws were also used in June 1931 in St. Clarksville, Ohio. There, five men were charged under Ohio's syndicalism law. In their case, the crime was circulating radical literature among miners who were on strike.[26]

Pointedly, criminal syndicalism had also been invoked amid the Harlan mining violence. There, author Theodore Dreiser, a communist supporter acting as a representative of the National Committee for the Defense of Political Prisoners, was arrested. Dreiser would be charged with criminal syndicalism in November 1931 for traveling to Kentucky to support the strikers.[27] While Dreiser's charges would ultimately not be pursued, the indictment underscored the routine use of criminal syndicalism and criminal anarchy statutes as instruments to attack communist activity.[28]

The Unemployed

Among the most onerous impacts of the Great Depression was massive unemployment. At its worst in 1933, 24.9 percent of the country's total workforce, 12,830,000 people, were out of work.[29] This took place at a time when there was no unemployment insurance, federal housing assistance, food stamps, Medicare, or Medicaid. For those out of work, the deprivations were immediate. Homelessness, hunger, and illness would quickly take hold—with only the thinnest of aid via religious and private charities to offset the misery.

It was in these conditions that the CP stepped into the breach. On March 6, 1930, the party undertook a national campaign of marches and rallies under the banner of supporting the unemployed in an "International Unemployment Day"—demanding "work or wages." The most contentious of the demonstrations took place in New York's Union Square. There, a core of around two thousand communists led a rally that drew an estimated thirty-five thousand people. The entire event would descend into a police riot when demonstrators attempted to march.

The police had put the organizers on notice, with the NYPD commissioner telling William Z. Foster, "If you attempt to proceed to City Hall in any great number we will not only break up the parade, but we will arrest every one of your leaders." He then concluded ominously, "If you march to City Hall you must take the consequences." It was not an idle threat.[30]

What followed was a police riot, one the press attempted to blame on the organizers. However, their very description showed it to be otherwise. As *The New York Times* reported, "Hundreds of policemen and detectives, swinging nightsticks, blackjacks and bare fists, rushed into the crowd, hitting out at all with whom they came in contact, chasing many across the street and into adjacent thoroughfares and rushing hundreds off their feet . . . a score of men were sprawled over the square, with policemen pummeling them." The ferocity of the violence also comes through in the following account: "Several policemen jumped upon a man, kicked and beat him and even after he got up and ran they followed him, administering punishment." Another incident described how a policeman "in civilian clothes, wearing a sheepskin coat and carrying a long yellow nightstick was particularly active. He ran wildly; swinging his stick in all directions, striking whomever he could reach and dispersing hundreds in hysterical flight."[31]

It was not just adults singled out. Pointedly, schools had actually dispatched truant officers to the rally so that students "were rounded up and escorted off the square . . . escorted to their homes, where summons were issued to their parents for appearance in court today to explain the absence of their children from school."[32] Eleven parents were in turn dragged into court and fined from five to ten dollars—a considerable sum in the Depression; the fines varied depending on how many of their children took part.[33]

While the police violence in New York was the largest to take place in this period, it was not the most extreme. An even more deadly incident

FIG. 3.1 American Communist Party leaders William Z. Foster, Robert Minor, and Israel Amter at the time of their arrest in New York City in conjunction with International Unemployment Day, March 6, 1930
Photo published in *Labor Defender* 5, no. 4 (April 1930): 64

occurred in March 1932. In that instance, a demonstration of unemployed marched to the gates of the Ford Dearborn plant in Detroit. When they arrived, they were fired on by police. Five people were killed, and another fifty were injured.[34] The incident, originally called the Ford Hunger March, was from that point on called the Ford Massacre.

Pursuing Foster

Much in the way Benjamin Gitlow and Charles Ruthenberg were pursued in the previous decade because they were communist leaders, authorities targeted William Z. Foster, who had become general secretary of the party in 1929—this after a factional battle with Jay Lovestone, who would be expelled from the party.

Foster—along with Robert Minor and Israel Amter—was put on trial for his role in the demonstration in Union Square. All three men would be convicted of unlawful assembly. They were given indeterminate sentences of up to three years. As a result, Foster spent six months imprisoned on New York's Hart Island, where he was assigned to the degrading position of custodian of the warden's basement.[35]

That was not, however, the end to his troubles. He would also be singled out for taking part in the Ford Hunger March, when he gave a speech the day before the Dearborn killings. In that instance, he was arrested with four others and charged with criminal syndicalism. While the charges would eventually be dropped, they were nonetheless used by New York authorities to keep him from traveling out of state as a condition of his parole.[36]

Foster again confronted imprisonment, this in 1933 as he mounted a campaign for president. When he attempted to give a speech in Los Angeles in June of that year, he was surrounded by police as he exited his car. He was then arrested.[37] On the heels of that incident, he was arrested again, this time in August in Lawrence, Massachusetts, when he attempted to speak.

Not surprisingly, all this took its toll. After the Massachusetts arrest, he suffered a physical and emotional collapse. While the strain in no small way came from his dogging by authorities, he was also suffering from severe angina pectoris, a condition that in certain periods confined him to bed. Seeking relief, he would travel to the Soviet Union that fall for treatment.[38] By that point, however, Earl Browder had assumed leadership of the CP. As such, the focus was off Foster for the moment. By the end of the following decade, it would return.

Local Red Squads

While the FBI played the federal role in pursuing communists, most major cities within the United States had their own political police entities, known popularly as "red squads." In New York, the division was called the Radical Bureau—an offshoot of the city's Bomb Squad. In Philadelphia, it was known as the Radical Squad, in Chicago, it was called alternately the Industrial Unit, the Intelligence Division, and the Radical Squad, and in Los Angeles, it went by the name of the Intelligence

Division.[39] Regardless of the name, these agencies—though nominally independent—complemented the work of the Bureau of Investigation.[40]

In Chicago, the red squad routinely harassed demonstrators, particularly those organized by the CP's Unemployment Councils. As historian Thomas Aiello describes, "Police lieutenant Make Mills' Radical Bureau would drive patrol cars into the assembled crowds, clubbing the participants or (in a few instances) shooting at the protesters." Similarly, the Philadelphia red squad "repeatedly broke up demonstrations, brutally beating protesters with nightsticks and executing mass arrests." Things were no different in Detroit, where the Special Investigation Bureau "attacked a hunger march organized by the Auto Workers Union, using tear gas, mounted charges, and clubbings." That effort against the auto workers "culminated in early 1933 with police shootings, beatings, mass arrests, and mistreatment of prisoners."[41]

These units would continue their operations over the ensuing decades. Their chief mission was in pursuing radicals, especially communists.

Harassment and Arrests

While many of the measures against the communists in the early Depression years were extraordinary, they were surrounded by routine—if unrelenting—harassment. For example, in New York, where communists had their greatest numbers, arrests at demonstrations were commonplace. In December 1929, one incident involved sixty communists, twenty-eight of them women, who were arrested for disorderly conduct for picketing a shoe company on Manhattan's Twenty-Sixth Street.[42] Another demonstration, this one in Washington, D.C., in December 1931, saw fourteen demonstrators given six months in jail for an unpermitted march, which sought to present a petition to President Herbert Hoover.[43] In upstate New York in February 1932, two men and four women were "accused of being communist leaders" after disrupting a town council meeting in North Tonawanda, a town just north of Buffalo.[44] Later that year downstate in New York City, a demonstration at a relief bureau in Manhattan was broken up by club-wielding police. Eight people were arrested. The media "attributed the trouble to communists."[45]

The picture that emerges in all this is one of communists and those they were working with routinely landing in jail, facing police clubs, and characterized as intransigent troublemakers for engaging in rather ordinary political protest—all of which was in turn trumpeted in the media. There was

FIG. 3.2 May Day, Union Square, New York, 1933
Underwood and Underwood, photographer, *Communists' Party Demonstration in Union Sq. May Day 193?*, Union Square New York, ca. 1930 [between and ca. 1940], photograph, https://www.loc.gov/item/2012646317/

even one news item claiming the radicals wanted "more and more Communists going to jail in order to spread their doctrine and gain recruits." This conclusion was based on the press mischaracterizing statements at a meeting where someone said people should be ready to "go to jail if necessary to further the cause."[46]

It is noteworthy here that the major organizational instrument for defending communists, the International Labor Defense, itself was a target. The organization, begun in 1925, defended not only communists but also labor organizers and was involved in cases involving lynching.[47] As such, it ran smack up against the repressive operations of various local and federal reactionaries. Writing in *The Philadelphia Tribune*, the presiding judge of that city's Common Pleas Court editorialized against the organization:

> The International Labor Defense (ILD) is a Communist proselyting affair that gathers in non-Communists and converts them to Communism. Because it is a proselyting affair it mendaciously says it is not Communist for any of those it wishes to fool would not join an openly Communist concern nor would many of the suckers whom its grafting leadership wish to fleece. The Communist leaders even change their names to cover up their past. Thus the Communist Commissar for Foreign Affairs, corresponding to our Secretary of State, calls himself Litvinoff when he is a former bank robber named Finkelstein and he has had other aliases.[48]

Such maligning of a legal defense organization was indicative of the hostility—and difficulties—confronting the communists as they contended with the criminal justice system.

***

As the short-lived Roaring Twenties gave way to global depression, plunging the world into dangerous and uncharted waters, the communists proceeded as if there was an opportunity for revolution. The authorities in the United States, by contrast—confronting the fact that for a considerable swath of the population, their social-economic system was simply not working—pushed back reflexively and hard. As the Depression continued, the communists would extend their reach while they broadened their basis of unity. That increase in strength would be met by continued and, in many ways, more strategic repressive efforts.

4

Marginalized in the Mainstream (1934–1939)

> We in the Democratic Party have not been content merely to denounce this [communist] menace. We have been realistic enough to face it. We have been intelligent enough to do something about it.
>
> **FDR**, 1936

The period of the middle thirties was one in which the communists—bruised and battered by their Third Period ultraleftism—sought to work in alliance with a broader array of political forces than they had heretofore undertaken. Along the way, they sought to redefine themselves as the embodiment of the highest ideals of freedom and democracy in the United States. At the same time, they positioned themselves on the cutting edge of several labor and civil rights struggles, encountering harsh pushback from hostile and reactionary forces in the process. While they might have objectively sided with the Roosevelt program of liberal social-democratic reforms within the United States, they did so as a barely tolerated ally.

A New Period

The Third Period of imminent revolution the Comintern declared in 1928 ended abruptly when Adolf Hitler assumed power in Germany in 1933. To their peril, the communists and social democrats of Germany held to the idea that the Nazis were a temporary phenomenon. As *The New York Times*, profiling German Communist Party (KPD) leader Ernst Thälmann in 1932, reported, "The Communists look on Hitler's possible accession to power as the beginning of their dawn. They expect complete failure from him and disillusionment in his party, with resultant defections."[1] Similarly, the Social Democratic Party of Germany (SPD) held the view, as defeated SPD candidate Karl Höltermann optimistically told the press in 1932, "After Hitler, our turn."[2] It was one of the worst—if not *the* worst—presumptions in history.

That the communists and social democrats had been targeting one another intensely in the preceding years was no small factor in Hitler's success in ascending to power. As historian Richard J. Evans notes, writing about the immediate aftermath of Hitler's ascension, "Neither the Communists nor the Social Democrats did anything to coordinate protest measures on a wider scale. Although the Communist Party did immediately urge a general strike, it knew that the prospects of one occurring were zero without the cooperation of the unions and the Social Democrats who were unwilling to allow themselves to be manipulated in this way."[3] Locked in acrimony with one another, the two forces on the left unintentionally cleared the way for Hitler's seizing the mechanisms of the state.

Hitler's consolidation of power was a disaster for the communists in Germany and internationally. Among other things, it led to Thälmann's incarceration for eleven years in various prisons, including Moabit, Hanover, and Bautzen—mostly in solitary confinement. In 1944, he was transferred again, this time to Buchenwald. On August 7, he was shot to death in that camp's crematorium.[4]

These events impelled the Communist International to reassess their stance. General Secretary of the Executive Committee of the Comintern Georgi Dimitrov—himself tried but acquitted by the Nazis, accused of having a role in the February 1933 Reichstag fire that ushered in major repression in Germany—was at the forefront of the new thinking.[5] In Dimitrov's view, "It is necessary to strive at the same time both for short-term and for long-term agreements that provide for *joint action with Social Democratic Parties, reformist trade unions and other organizations of the working people* against the class enemies of the proletariat."[6] Put plainly, the social democrats were no longer to be targeted as social fascists and the prime enemy. This was the basis for a broad antifascist front. In the United States, this came to be known as the Popular Front period. Embracing the new political line, CP General Secretary Earl Browder put forward the slogan "Communism is Twentieth-Century Americanism."[7]

The communists were now willing to play nice with liberally inclined mainstream political and social forces. This would result in huge gains for the organization. It did not, however, mean the end of their being a prime target of the myriad repressive forces in the United States.

SF General Strike

While the global economic crisis had impelled Germany into the extremist grip of the Nazis, in the United States matters continued to play out within the standing social and political order. What this meant was an abundance of social and labor protests. While such actions were in no way as suppressed as they were in Hitler's Germany, they did nonetheless confront harsh repression.

On May 9, 1934, West Coast longshoremen, centered in San Francisco, went on strike, closing the key port of San Francisco and other ports on the West Coast. After nearly a month of strike, on July 5, the employers of the Industrial Association tried to force open the ports by having police move on picketing strikers. What followed was lethal violence, when police fired into a crowd, killing two on the spot—another would die later—and injuring more than a hundred others.[8] The incident, which came to be known as Bloody Thursday, triggered a general strike that lasted until July 19.[9]

In the wake of the strike, the authorities arrested fourteen communists in Sacramento and charged them under the state's criminal syndicalism law. What followed in early 1935 was a four-month trial. Of the fourteen tried, eight were convicted and six were acquitted. Those convicted were sentenced from one to fourteen years, though those sentences would be overturned on appeal.[10]

Through the course of the strike and its aftermath was a campaign of anticommunism. Emblematic of this was a *Los Angeles Times* article titled "Trial Shows Red Menace Grips State." Ostensibly about the trial, the piece used it as a forum to rail against the communists: "The Communist party in California has become a menace to organized government, the extent and importance of which is not realized by the public at large." The piece also cast aspersions on the party's defense lawyer, Leo Gallagher. As it pointed out, Gallagher was part of a committee that went to Germany to defend communists charged with burning the German Reichstag. In their view, this was problematic: "He is reported to have immediately gotten into trouble with the Nazi authorities and was excluded from the trial. He was expelled from Prussia as an 'enemy of the state.'" The inference was that he had a reputation for disorder, this for having the insolence to defy the decorum of the justice system in Nazi Germany.[11]

At the center of events in San Francisco was the leader of the International Longshoremen and Warehousemen's Union, the Australian national Harry Bridges. While Bridges was not tried for the general strike, he would be pursued unrelentingly over the course of the ensuing two decades. In the view of the authorities, he was a secret member of the Communist Party, and they wanted to deport him. Unfortunately for them, try as they might, they were never able to provide the necessary proof of such membership.

From Scottsboro to Harlem

On March 25, 1931, a fight broke out between a group of white and Black teenagers riding a freight train in northern Alabama. The Black teenagers, whom the whites were trying to kick off the train, however, prevailed. Stung, the whites then complained to the local sheriff, who organized a posse to meet the train and arrest the teenagers in Paint Rock, Alabama. Things escalated from there. Two young women, who were also on the train, then leveled the charge that they had been raped by the Black boys—a hanging offense in the Jim Crow South. What followed was a trial in Scottsboro, Alabama, leading to a conviction and death sentence for all but one of the teenagers—a thirteen-year-old. Under usual circumstances, that would have been the end of things. However, the CPUSA, through its legal arm of the International Labor Defense (ILD), took up the case and would lock onto it throughout the remainder of the decade—saving the young men from execution, if not imprisonment.[12]

At issue in the Scottsboro case was not simply the fate of these teens but the existing Jim Crow strictures and white supremacy in the United States. The CPUSA was especially active in taking the cause of this case to Harlem, the nation's preeminent Black community.

In November 1934, they attempted to hold a rally of the ILD in honor of one of the mothers of the Scottsboro defendants, Ada Wright. Wright had come up from Alabama, where she had visited her sons Roy and Andy. Police, however, after demanding to see a permit, drove a car into the crowd and lit a tear gas grenade. In response, people pelted them with "stones, fruit, eggs, and sticks." The mini riot lasted only an hour; however, it not only was troubling for the powers that be at the time but also presaged a much larger incident the following year.[13]

On March 19, 1935, a Puerto Rican boy named Lino Rivera was caught shoplifting a knife at the Kress Five and Dime store on 125th Street in Harlem—a store that had been the site of controversy by community forces for its failure to hire Black workers. After being caught in the act, workers in the store forcibly removed Rivera and turned him over to police at the front of the store. The police, in turn, took him into the cellar—out of sight of the gathering crowd. Unbeknown to those on the scene, the boy had been released out the back of the store. However, a rumor quickly began to circulate that he was being beaten.

What ensued was a riot, the likes of which had been unseen in the United States. Historian Mark Naison described the scene, "As squads of mounted and foot patrolmen charged into the crowd, enraged Harlem residents threw rocks and bottles at store windows and police. Each time police charged into the crowd, by now numbering 3,000, it dispersed into the side streets, returning to 125th Street when the police retreated." The melee lasted for a half hour before the police cleared 125th Street, "but not before every store window between 7th and 8th avenues had been smashed by the crowd."[14]

While the initial confrontation subsided, further rumors circulated claiming the boy had died. As a result, renewed violence would continue throughout the night, with people showering the police "with missiles from roofs, hallways, and windows." By the time the violence ended, one person was dead, several others were seriously wounded, and over two hundred others were injured or arrested.[15]

The communists, who were actively organizing in the neighborhood, were fully in the mix of events. Amid the riot, "black and white Communists circulated throughout the crowds, trying to prevent the outbreak from assuming an anti-white character and to stop suicidal confrontations between Harlemites and police."[16] Despite those efforts, the powers that be sought to lay blame for the violence on the communists. Manhattan District Attorney William C. Dodge initiated police raids on party offices in pursuit of evidence for criminal anarchy indictments. Dodge hurled the accusation in the press that "two hours after that boy stole that knife the Reds had placed inflammatory leaflets on the streets." He went on to proclaim, "The Reds have been boring into our institutions for a long time, but when they begin to incite riots, it is time to stop them."[17]

As things developed, the authorities were forced to back off from their more incendiary claims—the situation remaining considerably volatile. Instead, they were compelled to appoint a commission to investigate the conditions that led to the riot. However, the fact that their initial impulse was to attack the communists was revealing of what the party and its supporters were confronting—this in a situation where they had shifted their politics in a far more accommodating position to the status quo.

Little Steel and Local Politics

Where the violence in Harlem was a spontaneous reaction to an incident of perceived police violence, the labor front saw deliberate murderous violence. This occurred in a struggle revolving around the "Little Steel Strike," so named because it targeted companies apart from the behemoth U.S. Steel.

On May 30, 1937, police attacked workers and their supporters as they were attempting to set up a picket outside a Republic Steel plant in Chicago. In a violent scene—captured on film—police attacked demonstrators, opening fire and killing ten and injuring about one hundred others. The police would claim the violence was the fault of the communists. However, a later congressional investigation established that the major share of the violence came from the actions of the police. Only a few workers on the scene were, in fact, political leftists.[18]

Communists were, however, deeply involved in the larger labor dispute. In Ohio, where Republic Steel's headquarters was located, Communist Party member and Congress of Industrial Organizations (CIO) union official Gus Hall was stripped of his position because of his role in the strike. Notably, the party was not attempting to hide their role in this conflict. This comes through in response to charges of communist subversion offered by Phil Bart, the secretary for the CP in Ohio's Mahoning Valley. As Bart wrote in a flier, "Of course, the Communist party and its members in the steel mills participated in the drive to organize steel and all other unorganized industries. The Communist party joins with all democratic forces in the struggle against reactionaries."[19] The reference to democratic—versus fascist—forces was in line with the Popular Front doctrine of the Comintern.

Such openness no doubt amplified the communists being targeted. In Hall's case—this at the time of his dismissal from union office—he was sitting in jail. This was for having been accused of being part of a "dynamite ring" that was said to target company property. As sensational as that charge was, the reality appears to have been more modest. In the end, Hall was given a five-hundred-dollar fine. While that was not an inconsequential sum, it hardly corresponded to someone accused of leading something as ominous as a "dynamite ring."[20]

On another front, the American Legion led a drive to remove Simon W. Gerson, a party member who had a position they considered too close to an elected official. In 1938, Gerson was the assistant to Stanley Isaacs, the borough president of Manhattan. Incensed by this development, the legion commander, Jeremiah F. Cross, spearheaded an attack that included leveling a lawsuit. As part of this effort, Cross put out a call for people to send telegrams and letters to the New York mayor and governor proclaiming the "Communists, Fascists or Anarchists must be summarily dealt with."[21] While Gerson was able to keep his job, it was only through a bureaucratic sleight of hand by way of his boss, making him his "Confidential Examiner" rather than his assistant.[22] While Gerson was able to retain his position, it would continue to be a source of controversy for both him and his boss.[23]

Meantime the New York legislature passed the McNabe bill, which called for banning from public office, civil service jobs, or work in schools anyone "who prints publishes or sells any paper or document advocating 'subversive doctrines'" or becomes a member of any organization "formed to teach or advocate the propriety of the doctrine of criminal anarchy or communism." While there was opposition to this measure, the issue they had was not with its effort to curtail communism. Rather, as State Senator

Julius Berg said, "It will result in the making of a thousand Communists for every one it keeps out of office."[24] The bill would be vetoed by New York Governor Herbert H. Lehman, who struck a similar tone: "The fight against communism, which I abhor fully as much as you do, would not be advanced by the provisions of the bill."[25]

Culture and the Popular Front

It was in this period, as well, that the CP sought to work in closer alliance with various artists and in cultural undertakings. The powers that be, such as they were, were aware of this and keeping watch. Two notable figures are exemplary in this regard.

In the 1930s, the composer Aaron Copland was a member of the CP-supported Composer's Collective, along with people such as Charles Seeger—Pete's father—Marc Blitzstein, Elie Siegmeister, Earl Robinson, and others.[26] Copland was also suspected of being a party member and as such was an object of scrutiny of the FBI, Congress, and right-wing media. In the early 1950s, he would land on the bureau's radar when Louis F. Budenz, a National Committee member who renounced communism and went on to become a government witness, told the FBI that Copland was someone he knew as a concealed communist.[27]

Another figure who would encounter difficulties after gaining prominence during the Popular Front era was the music advocate and producer John Hammond. It was during the Popular Front period that the estimable Café Society opened in New York in 1938. The club was a bohemian venue, its slogan being "The Wrong Place for the Right People," and it showcased cutting-edge music to a multicultural audience. The club had been started by Barney Josephson, a onetime party member, who opened it with the financial support of Hammond. Hammond was a music enthusiast who, among other things, discovered Billie Holiday and would later bring Bob Dylan and Bruce Springsteen to public attention.

Hammond would land on the FBI's radar by way of a confidential informant a few years after Café Society opened. This was revealed in a letter by J. Edgar Hoover to his New York station chief. Quoting a confidential source, Hoover wrote, "One of the wealthiest Communist Party 'members-at-large' is John Hammond Jr., whose party name is Henry

Johnson. The Party practically controls Café Society, which is a Communist Party night club venture in New York, which maintains two night clubs, and they are great successes." Hoover signed off writing, "On the basis of this information, it is desired that appropriate investigation be undertaken."[28] An informant would later report that Hammond "comes from a very fine, rich family and is a charming, cultured gentleman" who "is particularly interested in negro music."[29] The bureau would later step back from that assessment: "Informants state HAMMOND is not Communist but 'fellow traveler.' Café Society Uptown and Café Society (Greenwich Village) owned and operated by BARNEY JOSEPHSON and OSCAR SCHIMMERMAN and not believed to be maintained by the Communist Party." Nonetheless, Hammond's file remained open.[30]

Copland and Hammond were just two of the scores, if not hundreds, of artists targeted and tracked by the bureau, people such as Alan Lomax, Pete Seeger, Woody Guthrie, Dashiell Hammett, Lena Horne, Edward G. Robinson, Will Geer, Charlie Chaplin, and others. The efforts against them would culminate in the Second Red Scare, and many of them would be hauled in front of the House Committee on Un-American Activities.[31]

Browder's Run for President

As part of its Popular Front line / antifascist stand, the CP tacitly supported the Roosevelt administration—this regardless of what the administration thought of them. Despite this, in 1936, they undertook a symbolic presidential campaign. Their candidate being the party's general secretary, Earl Browder, along with James Ford—an African American man—as his running mate.

The run was largely symbolic; the CP had no intention of disrupting FDR's attempt at reelection. As historian James J. Ryan points out, when Browder visited the USSR in 1936, "Dimitrov told him point-blank that a Comintern consensus backed FDR."[32] Regardless of their support for Roosevelt, they sought to use the electoral platform to popularize their larger agenda—one that had much in common with FDR's. The party's platform carried the slogan "For a Free, Happy and Prosperous America" and called for jobs at a living wage, unemployment insurance, higher taxes on the rich, defense of civil liberties, and full rights for Black people.[33] In

FIG. 4.1 Earl Browder, circa 1939
From *The Communist*, vol. 18, no. 9 (Sept. 1939), frontis photo plate, p. 2. Special issue: "Twenty Years of the Communist Party of the USA, 1919–1939"

the words of Ryan, it was a program that "could have come from liberal democrats."[34]

The problem is that the CPUSA was not the Democratic Party. As such, the Browder campaign confronted sharp pushback and authoritarian repression. For example, when he arrived in Atlanta in September 1936 on a campaign stop, he was met at the station by two police detectives. They told him he was to accompany them and threatened to arrest him "if he made any Communist utterances." Browder in turn canceled the appearance.[35]

Later that month he was unable to avoid arrest at a scheduled September 30 appearance in Terre Haute, Indiana. There too he was met by police detectives, who this time took him into custody on a vagrancy charge. City officials, who had threatened arrest in advance of Browder's appearance, issued a statement on his arrest, saying, "We are not going to allow Communism to become established in Terre Haute."[36] Browder would return to the city for a radio broadcast the following month. While he was not arrested, he was met by a mob of three hundred vigilantes who pelted him with rotten eggs and tomatoes, forcing him to leave the scene.[37]

For their part, the CP did not passively absorb these blows. Beyond calling out the attacks in their press, they appealed, futilely as it turned out, to the Roosevelt administration to intervene. The American Civil Liberties Union (ACLU) protested as well, this regarding the fact that the radio station WIRE and the Minneapolis station WTCN had suppressed airing Browder's appearances.[38] Along with this was *The Indianapolis Times*, who wrote, "The lawmen had tried to imprison the Constitution." Other newspapers struck a similar tone. One columnist writing free speech had been given "a swift kick in the pants."[39]

Such support notwithstanding, the attacks continued. When Browder appeared in Tampa, Florida, at the end of October, he was met with mob violence. At a rally there, fifteen members of the American Legion threatened to disrupt the rally. Despite the intimidation, Browder appeared. He began his speech saying, "There is one issue in this campaign. It is the defense of democracy." However, the vigilantes moved on the rally, physically upending the stage. While Browder was able to exit the scene unharmed, four people needed treatment at a local clinic; one of those was a woman suffering a blow to her face by the barrel of a gun.[40]

Antifascism and Spain

Beyond the specific targeting of Browder, the communists confronted arrest in other areas—including when their actions ran counter to the government's official geopolitical position of neutrality.[41]

In July 1934, eleven demonstrators were arrested at the German Embassy in Washington, D.C., this in a protest spearheaded by communists. The demonstration had sought to present a letter to embassy officials that denounced the persecution of the Jewish people under the Hitler regime.[42] A few months later, police again intervened against antifascist protesters. This occurred when the Italian, National Fascist Militia Band performed at Manhattan's Academy of Music. In that instance, police moved on the demonstration—which in part had been organized by communists. Press accounts described how, "Wielding clubs freely, 100 patrolmen under five sergeants put the crowd to flight while 75 mounted patrolmen, repeatedly charging the sidewalks, threw the belligerents into panic."[43]

Another fascist movement that would garner an even more determined opposition from the communists was that led by Francisco Franco in Spain. In 1936, civil war had broken out in Spain between governmental loyalists and insurgent fascists led by Franco. The Republican government garnered no support from Britain or the United States. As such, communists internationally mobilized to support the loyalists. The physical embodiment of that support came in the form of international brigades of volunteers—many of whom were party members, who traveled to Spain to battle the fascists. In the United States, the party was a key force in organizing the Abraham Lincoln Brigade, which joined similar "international brigades" from more than fifty other countries.[44]

Despite its progressive facade, the Roosevelt administration held firm to a policy of neutrality on Spain, a stand that objectively aided the fascists. Given that, when the administration became aware that American volunteers were entering the country to fight for the republic, Roosevelt's acting secretary of state, R. Walton Moore, declared that such activity was "unpatriotically inconsistent with the American government's policy of the most scrupulous non-intervention in Spanish internal affairs." In turn, he told the consul general of Spain to notify would-be volunteers that there were "statutes that bar Americans from enlisting within the United States or engaging to enlist for service in a foreign army and to the loss of American citizenship resulting from taking an oath of allegiance to a foreign State."[45]

A measure of the degree to which authorities opposed volunteers going to Spain can be seen by the fact that in April 1937, twenty-nine U.S. volunteers attempting to enter that country by first posing as tourists in France were taken into custody and had their vehicle confiscated.[46] Despite such threats, some 2,800 volunteered for the Lincoln Brigade. However, given the government's position, they first had to evade the authorities to be able to fight with the Republican army.[47]

The Dies Committee

Amid all this, a new anticommunist weapon appeared on the scene in the form of the House Special Committee to Investigate Un-American Activities (known after its chairman, Martin Dies, as the Dies Committee). The committee was created after a high-profile spy trial involving a domestic Nazi and a riot where Nazis attacked members of the American Legion. Officially, it was to investigate both fascists and communists, but it would be the latter that garnered the disproportionate focus.[48]

Writing in *Public Opinion Quarterly* in 1939, D. A. Saunders noted, "More than two months elapsed between the passage of the resolution by the House [establishing the committee] and the first move by the Committee. During this interval some criticism was voiced on the grounds that various Nazi agents were fleeing the country and important records were being destroyed in the interim." In other words, the fascists were given ample time to avoid subpoenas. Further, evidence of the committee's bias comes through in this observation by Saunders, "A speaker in an early June meeting of the American Patriots, a New York super-patriotic society, remarked that 'the Dies Committee is a good committee' and that those present need not fear its activities."[49] When the committee finally did begin hearings, Saunders notes that after a "cursory examination of Nazi activities, the Committee turned at once to Communism."

The Dies Committee had an investigatory staff of thirty men who operated out of six branch offices; a good deal of their information was then passed on to the FBI. A sense of the breadth of the intelligence making its way to the bureau comes in the committee's first published volume of its hearings. There it itemized "some 640 organizations and 438 newspapers as communist controlled," this along with 284 labor organizers and "perhaps 1,000 other individuals as CPUSA members." During the hearings,

John P. Frey, head of the AFL's Metal Trades Department, "personally named nearly 300 rival CIO organizers as Reds." Pointedly, the Dies Committee sent the names of the CIO organizers to the "chiefs of every police department operating a Red Squad."[50]

Roosevelt and the FBI

In 1936, FDR met secretly with J. Edgar Hoover and tasked him with stepping up efforts against U.S. communists and, to a lesser degree, Nazis. Investigating how the FBI came to hold its political police powers, some forty years later the Church Committee reported on the consequentiality of that meeting:

> On August 24, 1936, Director Hoover, representing the [Justice] Department in the Attorney General's absence, was summoned to the White House by President Roosevelt. As referenced in two memorandums by Mr. Hoover dated August 24 and August 25, 1936, the President "was desirous of discussing the question of the subversive activities in the United States, particularly Fascism and Communism." Hoover recorded that the President stated he had been concerned about the communist and fascist movements and that "what he was interested in was obtaining a broad picture of the general movement and its activities as may affect the economic and political life of the country as a whole."[51]

That meeting was never officially documented in a way that made it into the public presidential archives. As such, the only evidence of it comes by way of Hoover's memorializing it.[52] However, according to the Church Committee, aside from a reference to some earlier material, it made Hoover's focus clear: "It dealt exclusively with Communist activities."[53]

Further exemplifying this, according to his memo, Hoover told Roosevelt that "the West Coast longshoremen's union headed by Harry Bridges 'was practically controlled by Communists,' and that the communists 'had very definite plans to get control of' the United Mine Workers." He also recorded, "I told him [FDR] that my information was that the Communists had planned to get control of these three groups and by doing so they would be able at any time to paralyze the country in that they stop all shipping in and out through the Bridges organization; stop the operation of industry through the Mining Union of Lewis; and stop publication of any newspapers of the country through the Newspaper Guild." Hoover also recounted telling Roosevelt, "I had received information to the effect that the Communist Internationale in Moscow had recently issued instructions for all Communists to vote for President Roosevelt and against Governor Landon because of the fact that Governor Landon is opposed to class warfare."[54]

The picture that emerges is one of a debrief of the president on the specter of communism in the United States and the need to combat it. It was not FDR's final word on this. In November 1938, he again met with Hoover, this time on Roosevelt's secure presidential train. As historian Beverly Gage notes, in "Hoover's memo of the meeting, the president 'approved the plan which I had prepared.' Authorizing the FBI to take the federal lead in the effort to combat espionage, sabotage, and subversion on American soil." In real terms, that meant $150,000 (over $3,000,000 today) of funding for the bureau. In this way, the FBI's power had increased astronomically and would continue to expand thereafter.[55]

5

To War (1939–1945)

It has been said that some of you are Communists. That is a very unpopular term these days.

FDR, to American Youth Congress, 1941

On August 25, 1939—one week before German tanks rolled into Poland—the Communist Party in San Antonio tried to hold a public meeting. Despite support from the liberal mayor, who allowed them the use of the San Antonio Municipal Auditorium, they were violently shut down by a broad coalition: Baptist pastors, the American Legion, Knights of Columbus, the Junior Chamber of Commerce, the Catholic Daughters of America, the St. Anthony Society, the San Antonio Ku Klux Klan, the Texas Pioneers, the Exchange Club, and the League of Loyal Americans.[1]

The meeting was to have been led by the Mexican American communist Emma Tenayuca, who had been instrumental in a strike of mainly Mexican and Mexican American women working in the pecan industry.[2] It was, however, stopped before being able to start. After singing "The Star-Spangled Banner"—a hallmark of Popular Front–era communism—a mob, who had gathered outside, set loose a "barrage of bricks, stones, and bottles," smashing the windows of the auditorium. The rioters—shouting, "Lynch 'em," "Kill the reds"—forced the attendees to flee by way of an underground tunnel. After stopping the meeting, the mob, which had grown to anywhere between five and ten thousand, then turned their fury on the police, who responded with fire hoses and tear gas. In the aftermath of the assault, the local press called it "the greatest exhibition of mob violence and vandalism in the city's history."[3] It would not be the last, or even the most violent, assault on a communist gathering.

The period of 1939 through 1945 is generally considered a time of the greatest contortions of the American communists. It is one where they went from a Popular Front, antifascist stance to an aggressive antiwar position, quickly followed by a prowar stand—all within two years. At the core of the gyrations were the shifting geopolitical and diplomatic positions of the USSR. That country, attempting to avoid a full-on confrontation with Nazi Germany, first negotiated a nonaggression pact with Hitler in August 1939; then, when Germany nullified the agreement with its invasion in June 1941, the country bore the brunt of German attacks in World War II.[4] The CPUSA, a domestic political organization without state power, was caught in a bind. They had more ideological and political fealty to a foreign power than the country in which they lived. When their interests conflicted with their home country's, the hammer of the state came down. When they coincided, tensions abated. While the latter circumstance would come into play, it would not last.

Roosevelt Prepares

When Germany invaded Poland in September 1939, Franklin Roosevelt addressed the country, "I hope the United States will keep out of this war. I believe that it will. And I give you assurance and reassurance that every effort of your Government will be directed toward that end. As long as it remains within my power to prevent, there will be no black-out of peace in the United States."[5] It was a reassurance that, if read closely, was not all that reassuring.

In fact, the United States was actively preparing for war. As *The New York Times* noted two days after the invasion, the "feverish activity among departments concerned with military, naval and industrial preparedness continued today."[6] Those measures were followed by Roosevelt signing the Selective Training and Service Act in September 1940. The act mandated that all men between twenty-one and forty-five register for the draft.

Meantime, during his 1940 campaign for reelection, Roosevelt proclaimed, "I have said this before, but I shall say it again and again and again; your boys are not going to be sent into any foreign wars."[7] It was, as war preparations ramped up, a promise intended for the gullible. After winning reelection, Congress, with Roosevelt's support, passed the Lend-Lease Act. This move, allowing money and war material to flow to Britain, moved the United States one more step in the direction of entering the war. While the Japanese attack on Pearl Harbor, Hawaii—the U.S. territory seized in 1898—may have been a shock to most Americans, it reads historically as the culmination of years of the United States preparing to enter World War II.[8]

This was the backdrop for Roosevelt bestowing what were essentially wartime powers onto the FBI. Decades later, the Church Committee would report on a confidential directive he issued in June 1939. The directive instructed the FBI and military intelligence to conduct all investigations of "'potential' espionage and sabotage."[9] Beyond that, an interagency Delimitation Agreement, adopted in June 1940, "assigned most such domestic intelligence work to the FBI." That agreement, which would be revised in February 1942, also covered "investigation of all activities coming under the categories of espionage, subversion, and sabotage." The FBI, which had seen its domestic intelligence authority curtailed to a degree after the Palmer Raids of 1919–1920, now found themselves empowered to conduct all investigations "involving civilians in the United States" and responsible for keeping the military informed of "the names of individuals known to be connected with subversive activities."[10] While FDR's instructions did involve efforts aimed at the fascist forces the United States would soon be at war with, more consequently, they gave the FBI the wherewithal to increase its efforts against the Communist Party. It was this that would have the most lasting implications.

Imprisoning Browder

In the first phase of World War II, the Communist Party found itself sharply at odds with the Roosevelt administration. In advance of the September 1,

1939, invasion of Poland, the USSR had signed a nonaggression pact with the Nazi government—called the Molotov-Ribbentrop Pact after the respective foreign ministers of the USSR and Germany. The U.S. party, not surprisingly, supported the move by the Soviets. The United States, on the other hand, did not. As such, the group and its leaders were at cross-purposes with the aims of the U.S. government.

The general secretary of the CP, Earl Browder, had been in prison for his political stands before. In 1917, he was incarcerated for his antiwar work under the Espionage Act. He spent ten months in a Missouri jail before a temporary release in October 1918 while he mounted an appeal, which he lost. He was then sent to the federal penitentiary at Leavenworth in July 1919 and was not freed until November 1920.[11] It would not be the last time the party's leader saw the inside of a U.S. government prison.

On September 6, 1939, days after the German invasion of Poland, Browder appeared before the Dies Committee, where he was pressed on his views on loyalty to the Soviet Union. When asked about what his response would be if the United States were to go to war with the Soviets, he replied, "If it were possible for the American Government to do that, or if we assume that the American government should make an aggressive war against the Soviet Union, I would stand as absolutely opposing such a war, and as doing everything possible to stop it." By way of follow-up, Senate researcher J. B. Matthews asked, "Even to turning such a war into a civil war?" Browder responded, "Yes, sir; in every way I could to stop it. I cannot conceive, however, of America being an aggressor nation."[12] Given the position of the United States, this was, to say the least, a problematic answer. It appears, however, that Browder, who had appeared under subpoena, was operating under the influence of a good many illusions.

Those illusions were magnified when the committee—who knew he had traveled to the Soviet Union under a false passport—asked him about his trips. Browder, mistakenly thinking the statute of limitations had passed, admitted he had.[13] What followed was an indictment and trial, in the course of which the government presented evidence not only of one phony passport but of three—under the names Nicholas Dozenberg, George Morris, and Albert Henry Richards. They also had an expert witness testify that Browder's handwriting was on all the applications.[14] Unsurprisingly, he was convicted and sentenced to two years in federal prison, which he would begin serving in March 1942. He would remain there until the party's position shifted to one more in sync with that of the U.S. power structure.[15]

Roosevelt Addresses Youth

In the view of the right wing in the United States, FDR and the communists shared a certain common cause. It was a canard from which Roosevelt himself sharply disassociated himself many times.[16]

This was on sharp display on February 10, 1940, when the American Youth Conference, a group in which the Young Communist League (YCL) played an active role, staged a march to hear remarks from Roosevelt on the White House lawn. Greeting the young crowd cordially—who had marched amid an unobliging rain—Roosevelt said, "You who are attending this institute, whose primary aim is to obtain further knowledge of the democratic processes of American Government, are very welcome at the White House today." Then after delivering something akin to a campaign speech on how the economy was improving under his leadership shifted, telling the crowd, "Do not seek or expect Utopia overnight." He then turned to the Soviet invasion Finland two months earlier, "The Soviet Union, as everybody who has the courage to face the fact knows, is run by a dictatorship as absolute as any other dictatorship in the world. It has allied itself with another dictatorship, and it has invaded a neighbor so infinitesimally small that it could do no conceivable possible harm to the Soviet Union, a neighbor which seeks only to live at peace as a democracy and a liberal, forward-looking democracy at that." The remarks served as a firm rebuke, not only to the utopian vision of communism, but against the Soviet Union—the beacon of inspiration for U.S. communists.

That basis laid, Roosevelt proceeded to issue a caution, bordering on threat:

> It has been said that some of you are communists. That is a very unpopular term these days. As Americans, you have a legal and constitutional right to call yourselves communists, those of you who do. You have a right, peacefully and openly to advocate certain ideals of theoretical Communism. . . . As Americans you have not only a right but a sacred duty to confine your advocacy of changes in law to the methods prescribed by the Constitution of the United States—and you have no American right, by act or deed of any kind, to subvert the Government and the Constitution of this Nation.[17]

Not only were FDR's remarks menacing, his assertions about the freedom of advocacy were hollow. In little more than four months, Congress would pass a bill, which Roosevelt would sign, making it a federal crime to advocate the principles of communism.

A Storm of Laws

Weeks before the invasion of Poland, the U.S. government adopted the Hatch Act, officially known as Public Law No. 252, "An Act to Prevent Pernicious Political Activities." Named after New Mexico Senator Carl Hatch, the law aimed to keep perceived subversives from holding federal jobs. Section 9A (1) of the law showed it as an instrument directly aimed at communists: "It shall be unlawful for any person employed in any capacity by any agency of the Federal Government, whose compensation, or any part thereof, is paid from funds authorized or appropriated by any Act of Congress, to have membership in any political party or organization which advocates the overthrow of our constitutional form of government in the United States."[18] To enforce this provision, the legislation empowered the FBI to dig into the backgrounds of government employees, to determine whether they were organizationally compromised by the law.

The Hatch Act was followed in June 1940 by another measure targeting the radical left, the Smith Act—officially known as the Alien Registration Act. Ostensibly an immigration bill put forward by Virginia Democratic Representative Howard W. Smith, the law carried a stipulation with far wider applicability. Specifically, it made it a crime "to knowingly or willfully advocate, abet, advise, or teach the duty, necessity, desirability, or propriety of overthrowing or destroying any government in the United States." It also specifically defined certain types of speech as criminal, making it illegal to "print, publish, edit, issue, circulate, sell, distribute, or publicly display any written or printed matter advocating, advising, or teaching the duty, necessity, desirability, or propriety of overthrowing or destroying any government in the United States." Finally, it carried a provision making it a crime "to organize or help to organize any society, group, or assembly of persons who teach, advocate, or encourage the overthrow or destruction of any government."[19] Unlike the patchwork of state laws against such advocacy under the strictures of criminal anarchy and syndicalism, this was a federal act in effect in every part of the United States.

Finally, following the Smith Act, Congress and the president implemented a law specially designed to go after groups with foreign ties such as the German Bund and CPUSA. In January 1941, the Voorhis Act went into effect, requiring the "registration with the Attorney General of certain organizations, the purpose of which is to overthrow the government."[20]

With these laws, the government now had a slate of criminal justice instruments they could deploy to neutralize the CP. It would not be long before they were utilized.

Raids in Oklahoma

Congress may have enacted a federal law against advocacy, but states continued to wield their own ordinances. As such, on August 17, 1940, authorities in Oklahoma City—enforcing the state's criminal syndicalism statute—raided the Progressive Bookstore, the local offices of the Communist Party, and the homes of five suspected communists.[21] It was an undertaking that was stunning in its breadth and disregard for nominal rights. At the bookstore, authorities not only confiscated communist literature—and arrested customers and repairmen alike, who happened to be in the store—but also took copies of the U.S. Constitution, Carl Van Doren's biography of Benjamin Franklin, and the Bible.[22]

The books, however, were not the prime target. More importantly was the communist leadership in that state. In the aftermath of the raids, four prominent communists—Bob Wood, Alan Shaw, Ina Wood, and Eli Jaffe—were put on trial for violating the state's syndicalism statute. As written, the law made it illegal "to circulate or display printed matter or books that taught, advocated, or affirmatively suggested criminal syndicalism or sabotage."[23] The four would be convicted and sentenced to ten years in prison. Fortuitously, their sentences were overturned on appeal in February 1943, a point at which the party had abandoned its antiwar stance in favor of actively supporting the U.S. war effort.[24]

Smith Act in Action

While the syndicalism law still exuded power in places like Oklahoma, the federal Smith Act was about to get its inaugural use, though not against the CPUSA. On June 22, 1941, Hitler's armies invaded the Soviet Union, thus shredding the Molotov-Ribbentrop Pact and putting the Soviets at war with Germany. This in turn precipitated an immediate political line reversal for pro-Soviet parties throughout the world, including the CPUSA. This could readily be seen on the masthead of *The Daily Worker*, whose slogan went from the expansive "People's Champion of Liberty, Progress, Peace, and Prosperity" to the patriotic "National Unity over Fascist Enslavement."[25] Events may have impelled the CP to have turned on a dime, but the Trotskyists of the Socialist Workers Party (SWP) were another matter.

The SWP had no abiding sympathy for the Soviet Union of the 1930s and 1940s—not the least reason being their namesake, Leon Trotsky, having been assassinated in Mexico City in August 1940, apparently on the orders of the Stalin regime.[26] As such, they did not see the Nazi invasion of the USSR as a turning point in the character of the war—this in contrast to the CP, who saw the invasion as the moment the war transformed from an imperialist undertaking to an attack on socialism. For the Trotskyists, the war was essentially a mirror of the same terms of World War I, a conflict among imperialists set to redivide the spoils of the world. Even after Pearl Harbor, they held firm to this position. James Cannon, head of the SWP, made this clear: "The considerations which determined our attitude toward the war up to the outbreak of hostilities between the United States and the Axis powers retain their validity in the new situation." In their view, "the war upon the part of all the capitalist powers involved—Germany and France, Italy and Great Britain—[is] an imperialist war."[27] Not only was this a wooden and dogmatic position, it put them at cross-purposes with the aims of the United States government.

As such, their position dogged the Trotskyists—much in the way it had dogged the CP. Six months before the United States entered the war—and six days after Germany invaded the Soviet Union—the FBI and U.S. marshals raided SWP offices in Minneapolis and St. Paul. In the aftermath of the raids, twenty-nine SWP members, fifteen of whom belonged to Teamsters Local 544, were arrested. The group was indicted under the provisions of the Smith Act.

A trial quickly ensued, with the judge declaring five of the defendants not guilty before the start of the trial—one defendant tragically committed suicide before the proceedings began. The other twenty-three, however, proceeded to trial. On December 1, 1941, all those defendants were acquitted of "organizing armed revolution against the government." However, eighteen of them were convicted of sedition and conspiracy. They were then sentenced to twelve to sixteen months in prison. They began serving those sentences at the end of December 1943.[28]

For the communists, mired in the Soviet party's hatred of Trotskyism, this was of little concern. They did nothing to help. Rather, they heaped scorn on the SWP, slandering it as a "Fifth Column"—a secret enemy force—for Hitler.[29] It was a position that was as politically reprehensible as it was strategically wrongheaded. It would be only a few short years before the Smith Act was leveled against them.

Custodial Detention

Such legal measures and undertakings were hardly the only efforts in play against those standing in opposition to U.S. war preparations. One of the measures to flow out of Hoover and FDR's meetings further empowering the FBI—though its actual lineage is far from clear—was the development of a preventative detention list. This was a database of people the government considered problematic to its national security and, as such, candidates for putting in what could fairly be called concentration camps.

The mandate for the list does not appear to have been memorialized as a formal government document, but the Church Committee, many years later, offered a sense of its evolution. In 1940, J. Edgar Hoover asked then–Attorney General Robert Jackson for policy guidance concerning the FBI's "suspect list of individuals whose arrest might be considered necessary in the event the United States becomes involved in war."[30] What Hoover had in mind—and something FDR would implement, albeit against Japanese Americans—was the mass incarceration of enemies of the state. At the time, Hoover's list was called the Custodial Detention list.

Among its targets was the CP's National Board member Benjamin Davis. Little more than a month after the December 7, 1941, attack on Pearl Harbor, the FBI noted in Davis's file that he should "be considered for custodial detention given the existing emergency."[31] Also included on the list was West Indian native and Harlem communist Claudia Jones. There, the FBI's New York special agent in charge reported her custodial detention card had been added as of July 26, 1943.[32]

The scheme did not just consider prominent leaders. For example, in California, journalist and radio personality, Ed Robbin, was marked for detention. The reason for his inclusion being that he was a "CP news commentator, presenting reporting over local station daily."[33] In the cultural realm, the list included people such as the musicologist and assistant in charge of the Folklore Center of the Library of Congress, Alan Lomax. Included on the list was Almanac Singer Agnes "Sis" Cunningham. Also considered—though it is unclear if he was added—was John Hammond.[34] This was no small undertaking, and its breadth was shocking. By the mid-1950s, the list had grown to include over 25,000 names—of whom more than 11,033 were high-priority detention targets.[35]

Rapp-Coudert Committee

Another front in this period was education, with an effort on display via the New York State legislature, with Assemblyman Herbert A. Rapp and State Senator Frederic René Coudert—both Republicans—leading the charge. The objective was to drive communists and their supporters out of the public and university system, something done with a measure of success. Specifically, between 1940 and the end of World War II, the committee was responsible for driving fifty faculty and staff members out of their jobs in a "purge" of communists at the City College in New York.[36] Notably, one of those fired in this process was the preeminent labor historian Philip Foner, this from a position he held as a clerk in the registrar's office.[37]

The committee was also instrumental in jailing Morris Schappes, an English instructor at City College. Schappes was prosecuted for perjury for telling legislators that the communist unit at City College had only four members—the government claimed there were fifty. He also had told the committee that he was the sole editor of *The Teacher Worker*, a party newsletter on campus, while the government claimed he was one of ten. As such, his real crime was refusing to implicate his comrades in front of a committee set on driving them out of their jobs. For this, Schappes was found guilty in June 1941. He was given a sentence of eighteen months to two years in New York's Sing Sing Prison. After exhausting all appeals, he began serving his sentence in 1943.[38]

At War

Earl Browder was sitting in an Atlanta prison when Germany invaded the Soviet Union in June 1941. Now that the war was no longer considered by the CP as one between imperialists but a cause to defend the socialist Soviet Union, Browder's party was no longer on the wrong side of the United States' geopolitical position. As such, the repression, which had been increasing at an alarming rate, was dialed down—though it did not end.

Following the December 7, 1941, Japanese attack on Pearl Harbor, the United States fully entered into an alliance with the Soviet Union; this offered a significant respite for the CPUSA. In May of the following year, Soviet Foreign Minister V. M. Molotov visited FDR in Washington, D.C. That same month, Roosevelt commuted Browder's sentence, saying it would "promote national unity and allay any feeling which may exist in some minds that the unusually long sentence was by way of penalty imposed upon him because of his political views."[39] More accurately, it was a gift from the United States to their new ally, the Soviet Union.

Such was the situation when the United States officially entered the war. For the communists, the major way they saw supporting the Soviets was through supporting the U.S. war effort. Thousands of communists enlisted in the army—of necessity, dropping their party membership—while many others joined various government agencies in support of the war effort. While the powers that be allowed this, they did so without relinquishing their anticommunist sensibilities.

For example, the author Howard Fast went to work for the Army Morale Services Division based in New York. As such, he was investigated by the FBI, who reported, "That subject associates with Communists and appears to be active in reported communist-front organizations."[40] Similarly, musicologist Alan Lomax and writer Gordon Friesen were both investigated by the FBI under the Hatch Act for their suspected communist associations.[41] While the inquiries ultimately did not preclude these figures from serving the U.S. war effort, the investigatory results remained in their files and would be a point of reference during the far more repressive postwar period.

For those communists who entered the military, Military Intelligence was on the point for background checks, though they worked closely with the FBI on their results. A look through folk singer Pete Seeger's Military

Intelligence file, which had been sent to and incorporated into his FBI file, is exemplary. It notes that he was subject of a "disaffection investigation" after he "wrote a letter protesting and criticizing the California American Legion's resolution advocating deportation of all Japanese"—Seeger's wife, Toshi, was Japanese American.[42] While the CP, to their discredit, effectively supported FDR's detention, Seeger was unsurprisingly at odds with that position. The file also included interviews with his bunk mates, one of whom "stated [Seeger] was active in an organization called Japanese-American Committee for Democracy; that this organization bore every stamp of a Communist front organization."[43]

Military Intelligence also noted that Seeger was a "good friend" of Alan Shaw, Ina Wood, and Eli Jaffe, the defendants in the Oklahoma criminal syndicalism trial. His file also recorded, "Subject admits barely escaping 'being hooked into that round-up too.'"[44]

Also in Seeger's dossier was the fact that he was a member of the Almanac Singers, whose "lyrics were in keeping with the Communist Party line."[45] The reason the military knew all these things is that they were "intercepting" his letters—that is, reading his personal mail.[46] For Military Intelligence, while Seeger may have been allowed to serve in the army, he would only do so under the utmost scrutiny.

Such attention, considering the fact that U.S. communists were enthusiastically supporting the U.S. war effort, moved the government to back off its plans to detain communists. In 1943, Attorney General Francis Biddle ordered the Custodial Detention list to be abolished. In his view, it was "impractical, unwise, and dangerous." Given the CP was ostensibly an ally of the U.S. government, this made sense. J. Edgar Hoover, however, was not convinced. While he scaled back the project, he did not abandon it. Instead, he kept the records he had, renaming them the Security Index.[47] While for the moment official U.S. policy shunned such lists, it was a policy that would not live past the war.

The Short-Lived CPA

In February 1943, Soviet forces defeated German troops at Stalingrad and began the long road to pushing the invaders back to their home country. Stalingrad was a turning point in the war and the beginning of the end for Nazi Germany. Following that victory, Winston Churchill, Franklin

Roosevelt, and Joseph Stalin met in Tehran, Iran, to begin mapping out plans for the postwar world.

Sensing victory, Earl Browder projected a vision for how the communists would fit into that new world. In a speech, later reprinted in the pamphlet *Moscow, Cairo, Tehran*, Browder proclaimed, "The world has opened a new epoch in its history." In his thinking, the communists needed to "gather [their] full fruits for our country in a mighty strengthening of national unity to complete the war with honor and dispatch, and thus to reach the post-war reconstruction of the world under happier auspices than had hitherto seemed possible."[48] Following that buoyant logic, Browder would go on to be the architect of the dissolution of the CPUSA—one more nominal than substantive. In its place, he created the Communist Political Association.

The change was heralded in *The Daily Worker* of May 22, 1944, complete with a picture of a beaming William Z. Foster and Earl Browder. Pointedly, the article announcing the name change was written by party member Louis F. Budenz—someone who would soon become highly problematic for the communists. Budenz's piece presented the CPA as an American-friendly communist entity: "The Communist Political Association is a non-party organization of Americans basing itself upon the working class, carries forward the traditions of Washington, Jefferson, Paine, Jackson, and Lincoln under the changed conditions of modern industrial society."[49] It was language steeped in the ethos of Browder's "Communism is Twentieth-Century Americanism"—an outlook that did little to allay the hostility of the U.S. mainstream attitude toward them.

Whether party or association, this did not stop the FBI in its efforts against the communists. Throughout the short life of the CPA, they continued to lock onto the group and its leaders. This can be seen in the wiretap they had on Ben Davis's telephone. One exchange is exemplary—this between Davis and Eugene Dennis:

B: Hello. GENE?

G: Yes BEN.

B: This is BEN. GENE, REDACTED of the Council of African Affairs, has been in touch with Max Yergan [a Black communist] from San Francisco and he wanted her to take up something with some of our friends, so I'm asking her to come direct to you.

G: Well you made a mistake brother.

B: Why?
G: When do you want it?
B: Right away.
G: No can do.[50]

Eventually, the two agreed on a way to connect. Regardless, the intercept—despite attempts at circumspection by Davis and Dennis—is revealing as to how much attention the bureau was giving them and the information they were accumulating.

The CPA lasted all of a year. The project was forced to beat a hasty retreat in the face of an article published in April 1945 in the French Communist Party's newspaper, *Cahiers du Communisme*. The article, with apparent Soviet sanction, took the U.S. comrades to task, especially their leader: "If Comrade Earl Browder had seen, as a Marxist-Leninist, this important aspect of the problems facing liberty-loving peoples in this moment in their history, he would have arrived at a conclusion quite other than the dissolution of the Communist Party of the United States."[51] In other words, the name change, with the suggestion of it operating other than as a Marxist-Leninist vanguard, was not going to be sanctioned. In this, Browder had fundamentally miscalculated. The Soviet party—and its omnipotent leader, J. V. Stalin—was not going to countenance measures that could move parties away from the Soviet Union. The CP would need to be reconstituted, and Browder would have to go as its leader—a matter that would soon be in the offing.

Problematizing things further was the fact that the United States was not going to maintain its alliance with the USSR. Another paradigm would soon be put into effect: rather than a lasting partnership, there would be a decades-long cold war. In this, the U.S. communists would confront the greatest level of repression they had ever encountered.

6

Clampdown (1946–1947)

I do not believe in, and I am not a member of nor do I support any organization that believes in or teaches the overthrow of the United States Government by force or by any illegal or unconstitutional methods.

UNION OFFICER AFFIDAVIT MANDATED BY THE TAFT-HARTLEY ACT

The United States was victorious in World War II, but it was not the sole victor. It shared that distinction with the Soviet Union, which had far and away bore the greater share of sacrifice in achieving that victory. As things developed, the two countries that had been major allies were about to become bitter rivals. The CPUSA had occupied a space in between by supporting both countries. It would now, however, find itself in the unenviable position of operating within the most powerful empire in the world, one now having nuclear weapons, as it squared off against the country to which the party held ultimate loyalty. All the efforts against the group, up to and including the post–World War I repression, would pale in comparison to what was to come.

The Cold War Begins

Historically, Martin Dies does not have the same consequentiality of a J. Edgar Hoover or Joe McCarthy, but his role in articulating the post-war framework of anticommunism is notable. This stands out in a letter he wrote to FDR's successor, Harry S. Truman, in 1946. In it, he outlined seven things the president ought to do to bring the communists to heel. They were measures to deport alien communists, mandating the registration of communist organizations, refusing to recognize unions that have communist officers, barring communists from other countries from entering the United States, firing communists holding public jobs, revoking the citizenship of any naturalized U.S. citizen found to be a communist, and compelling the CIO to purge any of its officers who were communists.[1] Taken as a whole, it was akin to a master plan for the ruination of domestic communism.

Truman did not answer the letter, but his attorney general, Tom Clark, did. Clark wrote, "You may be sure we are watching these groups and every effort will be made to prosecute successfully whenever a federal violation occurs." He added that there were federal laws to deal with "persons who advocate the overthrow of the government by force and violence and all these agencies have been activated to see that their provisions are carried out."

While the response was polite, it did not suggest an administration geared to implement Dies's suggestions. Despite that restrained tone, however, Truman and the political apparatus he headed would do exactly that. Over the next few years, the president and Congress would embark on a full-on confrontation with the Soviet Union. Hand in hand with that, they would launch a major offensive against U.S. communism. Dies's proposals, officially or not, would be implemented.

Truman's anticommunist offensive kicked off by way of a speech on March 12, 1947, now heralded as the announcement of the Truman Doctrine. The speech was ostensibly a proclamation on the part of the United States that it would not tolerate any further Soviet gains in Europe. The specific fault line was the civil war in Greece between communist forces on one side and Great Britain and the U.S.-backed Greek government on the other. The United States came firmly down on the side of anticommunist forces. As Truman declared, "The free peoples of the world look to us for support in maintaining their freedoms." Specifically, he asked Congress for $400 million to aid these countries.[2] The speech was only the beginning of a larger geopolitical stance. Among other things, it would include the Marshall Plan, which infused $13.3 billion in funds (about $178 billion in 2024 dollars) to bolster Europe against communism.[3]

For its part, the USSR pushed for political control through its agents in Poland and via a coup in Czechoslovakia. It also, in October 1947, established the Communist Information Bureau (Cominform) to fill the gap left by the Comintern, which had been disbanded during the war. All of this effected a dramatic shift away from the alliance that had joined the United States and the USSR during World War II.

The relationship had shifted from allies to adversaries. As Truman would say, "I have been fighting communism not merely as a contemptible minority where it is, in a land of freedom, but wherever it is marching or menacing power in the world."[4] Such were the geopolitical underpinnings of the full-on assault against domestic communists.

Commanding Allegiance

Truman followed up his anticommunist proclamation in March 1947 with Executive Order 9835, which came to be known as the Loyalty Order. This was a measure designed to purge communists from working at any level in the expansive executive branch of the federal government. The language of the order was direct, prohibiting "advocacy of revolution or force or violence to alter the constitutional form of government of the United States." To enforce it, the order mandated that the heads of every department and agency in the executive branch—using HUAC and FBI files—were "personally responsible for an effective program to assure that disloyal civilian officers or employees are not retained."[5]

A sense of how this worked in the real world can be seen in the case of labor folklorist, Aaron "Archie" Green. According to an FBI report, Green had been under a Hatch Act inquiry while working at the Veterans Administration—this around August 1947. That investigation was cut short due to personnel cutbacks—he was laid off.[6] However, in 1948, when he applied for a job with the U.S. Department of Labor, he then came under the auspices of the Loyalty Order. As a result, the Civil Service Commission directed the FBI to launch an investigation, relying on an informant who was "not willing to appear before a Loyalty Hearing Board or to furnish a signed statement." Among the evidence, the FBI reported, "[Informant] Advised that in October 1943 MAYER FRIEDEN, a delegate to the 1943 National Convention of the YOUNG COMMUNIST LEAGUE, was instructed by STEVE NELSON, at that time Chairman of the COMMUNIST PARTY of Alameda County, now a member of the National Board of the COMMUNIST PARTY, to contact ARCHIE GREEN concerning the new organization of the YOUNG COMMUNIST LEAGUE when he returned from the Convention."[7] The report on Green's loyalty investigation runs twenty-two pages, citing numerous times at which an unnamed informant had interactions with or witnessed Green participating in YCL activity. Reading through the file, it becomes clear that the loyalty oath was a boon to the legal ability of the FBI to increase its pursuit of communists and their supporters.

Green, however, was just one of many subjects of this governmental purge. By September 1948, 883 federal employees had quit their jobs rather than face trial associated with such investigations. These resignations, essentially soft firings, were facilitated in no small part by the FBI, which had initiated 6,344 undercover investigations. The level of scrutiny was far beyond the actual presence of communists working for the federal government—and even if they did hold positions, it hardly proved subversion. A sense of how overblown the issue was can be seen by the fact that as of September 1948, only one person in the executive branch was under investigation, along with one person in the Smithsonian Institution. Beyond that, the investigations were spread over agencies such as the Civil Aeronautics Board, the Agriculture Department, and the Post Office.[8] While the claim was that this was needed to bolster national security, the sweeping and undiscriminating nature of the program shows it as being fundamentally about removing those who held what the government considered a pariah ideology.

Taft-Hartley

Following on the loyalty oaths was a congressional measure to drive communists out of leadership positions in labor unions. The marquee of this effort was the 1947 Taft-Hartley Act. The law contained an array of stipulations and restrictions on union activity, including proscribing certain strike activity. It also, however, included provisions that put a knife into the heart of open communist participation in labor unions. While Truman vetoed the Taft-Hartley law, saying it was "deliberately designed to weaken labor unions," he did this by framing it in the context of the emerging fault lines of the Cold War: "As our generous American spirit prompts us to aid the world to rebuild, we must, at the same time, construct a better America in which all can share equitably in the blessings of democracy."[9] Regardless, Congress overrode his veto by a wide margin. Predictably, what followed was a purge of communists from some of the country's most vibrant unions.

The most lethal part of the law for Communist Party members was contained in Section 9 (h). That section required union officials to sign affidavits declaring they were not members of an organization seeking the "overthrow of the United States government by force or by any illegal or unconstitutional means"—that is, the Communist Party.[10] As Joseph Starobin, who had been foreign editor of *The Daily Worker*, would later explain, the choice for communist union officials "was to sign the non-Communist oath or resign from the Party. The former course led to the possibility of perjury proceedings by the government. The latter meant that the Party would lose important union leaders. Whichever choice the left took, the Taft-Hartley law favored anti-Communist opposition within the unions."[11] The results were predictable. While initially there was resistance to this stipulation by the leadership of the CIO and United Mine Workers, that quickly gave way to acceding to the new rules.[12] As such, communist union leaders were confronted with the hard choice of quitting the party or resigning their union office.

One can see the effects of this in the FBI file of Jack Spiegel, a longtime party member based in Chicago and an officer in a CIO union, the United Shoe Workers of America. Spiegel was compelled to sign a noncommunist affidavit in June 1953, something he then had to reaffirm in the years that followed.[13]

His affidavit, a copy of which is contained in his FBI file, shows that he had to reaffirm his claim at least through 1965. Reading through it, it appears the FBI had trouble ascertaining definitively that he remained a party member after having signed the document. The last relevant entry in his file from April 1965 reads, "Confidential informants advised that they were unable to furnish any current information regarding Communist

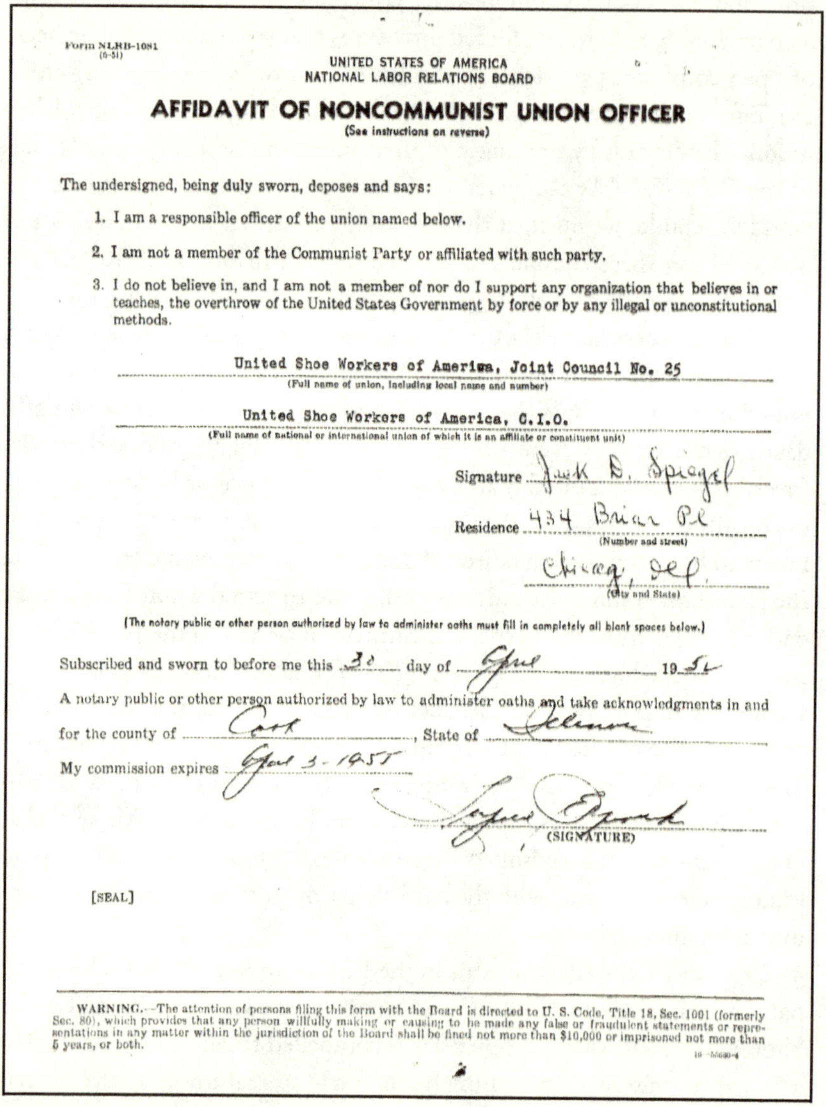

Form NLRB-1081
(6-51)

UNITED STATES OF AMERICA
NATIONAL LABOR RELATIONS BOARD

AFFIDAVIT OF NONCOMMUNIST UNION OFFICER
(See instructions on reverse)

The undersigned, being duly sworn, deposes and says:

1. I am a responsible officer of the union named below.
2. I am not a member of the Communist Party or affiliated with such party.
3. I do not believe in, and I am not a member of nor do I support any organization that believes in or teaches, the overthrow of the United States Government by force or by any illegal or unconstitutional methods.

United Shoe Workers of America, Joint Council No. 25
(Full name of union, including local name and number)

United Shoe Workers of America, C.I.O.
(Full name of national or international union of which it is an affiliate or constituent unit)

Signature Jack D. Spiegel

Residence 434 Briar Pl
(Number and street)

Chicago, Ill.
(City and State)

(The notary public or other person authorized by law to administer oaths must fill in completely all blank spaces below.)

Subscribed and sworn to before me this 30 day of April 19 54

A notary public or other person authorized by law to administer oaths and take acknowledgments in and for the county of Cook, State of Illinois

My commission expires April 3-1955

[illegible]
(SIGNATURE)

[SEAL]

WARNING.—The attention of persons filing this form with the Board is directed to U. S. Code, Title 18, Sec. 1001 (formerly Sec. 80), which provides that any person willfully making or causing to be made any false or fraudulent statements or representations in any matter within the jurisdiction of the Board shall be fined not more than $10,000 or imprisoned not more than 5 years, or both.

16—56680-4

FIG. 6.1 Union official Jack Spiegel's noncommunist affidavit
Spiegel, FBI file

Party membership or activity on the part of SPIEGEL."[14] In Spiegel's case, he retained his activism and association with the CP—though whether he continued as formally a member is unknown.[15]

While Spiegel's case was largely one of dodging a bullet, the larger impact on the party was devastating. This was on its most extreme display in their being purged from the CIO. This happened in the fall of 1949, when the CIO—an organization the communists had played an important role in building—began expelling communist-led unions. First came the United Electrical Workers and Farm Equipment Workers in the fall of 1949; this was followed in February of the following year with the expulsion of the Mine, Mill, and Smelter Workers, United Office and Professional Workers, and the Food and Tobacco Workers.[16]

The purges were aided by the testimony the CIO had solicited from union members hostile to the communists. One of these was Kenneth Eckert, himself a former communist. Eckert denounced his former comrade Maurice Travis as a communist to a CIO committee, despite the fact that Travis had quit the party to keep his union position. In 1952, Eckert would repeat his CIO testimony to the Senate, thus putting the matter into the wider public record:

QUESTION: Do you know Maurice Travis?
MR. ECKERT: Yes.
QUESTION: Do you know Maurice Travis as a member of the Communist Party?
MR. ECKERT: Yes.
QUESTION: Have you attended Communist Party meetings with Maurice Travis?
MR. ECKERT: I have attended many party meetings with Maurice Travis.[17]

The Senate then put into evidence the fact that Travis had announced in a union newsletter that he had quit the party. As their account characterized things, "The article was in substance an apology by Travis for resigning from the Communist Party to comply with the non-Communist-affidavit provisions of the Labor Management Relations Act of 1947."[18] Put in this way, Travis may have quit the party, but he had not dropped his allegiance to it.

While Travis was able to avoid perjury charges, his colleague Clinton Jenks—accused by a government informant of still being a member—was not as lucky. Based on the testimony of former communist and FBI informant Harvey Matusow, Jenks was convicted and given a five-year sentence for falsifying his affidavit. Matusow would later recant his testimony—and himself go to prison for perjury—and the Supreme Court, in 1957, would overturn Jenks's conviction.[19] Regardless, before the matter was resolved, Jenks had to endure three years in prison.[20]

Deportations

In this full-on push, the government drew on one of its most effective instruments in its repressive toolkit: deportation. Communists who were not U.S. citizens were easy targets, having no legal claim to be in the United States.

Specifically, the authorities employed the Immigration Act of 1917. The language of the law is soaked with the prejudices of the era, prohibiting "imbeciles, feeble-minded idiots, insane, etc. persons, epileptics, insane persons." Added to that, however, were undesirable political émigrés such as "anarchists, or persons who believe in or advocate the overthrow by force or violence of the Government of the United States."[21] Using that stipulation, immigration authorities were able to arrest nearly one hundred communist non-citizens in 1947 alone.[22]

Among those targeted was J. Peters (a.k.a. Alexander Stevens), a Hungarian-born communist U.S. authorities were keen to expel from the country. Peters was famous for authoring the *Manual of Organization*, a pamphlet cited by anticommunists as the smoking gun of the communists' conspiratorial nature. He was also implicated by Whittaker Chambers (more on him later) as being head of the communist underground; the two would famously meet at a HUAC hearing in 1948, where Chambers, who claimed Peters was his spy handler, identified him.[23] Peters would be arrested in October 1947, with efforts to stave off his forced return to Hungary being fruitless. He left the country in May 1949—or, in the sarcastic headline of *The New York Times*, "Alien Communist Deports Himself."[24]

Another target of immigration authorities was Gerhart Eisler, accused of being a Comintern official and spy operating in the United States. He was taken into custody by U.S. marshals on a presidential warrant in March 1947. Eisler was arrested under the Enemy Alien Act of 1798, which held that those from a "hostile nation" during wartime are considered enemy aliens.[25] He was convicted of contempt of Congress for refusing to cooperate with HUAC and lying on his immigration papers. Out on bail and sentenced to one to two years in prison, he fled to England. Earlier, his brother, the composer Hanns Eisler, was similarly pursued. In February 1947, after a brief hearing, Eisler was ordered deported. Rather than fighting to stay, he returned to the newly constituted German Democratic Republic in March 1948.[26]

Along with such high-profile figures were noncitizen labor activists. After visiting Canada in January 1948, Charles A. Doyle—a British native and international vice president of the United Gas, Coke, and Chemical Workers—was refused reentry into the United States. Then there was John Santo (who would later renounce communism) of the New York Transport Workers Union. He was charged in 1947 with illegal entry to the United States and forced to return to Hungary two years later.

Such targeting would continue well into the next decade. In its 1952 Annual Report, the Immigration and Naturalization Service (INS) reported, "The fiscal year saw 178 subversive aliens arrested under deportation proceedings." Along with this was the referral of thirty-eight cases to the Criminal Division of the Department of Justice for revocation of citizenship. As the INS happily reported,

> The vigorous program looking toward deportation has resulted in the institution of deportation proceedings in a gratifying number of cases. A few of the more prominent aliens were Vera Hathaway, wife of the former editor of the "Daily Worker"; Max Young, international representative of the Young Communist International; Israel Blankenstein, a charter member of the Communist Party of the United States; Anita Cohen Boyer Field, wife of the alleged "angel" of the Communist Party; Felix Kusman, former bodyguard to Gerhart Eisler; and Gordon Barrager, communist functionary in the transportation field.[27]

Barrager, it should be noted, was president of Local 252 of the New York Transit Workers Union. He was seized by immigration authorities amid a strike of Long Island bus drivers and deported to Canada. Likewise, Ferdinand Smith, secretary of the National Maritime Union and member of the CIO executive board, was arrested in February 1948 by immigration authorities. He would repatriate to the British West Indies in 1951.[28]

Finally, there was the extensive campaign against Australian native Harry Bridges. Bridges had landed on the radar of the authorities during the San Francisco general strike of 1934. Among the efforts to remove him from the country was a 1940 bill passed in the U.S. House of Representatives—

which the Senate failed to approve. While Bridges was able to attain U.S. citizenship in 1945, it was only after fighting through a deportation appeal to the Supreme Court. Despite this, in 1950, he was convicted on perjury charges for denying he was a communist. That decision, however, was reversed by the Supreme Court in 1954.[29]

Revitalizing the Security Index

The Custodial Detention list had officially been put on hold while the communists and the Roosevelt administration were in common cause against Hitler. With the end of that conflict and the ascent of the Cold War, the list was given a new life.

In 1946, as the Church Committee would later recount, Hoover brought the new attorney general, Tom Clark, up to speed on the state of the detention list, now called the Security Index. It is unclear why Clark had approached Hoover for such a status report, and Hoover did not make known to Clark that the list had never really gone away; regardless, Clark does not appear to have asked too many questions. The new situation, which held the potential for a war with the USSR, required the United States to plan accordingly—including having a contingency for detaining communists.[30]

And it was mainly communists on this Security Index. A clear sense of this comes by way of a 1950 report to Congress. At the time, they were considering a package of anticommunist legislation by way of the McCarran Act (for more on the law, see chapter 8), which carried a stipulation under the heading, "The Emergency Detention Act of 1950." According to the bill, "There exists a world Communist movement which in its origins, its development, and its present practice, is a world-wide revolutionary movement whose purpose it is, by treachery, deceit, infiltration into other groups (governmental and otherwise), espionage, sabotage, terrorism, and any other means deemed necessary, to establish a Communist totalitarian dictatorship in all the countries of the world through the medium of a world-wide Communist organization."[31] Such people would now be subject, if an emergency order were issued, to involuntary detention. The numbers affected were in the thousands. As the FBI reported at the time, of the 11,930 people on the Security Index, 11,491 were affiliated with the Communist Party. The next largest group was the Socialist Workers Party with 380, followed by the Nationalist Party of Puerto Rico with 77, the Independent Socialist League with 45, the Proletarian Party of America with 6, the Independent Labor League with 2, and the Revolutionary Workers League with 1.[32] By any meaningful definition, this was a communist detention index.

Hollywood Ten

The story of the Hollywood Ten—eleven if one includes Bertolt Brecht, a non–U.S. citizen who left the United States soon after testifying before HUAC—has become something of a cornerstone of the Second Red Scare. The men, most of whom were writers, were Alvah Bessie, Herbert J. Biberman, Lester Cole, Edward Dmytryk, Ring Lardner Jr., John Howard Lawson, Albert Maltz, Samuel Ornitz, Robert Adrian Scott, and Dalton Trumbo—all known, by the FBI anyway, as communists. After being called in front of the HUAC in the fall of 1947 and refusing to answer questions (though Dmytryk would later appear a second time and cooperate), they would be cited for contempt of Congress.[33]

According to the hearings and the media that popularized them, the issue was the matter of communist influence in films. It was a straw man. As studio head Louis B. Mayer told the committee, any problem with communists getting their ideas into films, *if* they even existed, would have been a mean feat: "The only ones that I would have to worry about are the producers, the editors, the executives because our scripts are read and re-read by so many of the executive force, producers and editors that if you looked carefully at 1,200 or 1,500 pictures I produced with my people out at the studio you would be surprised how little you could possibly point to, even now, when we are on the lookout for it, particularly at this time."[34] Given that, hauling these men before Congress and the bipartisan consensus to indict them for contempt, followed by conviction and imprisonment, was nothing short of a purge.

The hearings did not come out of nowhere. The FBI had been monitoring communists in Hollywood for some time as part of their wartime agenda to track loyalty. For example, Adrian Scott was a screenwriter who wrote the 1943 Cary Grant film *Mr. Lucky* and later was a producer on the Raymond Chandler film adaption *Murder, My Sweet*. Scott had joined the Communist Party in 1944. We know this because—according to his

FBI file—the bureau had an informant operating within the Hollywood writer's circle.

Scott's informant was quite specific, as outlined in one report,

> Source A, whose reliability has been well established, stated that during the days of the CPA [Communist Political Association] the subject [Scott] was a member of the "Special Group," holding the 1944 CPA card 46,832. This informant was also able to relate that on November 27, 1944 the subject was issued a 1945 CPA card 47,200. This source stated that the subject is presently assigned to the Davis Branch of the Cultural Section. This Branch is composed of ten of the most prominent Communists in the Motion Picture industry, and it is believed that this branch very rarely meets because it is known that several members of this Branch fear disclosure.[35]

What the report makes clear is how the HUAC hearings were able to include meticulous reporting on the Hollywood Ten's party membership, specifically their party membership cards—the gold standard of evidence for the government proving communist membership.

This and the fact that the men refused to answer questions put them in an untenable position legally. As such, beginning in 1950, they would spend between six and twelve months in prison. On release, they confronted a situation where their careers and reputations in Hollywood were in tatters.[36]

Hollywood informants did not limit themselves to those working behind the scenes. For example, as one FBI report records on several prominent Hollywood actors, "Edward G. Robinson has been identified as a Communist by Informant REDACTED. Charles Chaplin, according to REDACTED, may or may not be a member of the Communist Party. However, REDACTED has stated that Chaplin has financed the West Coast Communist newspaper 'People's World.'" Further, "John Garfield, according to the informant REDACTED has been affiliated with the Actors Laboratory, the Young Communist League, the Hollywood Anti-Nazi League, the Hollywood Democratic Committee, and the Hollywood Independent Citizens Committee for the Arts, Sciences and Professions."[37] With such inside information, these celebrities confronted the harsh spotlight of anticommunism, a phenomenon that was only increasing in momentum.

In later HUAC hearings, scores of actors and filmmakers were coerced into renouncing past associations or sympathies with communism—and implicating their colleagues. Among them were the choreographer Jerome Robbins—who cooperated after being threatened with his homosexuality being exposed—actor Lee J. Cobb, screenwriter Budd Schulberg, and fellow screenwriter Martin Berkeley, who named at least 150 people.[38]

Arguably the most notable of these was director Elia Kazan. Kazan not only informed on his former comrades but made the film *On the Waterfront*—with a prominent role for Lee J. Cobb. That film is a sympathetic portrayal of the plight of a government witness, albeit framing the story as an agonizing but righteous struggle against a mob-controlled union. Pointedly, the Academy of Motion Pictures Arts and Sciences awarded it eight Oscars, including prizes to actor Marlon Brando, screenwriter, Budd Schulberg, and director Elia Kazan.[39] In doing so, the mainstream of Hollywood sent a strong, if somewhat nuanced, message on where it stood on cooperating with the HUAC.

Defectors, Informants, and Spies

Notably, and to their detriment, the Communist Party attracted no small number of fringe, conflicted, and disturbed characters. As the postwar clampdown began to flower, they would reveal themselves in troublesome and problematic ways.

One of the most problematic of these was Louis F. Budenz. Budenz had not simply been a communist; he had been a member of the group's National Committee, a body on which he sat for a decade between 1935 and 1945. Before becoming a communist, Budenz had been steeped in Catholicism, having been trained by the Jesuits of St. Xavier University in Cincinnati and St. Mary's College in Kansas.[40] Having nonetheless found a home in the Communist Party and the later Communist Political Association, Budenz would have a crisis of faith in communism at the point Earl Browder came under criticism. As a result, he would quit the party and leave that ideology behind. He did not, however, just leave to lead a quiet life. Instead, under the tutelage of New York Bishop Fulton Sheen, he returned to the Catholic Church and became a vociferous anticommunist.[41]

Budenz's former leading position, coupled with his return to religion, was welcome fodder for anticommunist press coverage. In October 1945, *The New York Times*, reporting on the fact that he had taken a teaching position at Notre Dame, noted that his desertion was predicated on his belief that communism destroyed "the thinking and integrity of the individual."[42] With such a position he sought not only to restore his own individuality but to destroy, willfully or not, the lives of his former comrades. In that testimony before the HUAC in November 1946, Budenz claimed that every member of the American Communist Party—which counted anywhere from eighty to one hundred thousand members—was "a part of a Russian fifth column."[43] In his view, these were not just people he disagreed with but enemies of the American state.

What is noteworthy about Budenz, and a fact likely lost on him, is that before his defection, the FBI considered him as someone hostile to the United States. In 1941, they marked him as a candidate for "custodial detention in the event of a national emergency."[44] Had he not defected from the party, he may well have been imprisoned himself.

Budenz was one of several high-profile defectors who stepped forward in the mid to late 1940s, a period in which paranoia of communism—particularly of communist spies—was getting considerable media attention. For example, readers of *The New York Times* on August 4, 1948, were confronted with the lead story, "Red 'Underground' in Federal Posts Alleged by Editor." That piece detailed the revelations of Whittaker Chambers, who claimed there was a secret cell of communists working in government posts. Chambers was a former underground communist courier—someone whose task was to operate outside the purview of the authorities—who had become an editor at *Time* magazine. He claimed that a State Department employee named Alger Hiss was a secret communist. Hiss would eventually go to prison, not for being a communist, but for lying to Congress. Regardless, the specter Chambers presented of conspiratorial communists infiltrating the U.S. government would animate the HUAC and the anticommunist right in the years going forward.[45] That such infiltration was, to the degree it even existed, minuscule and marginally impactful was beside the point.

Chambers's revelations came one week after another former courier, Elizabeth Bentley, made the news. Bentley was described in the media as a "one-time espionage agent" who was portrayed as a conduit of information to the Soviet Union.[46]

Budenz, Bentley, and Chambers would be joined by people such as Herbert Philbrick, Matt Cvetic, Boris Morros, Angela Calomiris, and Maurice Malkin. Most of these informants and former communists would attain a type of celebrity—lauded for having infiltrated or broken with communism.

That there were so many is a testament to the attraction of certitude the party offered. It also suggests the CP was not all that discriminating—much as it may have thought otherwise—in whom it allowed to join and take on sensitive tasks.

Many of these informants would testify to or make exaggerated claims about the party's secret apparatus. While this had a certain shock value for the American public, given everything the CP had confronted since the days of the Palmer Raids, it is hardly a surprise they had mechanisms in place that sought, however fraught, to operate outside the purview of the authorities. It is also not surprising in the context of World War II, when the Soviet Union confronted an existential threat from Nazi Germany, that some communists were willing to go to extremes—including breaking U.S. espionage laws—to defend "the land of socialism." This is not to endorse such activity but to add the too often missing context. There was a rationale for certain communists doing what they did.

Regardless, the spy scare of the 1940s and 1950s was one more element in the marginalization and suppression of communism organizationally and ideologically. It would remain a component going forward. This was a juggernaut that was just getting started.

7

Decapitation and Violence (1948–1949)

That from on or about April 1, 1945, and continuously thereafter up to and including the date of the filing of this indictment, in the Southern District of New York. . . . The defendants herein unlawfully, willfully, and knowingly, did conspire with each other, and with divers other persons to the grand jurors unknown, to organize as the Communist party of the United States of America.

INDICTMENT OF THE CPUSA LEADERSHIP, 1949

While the president and Congress were serving up new laws and orders to purge communists from government positions and in the larger U.S. society, the criminal justice system was also called to action, targeting the communist's leadership for incarceration. In parallel to these statist initiatives were significant manifestations of extralegal political violence. As such, anyone laboring under the illusion, as in the previous Red Scare, that this episode of sustained anticommunism would soon abate would be perilously mistaken. It was not, however, as the communists assessed, a bellwether of Hitler-type fascism arriving at American shores. Rather, given the imperatives of the Cold War, it was the end of any tolerance—as threadbare as that had always been—for the Communist Party as a legitimate entity.

On March 30, 1947, less than two weeks after the Truman Doctrine was announced, Eugene Dennis, general secretary of the Communist Party, voluntarily appeared before Congress. His appearance was to have been an opportunity to speak out against legislation that would criminalize the Communist Party. Congress, however, had other things in mind.[1]

Rather than eliciting Dennis's views on repressive legislation, the committee blindsided him with the accusation that he had falsified his Selective Service application. Specifically, they interrogated him as to his identity, knowing full well his birth name was Francis Waldron, not Eugene Dennis. With film cameras rolling, Dennis attempted to get out of the snare by stridently declaring "Dennis" as his identity. The problem was—as the congressmen well knew—that "Dennis" was the alias he assumed after jumping bail in 1930, for a conviction for his role in leading an unemployment demonstration in Los Angeles.[2]

The same day that Dennis testified, J. Edgar Hoover also appeared, saying that the Communist Party constituted a "fifth column if there ever was one." In his view, the group's aim was "the overthrow of our government." Hoover's testimony would be the highlight of the next day's news coverage, thus amplifying his conspiratorial proclamations.[3] Pointedly, Hoover opposed criminalizing the Communist Party. This was not out of sympathy or fealty to civil liberties but because, in his words, "I would hate to see a group not deserving the category of martyrs made martyrs by some law which might later be declared unconstitutional." He also likely did not want to cede the intelligence his organization had accumulated against the communists. Openly criminalizing the group would have made public many of the secrets garnered and the informants used by the FBI.

Hoover's testimony aside, the media proceeded to conduct background research on Dennis's identity. At the same time, the courts snapped into action, putting him on trial for contempt of Congress for refusal to appear a second time. The results were not good for Dennis. On June 25, he was convicted and sentenced to a year in prison. U.S. Attorney John W. Fihelly made clear the government's objective: "Dennis had set himself up as a symbol of the Communist party—as being bigger and greater than the United States Government. . . . God help the day when Dennis or anyone else gets away with that."[4] The government, it appears, was out to make Dennis a symbol of their bigger and greater power.

Decapitation

The Dennis incident was a prelude to a far bigger effort by the government. Little more than a year after Truman announced his global anticommunist doctrine, the criminal justice system—with a big assist from the FBI—moved to remove the leadership of the CPUSA from the political scene.

On July 28, 1948, the bulk of the Communist Party's top leadership was rounded up and taken into custody. *The New York Times* described the scene of the initial arrests: "Six FBI men walked quietly into the discussion [underway] on the ninth floor of Communist headquarters, showed their badges and merely said. 'You are under arrest.' Gray-faced [William Z.] Foster and his companions did not seem particularly astonished. They got up from their chairs, walked to the elevators with the Federal agents, and at the curb entered two automobiles that took them directly to the Federal Building."[5]

Arrested that day in New York, along with Foster, were National Board members Henry Winston, John Williamson, and Jack Stachel; New York City Council Member Ben Davis; and Eugene Dennis—the FBI apparently timing the raid to grab as many leaders at once as possible.

Arrested separately were Robert Thompson, National Board member and chairman of the New York State Party; Irving Potash, head of the Needle Trades Workers Industrial Union; and *Daily Worker* editor John Gates. Those leaders would turn themselves in separately. Outside of New York, Gus Hall, chairman of the Ohio Communist Party, surrendered in Cleveland; Gil Green, head of the party's Chicago district, turned himself in there, while Carl Winter was arrested in Detroit.[6]

After the arrests, things moved swiftly. Ten of the arrested were put on trial—Foster's case was separated due to his frail health. The trial opened on January 17, 1949. At its core, the government's case revolved around a federal indictment that invoked the same principles that had sent communists to prison in 1920 under state statutes but had also been leveled at the Socialist Workers Party by way of the Smith Act, the charge being advocating and teaching the principles of revolutionary communism. Specifically, the Smith Act made a criminal of "whoever knowingly or willfully advocates, abets, advises or teaches the duty, necessity, desirability, or propriety of overthrowing or destroying the government of the United States."[7]

The particular line of attack by the government stemmed from the group's abandonment of the short-lived Communist Political Association and its reconstitution of the Communist Party. That explains the indictment's wording: "From on or about April 1, 1945, and continuously thereafter up to and including the date of the filing of this indictment . . . the defendants herein, unlawfully, willfully and knowingly did conspire with each other, and with [diverse] other persons to the grand jurors unknown, to organize the Communist party of the United States of America a society, group and assembly of persons who teach and advocate the duty and necessity of overthrowing and destroying the Government of the United States by force and violence."[8] The crime, as had been true with the bulk of syndicalism and criminal anarchy cases, was not engaging in revolutionary or violent activity but advocating and teaching the revolutionary doctrine of communism.

The party's defense, to their detriment, did not challenge the government based on its nullifying the principles of free expression enshrined in the U.S. Constitution. Instead, they argued—contrary to what the government claimed—the violent overthrow of the government was anathema to their organization. In this, they pointed to their constitution, which said, "Adherence to or participation in the activities of any clique, group, circle, faction or party which conspires or acts to subvert, undermine, weaken or overthrow any or all institutions of American democracy, whereby the majority of the American people can maintain their right to determine their destiny in any degree, shall be punished by immediate expulsion."[9] While this clause in the communists' program problematized the government's case, it did not defeat it.

The problem was that, for all their claims to the contrary, the communists could not separate themselves from their doctrinal bedrock. In fact, the government had works such as the *Communist Manifesto*—with its declaration "let the ruling class tremble at the communist revolution"—read into the trial transcript. That, along with a judge, Harold Medina, who was hostile to the defendants throughout the trial, made a conviction an all-but-foregone conclusion.

On October 14, 1949, a jury handed down guilty verdicts on all the defendants. In turn, the judge sentenced the men to five years in federal prison, except Robert Thompson, who was given a marginally lesser three years because he was a decorated war veteran.[10] Along with this, five of the defense attorneys, who routinely sparred with the judge throughout the trial, garnered contempt convictions. While the attorneys appealed their sentences, which ranged from three to six months, after three years of challenges, the Supreme Court upheld the convictions.[11]

Likewise, the appeals of the defendants were defeated. After going all the way to the Supreme Court, their appeals were denied. In 1951, six of the men would begin serving sentences. Gus Hall, Henry Winston, Robert Thompson, and Gil Green, however, would fail to turn themselves in. In the words of the party, they became "unavailable."[12] According to the government, however, they were fugitives—and a massive manhunt ensued.

Whether in prison or on the run, the result was the same. The government had successfully severed the top leadership from the body of the CP. It was only the beginning.

Driving Davis from Office

The Smith Act trial had a twofold impact on defendant Ben Davis, the African American New York City councilman from Harlem. Davis had come to communism in 1933 in Atlanta after defending Angelo Herndon, a Black nineteen-year-old YCL organizer. As such, he had encountered his share of the hard bite of racist attacks.[13] Davis stood for reelection in 1949, and the race would become a forum for anticommunism. He would be defeated by a three-to-one margin—63,030 to 21,962. His opponent, Earl Brown, hailed the outcome as "an overwhelming victory for Americans," proclaiming the results "should answer once and for all the false charge that my people [Brown was also Black] want communism—or any part of it."[14] Davis's defeat was cause for celebration among those who despised communism and the idea of a Black communist in an important political position.

The electoral defeat followed close on the heels of his Smith Act conviction. The consequence of that meant that he was barred from even voting.[15] Matters, however, did not stop there. After the conviction, the city council moved to expel him, though he still had until the end of the year to serve out his term. After refusing to let Davis speak in his defense—or participate

FIG. 7.1 Robert Thompson and Benjamin Davis during Smith Act trial, 1949
New York World-Telegram & Sun, photo by C. M. Stieglitz

in the vote—the council voted 15–0 to remove him from office.[16] He was thus stripped of his remaining privileged platform.

As a Black communist, Davis was the target of particularly vitriolic attacks. This comes through tellingly in an FBI memo, where it is reported,

> On March 9, 1949, REDACTED, staff writer of the "World-Telegram" advised the writer [of the FBI memo] that the subject spends considerable time with a woman named REDACTED residing in a top floor apartment . . . and has told the informant that the subject is the father of the child. REDACTED [the *World-Telegram* journalist] stated that he intends to publicize this information in the "World-Telegram" but given the possibility of a libel suit, would like to verify the facts first. Since the information may be of value on cross-examination of DAVIS, should he testify at the Communist trial, REDACTED submitted it to this office.

As a result, the New York office responded by saying, "The information would be submitted by him to United States Attorney JOHN F. X. MCGOHEY."[17]

The bureau, as this reveals, was willing to use anything available to it to sink Davis. While the issue of adultery does not appear to have come up at the trial, it was indicative of the efforts against Davis, which would continue and intensify when he eventually emerged from prison, especially when the bureau adopted an even more aggressive campaign of underhanded methods with its Counterintelligence Program (COINTELPRO).

Political Violence

While the fall of 1949 saw the legal machinery grinding away in the Smith Act trial, it was soon to be accompanied by a shocking episode of political violence in Peekskill, New York. That event, however, had been preceded by several disturbing and violent episodes.

In the fall of 1948, Robert Thompson was on his way to see a neighbor and fellow communist in the Sunnyside area of Queens when he was attacked by two men, while a third waited in a car. According to *The Daily Worker*, "One of the men grabbed him and spun him around. Thompson was then slugged on the head. Thompson, who holds an Army medical discharge for malaria incurred in the Pacific war, fought back." He was, *The Daily Worker* reported, "beginning to get the better of the men when he was stabbed in the stomach. The men then ran off, apparently believing their mission had been accomplished."[18]

While Thompson's injuries were serious, he recovered from the attack. It was not, however, the last incident. Less than two months later, a neighbor of Thompson's, who claimed to be a "freelance private detective," secretly entered his home while he and his wife were out. The couple's babysitter, however, discovered the man, Robert Burke, was in the house—apparently in the child's room—and called the police. He was then arrested and charged with molesting the couple's seven-year-old daughter. Burke would later claim he had gone to the house to denounce Thompson as a communist. Whatever the fuller story behind this troubling incident, Thompson called out the violation of his home as a political attack. As he said, "[It was] a direct consequence of the failure to arrest and punish the assailants who tried to take my life on September 23."[19] These would not be the last assaults.

The attack on Thompson took place during the period of the 1948 election. This was a time when the CP was working in a coalition with Progressive Party candidate and former vice president under FDR, Henry Wallace. While Wallace was in no way a supporter of communism, his platform called for working with, rather than against, the Soviet Union.[20] As a result, he was branded as a communist supporter and treated as such.

None other than Harry Truman disparaged him, saying, "The fact that the communists are guiding and using the third party shows that this party does not reflect American ideals."[21] Further, as recorded in one paper in Truman's archive, "Henry Wallace is a catalytic for Communism. By his candidacy for the presidency on the third-party ticket, he has precipitated the 'red' element in the CIO so that all may see it and readily identify it."[22]

Perhaps not surprisingly, Wallace too was attacked as he campaigned. While campaigning in North Carolina, over the course of five stops, he was repeatedly pelted with eggs, tomatoes, peach stones, and green peppers—this by men who shouted, "Chase the n----- lovers out of town," the racist vitriol a result of the Wallace campaign refusing to bow to Jim Crow strictures, including having segregated rallies.

The symbolic violence aimed at Wallace was accompanied by a physical attack: a knife assault on Wallace's bodyguard, James D. Harris, a navy veteran who had served in the Pacific. Harris was stabbed twice in the arm and six times in the back. While his wounds turned out not to be fatal, it was not for lack of trying.[23] Just how vile the atmosphere was surrounding the Wallace effort can be seen in a column in the *Los Angeles Times*, with one piece suggesting events in North Carolina may have been masterminded by communists. By the article's logic, the attacks could have been staged to elicit sympathy for Wallace: "The demonstrations could have been arranged without Wallace knowing anything about it. The Commies in his entourage are a good deal smarter than he is and could keep him in the dark."[24]

Pointedly, another violent incident aimed at the CP—this in Louisville, Kentucky, in October 1948—presaged worse to come. The event was a planned interracial picnic organized by the Civil Rights Council, a CP-supported group. The event had to be canceled because of the threats of violence. According to a press report, the safety director, David A. McCandless, "had warned the civil rights group that there would be arrests 'if white and Negroes intermingle at the picnic.'" He also claimed that a "Communist goon squad was ready to incite a race riot."[25] The specter of anticommunist and anti-Black violence would not be avoided in an incident the following year.

Peekskill

In August 1949—amid the Smith Act trial—the organization People's Artists, which worked to popularize working-class and left-leaning musicians, organized a concert, headlined by Paul Robeson, as a benefit for the Harlem Chapter of the Civil Rights Congress.

At the time of the concert, Paul Robeson was one of the most prominent artists in the world, and certainly the most prominent one associated with the CP. Like the CP, however, he had been under intense political targeting in the immediate postwar era. Specifically, he had been the subject of attacks in the media for a speech he made in Paris where he said, "We reject any hysterical raving that urges us to make war on anyone. Our will to fight for peace is strong. . . . We shall support peace and friendship among all nations, with Soviet Russia and the people's Republics." For unclear reasons, the Associated Press modified the speech, quoting Robeson as saying, "It is certainly unthinkable for myself and the Negro people to go to war in the interests of those who have oppressed us for generations." The press in turn seized on this, characterizing Robeson's remarks as being anti-American. It also took him to task for having the temerity to speak for Black people in the United States.[26]

That incident was still in the news as the scheduled concert in Peekskill approached. The event, scheduled at the Lakeland Acres picnic grounds, was under fire. The *Peekskill Evening Star* set the tone:

> It appears that Peekskill is to be "treated" to another concert visit by Paul Robeson, renowned Negro baritone. Time was when the honor would have been ours—all ours. As things stand today, like most folks who put America first, we're a little doubtful of that "honor" finding the luster in the once illustrious name of Paul Robeson now almost hidden by political tarnish. . . . The singer is being presented by People's Artists "for the benefit of the Harlem Chapter of the Civil Rights Congress," according to posters appearing in the neighborhood. . . . It becomes evident every ticket purchased for the Peekskill concert will drop nickels and dimes into the till basket of an Un-American political organization.[27]

That editorial was accompanied by the actions of a group of reactionaries in a coalition called the Joint Veterans Council. They organized a march, which took place at 6 p.m. on the day of the scheduled evening concert. As it got underway, it grew to become a mob of five thousand. That mob in turn proceeded to lay siege to the grounds where the concert was to take place. What followed was the destruction of the stage and equipment and the beating of those on-site who were working to set things up. The attack lasted overnight, trapping all those there, including women and children who had come to help.[28] Robeson, who heard of the siege when he arrived by train, was convinced—against his protests—to return to New York City. The concert was canceled.

As a result, the event was rescheduled, this time for the afternoon of September 9 at the Hollow Brook Golf Course, a few miles north of Peekskill. To avoid a repeat of the previous incident, organizers dispatched a contingent of hundreds of union members and veterans to guard the stage. As a result, the concert—which included performances by Pete Seeger; pianist Leonid Hambro, who played pieces by Prokofiev and Ravel; and Sylvia Kahn, who sang "The Star-Spangled Banner"—went off without a hitch. As author Scott Martelle recounts, however, "The trouble began as the crowd left the concert grounds, some aboard chartered buses, others driving out in personal cars, passing through the sentry line [concert security] and then a cordon of police and temporary deputies. Just south of the golf course, several thousand vigilantes lined a narrow, banked section of the roadway, creating a lengthy gauntlet with the full help of state police troopers and the Westchester County sheriff's deputies."[29]

Among those to first encounter trouble were Smith Act defendants Ben Davis and Irving Potash. As Davis describes, "As we emerged slowly from the entrance to the golf course at a speed of three or four miles an hour, the car was [pelted] with rocks and stones, many of them too large to be hurled with one hand. They shattered the windshield in front of the driver, and the glass on the door panel on the left-hand side of the car immediately beside the driver. Several of the stones came through the windshield and glass door panels."[30] Black concertgoers were particularly singled out. The *Peekskill Evening Star* reported, "Two Negro soldiers were booed loudly when they walked into the concert. . . . One was struck in the face, and both hustled into the grounds to escape the angry demonstrators." Another witness reported hearing, "Every n----- bastard dies here tonight! Every Jew bastard dies here tonight!"[31]

Ronnie Gilbert, the female singer of the group The Weavers, described how she was jammed into a standing-room-only bus trying to get away from the concert area: "In the dusky light a young man in rolled-up shirt-sleeves stood at the side of the road a neat pyramid of rocks at his feet." He proceeded to choose a rock and, as Gilbert recounts, "wound up like a baseball pitcher, and fired at the bus, straight at us. A window smashed near me where I was standing. Everyone was screaming. 'Jesus, don't faint,' I told myself."[32]

As things turned out, the Peekskill Riot would be the worst incident of mass violence ever leveled against the CPUSA and its supporters. It was not, however, the end of the repression.

8

Prison and Pursuit (1950–1953)

> This is America's task today: If we are to survive as a nation: to kill these Communist germs and to increase the strength and vigor of American resistance.
>
> **J. EDGAR HOOVER**, 1950

The period up to and through the Smith Act trials constituted the first wave in a juggernaut against the Communist Party. Had it not been for the successful seizure of power by communists in China in 1949—then the most populous country on Earth—followed by the war in Korea, it is conceivable matters might have abated, at least to a degree. That, however, is not what happened. The coming to power by Mao Zedong and the Communist Party was a political earthquake in a world that had yet to recover from the calamities and disruptions of World War II.

Because of this, the years 1950–1953 would see the societal level of anticommunism assume a near-pathological character—best embodied in the person of Joe McCarthy. It would also see the extension of Smith Act prosecutions against a further cohort of communist leaders. Along with this was legislation that called for the registration of communists and revitalizing moves toward their mandatory detention. All this fed the FBI's mandate for pursuing the radicals, something they did with a particular zeal, including in the recruitment of alienated and disaffected former comrades.

John Lautner

The FBI had been following John Lautner for some time. Because of this, they knew that in 1948 he was part of the New York Review Commission, the party's mechanism responsible for internal security, including investigating charges against party members for violations of party discipline, and for ferreting out spies.[1] The irony here was that Lautner would falsely be accused of being a turncoat, impelling him to become one himself.

According to party member Jack Kling, who played a key role in the ensuing events, "through various channels, the Party leadership learned that he [Lautner] was a government agent planted in the Party organization." According to Kling, while he was given a party trial, "he denied he was a stool pigeon. But the facts at our disposal were so complete that the trial committee voted to expel him from the Party as a government agent."[2] Kling's telling came thirty-six years after the accusation. His post-event assessment—which omitted critical facts—was as wrong then as it was at the time.

The truth of the matter is that the suspicion of Lautner lay in international intrigue. Specifically, the communist government of Hungary was in the midst of a campaign to root out a "counter-revolutionary conspiracy." That conspiracy, it was claimed, was headed by the government's foreign minister, László Rajk. As a result, Rajk and others were tried, convicted, and executed in 1949. They were accused of being "Titoite" spies—Yugoslavian leader Josip Broz Tito having become anathema to the Soviet leadership to which the Hungarian party was loyal. Lautner had the misfortune of being a Hungarian American who had served in a minor intelligence capacity in the Balkans during World War II. As such, he ticked all the boxes of suspicion for the Hungarian party—who had requested a list of Hungarian American comrades. Because of this, they asked that he be instructed to come to Hungary, where he would likely be tried—and quite possibly executed—as a spy.

Unfortunately for the U.S. and Hungarian parties, at the point this was playing out the U.S. State Department had banned travel to Hungary, meaning Lautner was unable to leave the country. Failing that, the party opted for a plan B, deciding to try him in the United States. They then proceeded to lure him to Cleveland under the pretense of his being reassigned to a different political responsibility.[3]

In fact, he was being called to judgment by way of an internal trial. If Lautner's account to the FBI of his experience in Ohio is to be believed—and it reads as credible—what happened was both shocking and amateurish:

> When they arrived at the house it was dark out and [Jack] KLING told him to go down to the basement with the driver of the car, but KLING stayed upstairs. In the basement, according to the informant [Lautner], which was partitioned off with blankets and had the water running in the sink, were two Party men, one of whom told him to undress. The informant noted there were a half dozen rubber hoses there and on the table, there were some knives. One of the men was carrying a pistol. The driver and two unidentified individuals told him to sit down and wait and when he asked what was going on they told him he would soon find out.[4]

From there they got down to business: "JOE BRANDT [an Abraham Lincoln Brigade veteran], according to the informant [Lautner], then pulled out a blue-covered book concerning the RAJK trial and said very excitedly that he, the informant, must have learned the lessons of the trial and wanted to know how the informant sent his reports to the CIA." In Lautner's view, "they were ready to kill him that night but because they thought he had left KLING'S name at the CLEVELAND hotel they were afraid to do so." However, he also reported that "he was not touched or hurt in any way during the questioning," suggesting that, despite his suspicions, his interrogators were smart enough to not escalate things beyond the already problematic level on display in the basement.[5]

After leaving Ohio, Lautner returned home. When he got back to New York, he read in *The Daily Worker*, "[The] National Review Commission of the Communist Party has been conducting an investigation to determine how the FBI agents exposed in the Foley Square trial [the first Smith Act case] penetrated and functioned in the ranks of the Party." Lautner, in their view, was a snitch and was expelled from the party.[6] Compounding this, his wife, facing expulsion herself if she did not dissociate from her husband, divorced him. Given all this, the FBI, which read *The Daily Worker* religiously, saw an opportunity. They set out to interview Lautner, to feel him out and explore if he would be open to working with them.[7]

The agents sent to talk to him sought to "obtain detailed info. concerning secret party apparatus, underground operations, security methods of CP, USA and identification of individuals connected with above."[8] When they sat down to interview him, Lautner was forthcoming. Among the things he told them was that the purpose of the Review Commission "was to carry out and safeguard the political, moral and physical aspects of the Party membership, and was considered to be an arm of the State Secretariat." He also told them of disciplinary actions taken against perceived counterrevolutionary forces, such as Earl Browder and perceived Trotskyists, in the party.[9]

In the bureau's view, this was a good start. As Edward Scheidt, the New York special agent in charge, reported to headquarters, "During the course of subsequent interviews, detailed information will be secured from LAUTNER concerning various departments of the Communist Party, USA, together with his knowledge of the organization set-up of the Party as an illegal organization in this country."[10] All in all, it would constitute an intelligence windfall for the FBI.

Notably, the agents debriefing Lautner went through a list of prominent people, asking who their new informant felt was a member, or strong supporter, of the party. He did not disappoint. Among those he identified were the writers Lillian Hellman, Dashiell Hammett, Mark Blitzstein, and Howard Fast. He also named the folk singer Woody Guthrie as well as actors James Cagney, John Garfield, Will Geer, and Jose Ferrer; and the scholar W. E. B. Du Bois.[11] All this was substantial grist for the bureau's investigatory mill.

The Lautner Affair, as it came to be called, created major problems for the CPUSA. The actions they took against him—at the behest of their comrades in Hungary—backfired. Instead of rooting out a bad actor, they created a highly effective renegade. It was a stunning example of the Chinese folk saying of one "lifting a rock only to drop it on one's own feet."[12]

Korea and Atomic Secrets

The intelligence coup embodied in the flipping of John Lautner played out on the threshold of the United States getting into a shooting war with communist forces in the Far East. That war saw the U.S. government go from expanding the imprisonment of the leadership of the party to the execution of the low-level members Julius and Ethel Rosenberg.

The Korean War began on June 25, 1950, when North Korea sent troops into U.S.-occupied South Korea. Two days later, the United States entered the conflict. The Truman Doctrine, which called for challenging communist expansion, had now been realized in a war between the Soviet Union, the People's Republic of China, the Democratic People's Republic of North Korea and the Republic of Korea, and the United States and its United Nations allies. The Cold War had gone from a diplomatic and economic confrontation to a very hot shooting war.

That was the backdrop to the arrest by federal authorities in June 1950 of David Greenglass and the subsequent arrest, in July, of his brother-in-law, Julius Rosenberg, a communist and electrical engineer accused of passing atomic secrets to the Soviet Union. A month later, Ethel Rosenberg, Julius's wife and David's sister, was arrested on the same charges. Neither Julius nor Ethel worked on the Manhattan Project, which was developing the atomic bomb. David Greenglass, however, had. Greenglass was a communist and machinist at the headquarters of the Manhattan Project at Los Alamos, New Mexico. His wife, Ruth, also a communist, had recruited him to pass secrets to help the Soviets win the war. Arrested the previous month, Greenglass flipped, becoming a government witness—ostensibly to protect his wife. He in turn claimed his brother-in-law and sister, like him, had been the conduits for information passed to the Soviets.[13]

What followed, in rapid succession, was a prosecution, conviction, and death sentence for the Rosenbergs—hinging largely on Greenglass's testimony. On June 13, 1953, just shy of three years after Julius's arrest, the couple were put to death in the electric chair at the Ossining Prison in upstate New York.[14] It was an event that was both stunning and merciless, magnified by the fact that the executed couple left behind two young children.

The culpability of the Rosenbergs has long been a matter of debate—though there is now hard evidence that Julius worked to aid the Soviet Union.[15] Saying that, given the level of publicity and the Draconian response, one could be forgiven for thinking the couple played a major role in the Soviets obtaining atomic weapons. That was not the case. Tellingly, at the time of Rosenberg's arrest, J. Edgar Hoover said only of Julius that he was "an important link in the Soviet espionage apparatus"—link, rather than linchpin, being the key word.[16] As for Ethel, it is doubtful she had much to do with the matter at all. By the government's own admission, she was a target mainly to leverage Julius into confessing—such being the ruthless nature of the U.S. criminal justice system.[17]

The Rosenberg case, like the wider media fixation on atomic spies, belied an important point. The main problem was not that the Soviets had obtained the atomic bomb but that the United States had not only led the way in developing such weapons but had been the first power—and the only one—to use them against human beings.[18] Once that genie was out of the bottle, as the president himself conceded, another country obtaining such weapons was more or less inevitable. As Truman said when it became public that the Soviets had obtained atomic capability, "Nearly four years ago I pointed out that scientific opinion appears to be practically unanimous that the essential theoretical knowledge upon which the discovery is based is already widely known. There is substantial agreement that foreign research can come abreast of our present theoretical knowledge in time." Truman also made clear that "no single nation could, in fact, have a monopoly on atomic weapons."[19]

Put simply, the information passed to the Soviets by people such as Julius Rosenberg, David Greenglass, and Manhattan Project scientist Klaus Fuchs—the German physicist who passed on the most important atomic secrets—did not enable the Soviets to build an atomic bomb. It only accelerated an awful process—one in which the United States, through its development and use, had led the way.

The McCarran Act

Along with the Korean War and prosecution of the Rosenbergs, Congress adopted the Internal Security Act of 1950, or McCarran Act—named after its sponsor, Nevada Democratic Senator Patrick McCarran. The bill was quite specific in targeting the CPUSA: "To protect the United States against certain un-American and subversive activities."[20] The law included provisions for the mandatory registration of communists and included the creation of a Subversives Activity Control Board to enforce that. It also allowed the president to arrest and detain anyone who might be a threat of sabotage or espionage.[21] As a section of the law titled "The Emergency Detention Act of 1950" laid out, "There exists a world Communist movement which in its origins, its development, and its present practice, is a world-wide revolutionary movement whose purpose it is, by treachery, deceit, infiltration into other groups (governmental and otherwise), espionage, sabotage, terrorism, and any other means deemed necessary, to establish a Communist totalitarian dictatorship in all the countries of the world through the medium of a world-wide Communist organization."[22] The bill passed in the House 312 to 20 and in the Senate 51 to 7. While it was vetoed by Truman, the House reaffirmed the bill 286 to 48, and the Senate 57 to 10.[23] However, much in the way he opposed the Taft-Hartley Act, Truman's veto was not out of any sympathy with communism. Rather, he had concerns that it would undermine the United States' image globally. As he said, "It would help the Communist propagandists throughout the world who are trying to undermine freedom by discrediting as hypocrisy the efforts of the United States on behalf of freedom."[24] In a similar vein, *The New York Times* opined that the law was "unworkable and un-American." Such concerns from the likes of Truman and *The New York Times* were not small matters. The United States had a lot vested in promoting itself as the land of freedom in opposition to the nominally socialist countries that had sprung up after World War II. Unfortunately, the impetus and momentum for suppressing domestic communism trumped such concerns. More to the point, the criticisms of the hypocrisy of American freedom were more true than certain authorities in the United States were willing to concede.

As for the McCarran Act, it is worth highlighting a revealing aspect of the debate around the law that emerged. In editorializing about the bill, *The New York Times* wrote, "One of the fine features about a democracy is that errors can be rectified before it is too late. And so we may hope that some of the more unwise and impractical provisions of this law will in due time be modified by Congress in a moment of calmer thinking and more reasoned reflection."[25] Such was the thin gruel of American freedom—such an argument essentially said, Let repression reign for a time, and shunt it to the side later. It was a philosophy that served well the instituting of onerous repression at key moments while maintaining an overall facade of freedom.

Smith Act Ruling

Following the adoption of the McCarran Act, the Supreme Court, in June 1951, came down with a ruling upholding the conviction of the eleven defendants in the 1949–1950 Smith Act trial. Before the ink was even dry on that decision, the government announced the indictment of twenty-one more party leaders.

Those targeted all held key positions in the group. They were the head of the party's Women's Commission, Elizabeth Gurley Flynn; the former vice-presidential candidate and southern region director, James E. Jackson; the southern director of the party and national secretary of the party's Negro Commission, Pettis Perry; the assistant national labor secretary, Sidney Steinberg; the secretary of the party's Women's Commission, Claudia Jones; the secretary of the Public Affairs Department, Fred Fine; the chief theoretician, Alexander Bittelman; the head of International Publishers, Alexander Trachtenberg; the head of cultural work, Victor Jeremy (V. J.) Jerome; the national maritime coordinator, Albert Francis Lannon; the secretary of the defense commission, Marion Bachrach; a member of the national review (security) commission, Louis Weinstock; the party chairman of Western Pennsylvania, Arnold Johnson; a Marxist teacher, Jacob Mindel; the national education director, Betty Gannett; a veteran communist, William Wolf Weinstone; the chairman of the New York State Committee, Israel Amter; a member of the Civil Rights Congress, William Norman Marron; the former chairman of the Bronx Communist Party, Isidore Begun; the chairman of the New York State Legislative Committee, Simon W. Gerson; and the labor secretary, George Blake Charney.[26]

Those indictments were followed by similar actions aimed at the party's West Coast leadership: in San Francisco, William Schneiderman, Al Richmond, Carl Lambert, Albert Lima, Lorretta Stack, Oleta Yates, Ernest Fox, and Bernadette Doyle; and in Los Angeles, Phillip Connelly, Rose Chernin, Harry Steinberg, and Dorothy Ray Healey.[27]

Taken as a whole, those indicted constituted the most dedicated and experienced of the party's leaders. Pursuing them continued the process that had begun in 1949—removing the top leadership of the party with the aim of crippling the organization.

To the Underground . . . Again

All this amplified the panic building inside the CP, one that manifested itself in an ill-considered underground effort. In the CP's view, the McCarran Act signaled the time was five minutes to midnight. Gus Hall, writing in *The Daily Worker*, explained, "This is a sober warning and an urgent appeal. A warning that a gigantic build-up for an all-out assault against the civil liberties and human rights of the American people is nearly completed . . . A brief review of the home-front communiqués issued since the war communiqués began to arrive from Korea tells us that the hour is very late and the danger of bloody fascist terror very grave."[28] Another *Daily Worker* piece, citing a recent Hall speech, argued that the McCarran Act was "the 'legal framework' for the establishment of fascism, and the largest step yet taken in that direction in the U.S."[29] Such writing made clear that significant elements of the party leadership thought matters were on the brink of an overwhelming repression, one in which they would be the target.

That was the thinking circulating as the Supreme Court ruling paved the way for the initial Smith Act defendants to begin serving their sentences. As such, while John Gates, Eugene Dennis, Ben Davis, John Williamson, Carl Winter, Irving Potash, and Jack Stachel surrendered to prison authorities, Gus Hall, Henry Winston, Robert Thompson, and Gil Green did not. They instead jumped bail, with the aim of continuing political work underground.

***

With the underground initiative, it was Gus Hall who suffered the most immediate consequences. Hall, unlike Green, Winston, and Thompson who resolved to stay in the United States, attempted to leave the country. Rather than report to federal prison where he faced a five-year sentence, he fled to Mexico, his ultimate destination being the Soviet Union. Because of an informant, however, his underground days were short. He was arrested in a raid on his safe house in Mexico City soon after having entered that country. With matters of extradition and due process disregarded, Hall was quickly returned to the United States and put in custody. The result of this escapade was that he would have an extra three years added to his sentence.[30]

For his part, Robert Thompson was able to evade capture, at least for a time. However, in September 1953, he was arrested along with Sidney Steinberg—who had gone underground before the second Smith Act trial. The two were captured in a raid in California's Sierra Mountains.[31] In the melodramatic account of *Time* magazine, "Hidden by the underbrush, 16 other men closed in silently around [Thompson's] cabin. They looked like unshaven, jean-clad campers, but they were actually FBI agents, armed with pistols and carbines. When they had completed their circle, at a prearranged moment, five sedans carrying reinforcements rattled down a dirt

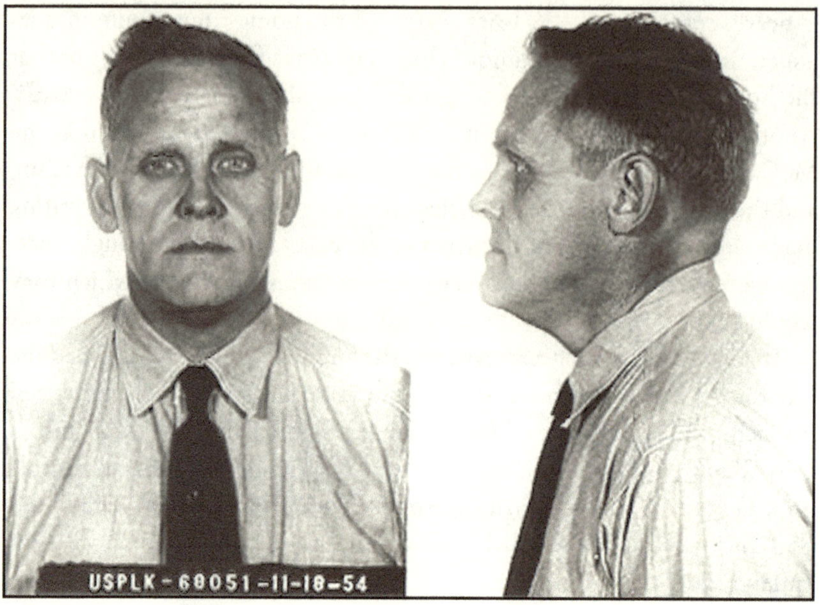

FIG. 8.1 Gus Hall photographed before he did time in Leavenworth, Kansas, 1954

road to a point 20 yards from the cabin. Slowly the G-men converged on the cabin." The raid was likely a result of the pair's support network faltering somewhere along the way, inadvertently giving up the fugitive's location.[32] For their part, the CP cast Thompson as a political refugee who had fled in the face of an outrageous conviction under the Smith Act.[33]

Henry Winston and Gil Green fared better. Rather than hiding in unfamiliar and isolated terrain, they kept close to the familiar turf of Chicago. As a result, they were able to evade capture for nearly five years. They surrendered in 1956, emerging in a far different world than the one they had operated in five years earlier.

***

A major problem for the communists in implementing their underground operations was the fact that John Lautner, now working as a zealous government informant, was able to supply the FBI with considerable information about the party's secret plans.

Among other things, Lautner described how the experience in Europe, including combating the suppressive measures of the Nazis, had informed the CP's measures. As he told the FBI in one of his debriefing sessions, he met with Robert Thompson in 1948, around the time of the Smith Act indictments, to sketch out a plan to go underground. According to Lautner, "THOMPSON mentioned that [William Z.] FOSTER had come back from Europe after a tour through the new democracies and that he had very valuable information concerning the history of the underground movement of Europe and all the problems that they were confronted with in Germany, Czechoslovakia, and Hungary." The CP, in other words, was not simply building on their experience from the previous decades but rather had access to measures their international comrades implemented to combat some of the most extreme repression meted out in the twentieth century.

As such, Lautner walked away from the meeting with Thompson with a better sense of how the New York apparatus would be organized. The New York State party "would be divided into three areas, consisting of the first area, New York County, [the] Cultural Division and some of the semi-legal apparatus already built, the second area consisting of Brooklyn, Queens, Bronx, Westchester County, and Nassau, and the third area the upstate area." Such information—while not rich in particulars, gave the FBI a basic grounding in what they were up against, this in the country's largest concentration of party members, New York City.

There *were*, however, particulars. Lautner reported that party leaders "THOMPSON, REDACTED, and NORMAN [William Norman Marrow] each were to name three immediate subordinates, with the result that one of these would know the other two and three people he appointed. In all, he would know five individuals, which was the extent to which one Party member knew about the others as being Party members. This principle worked all the way down through the county, regional, section, subsection and units." In this way, anyone apprehended by authorities could, at worst, reveal only a small number of comrades. Further, Lautner told the FBI that the "total groups in the state would amount to 1,093 and total number of members in the New York State Illegal Party would be 3,279."[34] For the FBI, this information was gold—unattainable in any other way except through such a highly placed defector.

Lautner's intelligence, however, was not limited to New York. He also gave the FBI an outline of the alternate national leadership to be called up if needed: "In addition, the informant believed that individuals would be brought from the Midwest and West Coast in the event the party becomes illegal, and individuals on the East Coast would go West in order that they could take up Party duties without having identified with the Party movement in the locality in which they are to work."[35]

***

Lautner's intelligence came amid the CP nullifying a huge chunk of its organization as a way of erecting an apparatus that could withstand heightened repression. As Joseph Starobin, who had worked as international editor of *The Daily Worker*, recounted, "Early in July 1951, the organizational department of the Party announced publicly that all those members who had not re-registered would be dropped from membership. A great many loyal although inactive members were in effect expelled. They were considered unreliable merely because they had not reasserted their party ties. This action was part of a theory that the American C.P. could only function in the years to come as a 'cadre organization,' a skeletal force because only such a force could withstand further repression."[36] While the group continued to exist as an open and public organization, "it was guided by a shadow leadership." According to Starobin, "The National Board, that is, the leadership elected at the 1948 and 1950 conventions, attempted by letters and through visits from family members to make suggestions and offer advice; most of these men were in different prisons. Their views were sometimes in complete contradiction to the opinions of the leaders at other levels."[37]

***

This underground effort was a different one from that undertaken in the period of the Palmer Raids. The party was much larger and its membership predominantly American-born, with deep ties to U.S. society. As such, the transition to the underground was much more disruptive. The move involved thousands of members who lived a quasi-illegal existence without really being illegal.[38] While party members and supporters operating in early 1950s America may have faced social ostracism and the consequences of loss of jobs and opportunities due to being communists, the reality was that the chief target of the authorities was not the broad membership but the group's leadership.

As such, for the party, the move underground was the worst of both worlds. Huge swaths of the members' efforts and financial resources were expended to protect leaders who, because of their fugitive status, were unable to offer the leadership required of a significant national organization. Along with all that, it created an opening for law enforcement, which now had an airtight legal justification for pursuing criminal fugitives.

Perhaps worst of all is that this was taking place in conditions—as repressive as they were—that in no way rose to the level of the Nazi terror that existed in 1930s Germany. The situation may have required extreme measures, but the measures implemented were not the ones needed.

Pursuing Fugitives

While the FBI knew in broad strokes how the underground was organized, they did not know all the specifics. As such, without strategically placed informants, they were at a disadvantage. In that respect, the group did have some success, particularly in the case of Gil Green and Henry Winston.

In his account, Green presents a clear picture of the mechanics of surviving underground. This included, contrary to the experience of Gus Hall and Robert Thompson, operating in areas where the party had a firm base of support. In their case, Green and Winston spent most of their time in the Chicago area. Their experience was also guided by a clear understanding of what they were up against. As he wrote, "We neither overrated nor underrated the FBI's ability."[39]

All of which led to a certain desperation on the part of the bureau. Their frustration manifested itself in their dedicating considerable resources to hounding Green's wife and three children. For example, when the family went to stay at their brother-in-law's lake resort near Chicago, agents laid siege to the place. According to Green's spouse Lillian, "[They] put a spotlight on our cottage at night. . . . They even followed the children when they went swimming and fishing." In another encounter—this in front of the children—agents issued a none-too-veiled threat: "We don't use guns much, but sometimes a man we're hunting gets shot. Now you wouldn't want that to happen to your husband, would you."[40]

Such measures were also leveled at the family of James Jackson, who had gone underground after being indicted in the second wave of Smith Act prosecutions. The harassment reached a level such that his spouse, Esther, wrote a letter to the editor of the *New York Daily Compass*. In it, she outlined the measures against her family: "My two children, aged 4 and 8, have been followed, threatened and intimidated constantly since June 20 when their father was indicted under the Smith Act."[41] Such extreme measures against family members would be appalling, regardless of the crimes of their spouses, but it is worth remembering that Green, Jackson, and Winston were not violent felons. They had been criminalized only for advocating and teaching the principles of communism.

Beyond harassing the fugitives' families, the government targeted the party's support apparatus. Given several communists had refused to show up for prison, the government used that as justification to target those who had organized bail for those convicted. As such, they demanded the Civil Rights Congress Bail Fund—which had helped post bond—disclose the names of all contributors. When the group refused—not wanting to make thousands of people vulnerable to persecution—the officers of the group were cited for contempt. In turn, author Dashiell Hammett; Director of Council of African Affairs Alpheus Hunton; activist and writer, and grandson of the Vanderbilts, Frederick V. Field; and Abner Green of the American Committee for the Protection of the Foreign Born were all given six-month prison sentences.[42]

TOPLEV

The move underground had given the FBI wide latitude to pursue communist fugitives. While they focused a good deal of energy on trying to locate them, they also used the opportunity to approach key members of the party they thought might have information to attempt to turn them into informants. This quickly evolved into a program in its own right. In September 1951, the bureau inaugurated an effort called TOPLEV, standing for Top Level, that sought to turn leading members against their organization. TOPLEV would come to be one of the most successful undertakings in informant penetration in the entire history of the FBI's efforts against the Communist Party.

In its early days, the program saw two dedicated agents assigned to approach CP members in each of the major cities the group operated in. A memo from 1952 outlines the program: "The accentuated need for live informants in all levels of the Communist Party must continue to be emphasized as well as the development of informants and American Legion informants which are also assigned to Agents on security work. The TOPLEV program, must, of course, receive the full attention of the two Agents assigned to it."[43]

Of note here, beyond the attention given to TOPLEV, is the less-than-casual relationship between the FBI and the American Legion.

The most commanding success of TOPLEV was the turning of Morris Childs into an FBI informant. Childs, an alienated party member who had been the *Daily Worker* editor and was closely associated with Earl Browder, was approached in the spring of 1952—at the suggestion of his brother, Jack Childs—by the FBI's head of counterintelligence in Chicago, Carl Freyman. Childs, who was sick and struggling at the time, would enter into a series of discussions with Freyman on why communism was a failed ideology, one that Childs ought to abandon. He also arranged for the ailing Childs—he suffered from a heart condition—to receive treatment at the Mayo Clinic. As Freyman would later say, "He cost us a lot of money at the time, but he was worth it."[44] Freyman's transactional assessment was nonetheless accurate. By the late 1950s, Childs would be the CP's liaison with the Soviets and Chinese and the FBI's most important resource inside the CP.[45]

A Culture of Anticommunism

Coinciding with all this was the propagation of a culture of informing. One missive in 1951 to J. Edgar Hoover was indicative of the type of response being generated from the depths of U.S. society: "I feel you would like to know a place that the eleven convicted Reds use to meet. . . . I will wager they are in this apt or the people know where they are. . . . These lousy reds have been meeting there for two years."[46] The report was duly followed up on and unsurprisingly turned out to be fiction. The point, however, is that this is what the FBI was soliciting.

No corner of U.S. society was omitted from the drive against communism. This can be seen in an editorial J. Edgar Hoover penned for the *Journal of the American Medical Association* in November 1950. In it, he called on physicians to embrace the scientific method to combat the "germ" of communism that was "attempting to infect the bloodstream of American life." In Hoover's view, Communist "germs spawned in the swamps of iniquity and terror, have blotted out, for one-third of the world's population, the sunshine of free thought, independent research, and unfettered inquiry." In order to oppose this, he said, "the physicians of America, by the very nature of their training, can render inestimable services in the ideological fight.

Medical science is interested in cause and effect, in careful diagnosis, detection of specific symptoms, and the prescribing of cures which will eliminate the cause of the malady. . . . The fight against Communism must be waged, if we are to win, on the same principles which have enabled the medical profession to render such magnificent services for the American people."[47] It was a stunning statement, not only because of its fascistic language, but in the fact that the American Medical Association saw fit to publish it.

For the FBI, such writing coincided with the specific objective of overcoming barriers to recruiting new informers. In 1952, they produced a paper to address this, titled "Stool Pigeon or Loyal Citizen," which sought to challenge the taboo of informing on friends and neighbors. Doing this, they pointed out that the FBI did not invent the concept of informing; in fact, as they explained, it went back millennia: "Even in the Old Testament we learn that Moses considered it just and necessary to send men into the Promised Land of Canaan to develop truthful information needed for worthwhile purposes." While that might read as laughable by today's standards, the fact was that a considerable swath of the American public in the fifties took their moral guidance from the Bible. Beyond that, the FBI's paper offered a primer on how informing, rather than being degrading, was a righteous act, and one incumbent on good citizens to undertake: "The common, ordinary citizen is morally obligated to convey to governmental authorities any knowledge he may have or is able to secure relating to a violation of his own laws."[48]

By contrast, the CP issued its own pamphlet titled *Stool Pigeon*, pushing the other way. In a *Daily Worker* editorial, Smith Act defendant John Gates was quoted saying, "It would degrade me in the eyes of my associates and the labor movement, in the eyes of the public and in the eyes of the jury to act as a common stool pigeon. . . . I do not want to have on my conscience the fact that any human being would lose his means of livelihood even his life because of any such information I might give."[49] Despite such pushback, the contestation around informants would continue going forward, with the communists generally coming out worse for wear.

Stalin Dies

The measures by the United States to neutralize domestic communism, while achieving a good deal, did not destroy it. The party continued, if as a diminished organization. However, historical events would have a far more devastating effect than anything Congress, the president, or the FBI implemented.

On March 4, 1953, Joseph Stalin died of a stroke. It was a milestone on which both the United States and the communists attempted to put their stamp. *The Daily Worker*, in a statement that would soon become problematic for them, wrote, "Humanity has lost the greatest man of our time."[50] *The New York Times* bent hard the other way, going so far as to lay World War II at Stalin's, not Hitler's, feet: "In his [Stalin's] account must be reckoned the guilt for the cynical deal with Hitler in 1939 which gave the go-ahead signal for the Second World War and its enormous sacrifices."[51] *The Baltimore Sun* offered a more sober, if more strategic, assessment: "Stalin's tyranny was only in part a personal tyranny. It was also the tyranny of an idea. That man, far from being the master of his fate, is its servant. Stalin is dead, His personal tyranny is ended. The tyranny of the idea lives on with so far undiminished strength."[52] Both the *Times* and *Sun*, however, agreed on one thing: there could be no retreat from anticommunism.

9

Disruption (1954–1963)

> For the present, our disruptive tactics will of necessity, be general in nature, that is, along the lines of "keeping the pot boiling."
>
> **FBI MEMO INAUGURATING ITS COINTELPRO SCHEME**

One could be forgiven for thinking that by 1954 the U.S. political apparatus had passed and adopted every conceivable piece of anticommunist legislation. They would have been wrong. In the summer of that year, Congress passed the Communist Control Act, a measure to officially outlaw the Communist Party. In announcing its passage, *The New York Times* proclaimed, "Congress Passes Softened Version of Communist Ban." The word *softened* was a reference to the rejection of a provision by liberal Senator Hubert H. Humphrey, who had introduced the bill with the support of Massachusetts Senator John F. Kennedy. Humphrey had wanted even membership in the group to be criminalized. That adjustment made, the bill was passed by an overwhelming majority, 79–0 in the Senate and 265–2 in the House.[1]

President Eisenhower, when signing the bill, took the opportunity to summarize the campaign against the Communist Party so far: "We have in the past 19 months stepped up enforcement of laws against subversives. As a result, 41 top Communist leaders have been convicted, 35 more are indicted and scheduled for trial, and 105 subversive aliens have been deported."[2] Congress may have passed a law making the party illegal, but the government had, in many ways, already done so.

McCarthyism

Despite the passage of the 1954 law, the drive against U.S. communism, which had been at a fever pitch since 1947, was losing momentum. Emblematic of this was the downfall of the poster boy for anticommunism, Wisconsin Senator Joe McCarthy.

McCarthy had forced himself onto the scene in February 1950 with a speech in Wheeling, West Virginia, where he falsely claimed to have a list of 205 people—later reduced to 57—who he claimed were communists working in the U.S. State Department.[3] What followed was three years of escalating accusations, thousands in the federal government losing their jobs, and an atmosphere of recrimination and paranoia, amplified and legitimated by huge swaths of the American media apparatus.[4]

McCarthy initially carried out his anticommunist work by way of speeches and testimony but later operated as head of the Senate Permanent Subcommittee on Investigations, all of which ran roughshod over the U.S. landscape between 1950 and 1953. However, he crossed a bridge too far during the televised sessions of what came to be called the Army-McCarthy Hearings of April–June 1954.

The pivotal moment of those hearings came when McCarthy sought to impugn the integrity of an attorney who had once worked for the National Lawyers Guild—a group with ties to the Communist Party—this despite a verbal agreement beforehand not to put the man's name into the record. When McCarthy reneged, he was confronted by attorney Joseph Welch, hired by the U.S. Army. Welch, after listening to the badgering and accusations of McCarthy, exclaimed, "You have done enough. At long last, have you no sense of decency." It was a made-for-TV moment that has since been canonized in U.S. culture as the point at which McCarthy lost his power.

McCarthy, however, was already on the ropes by the time of those hearings. In March, journalist Edward R. Murrow had signaled a certain consensus among influential authorities that it was time for McCarthy to go. In an editorial, he proclaimed, "This is no time for men who oppose Senator McCarthy's methods to keep silent."[5] By year's end, McCarthy would be censured by the Senate, a move that neutered him politically. It did not, however, hold him to any real account, nor did it end the myriad efforts against U.S. communism.

Civil Rights Versus Civil Liberties

On May 17, 1954, the U.S. Supreme Court ruled that schools could no longer be segregated by race, giving a huge impetus to the fight for civil rights, and signaling the coming to an end of the apartheid-like conditions of Black people in the United States. It was a milestone, but one that existed in parallel with one of the most repressive times in U.S. history.

By the end of 1954, forty-four states, including Alaska and Hawaii, had adopted laws on sedition, criminal anarchy, or criminal syndicalism or against the advocacy for violent overthrow of the government. Further, eleven states proscribed "subversive organizations" from using public schools for meetings.[6] These laws existed in an environment of the utmost hostility to communism.

Also in 1954, a poll by the Opinion Research Corporation asked if congressional committees hurt innocent people. Of those queried, 49 percent said yes. It then asked which was more important: to find out all the communists "even if some innocent people should be hurt" or to protect the rights of the innocent. A 58 percent majority said it was more important to uncover communists. Not surprisingly, most thought they should be stripped of citizenship and that the government should be entitled to tap their phones. They also thought it was a good idea "for people to report to the FBI any neighbors or acquaintances whom they suspected of being communists."[7] Taking into account the limitations of polls, the results were nonetheless shocking.

In his biography of Benjamin Davis, historian Gerald Horne noted, "I continue to find it mind-boggling that few scholars have noticed that in the 1950s civil liberties were being restricted while civil rights were being expanded and that Washington was prattling about 'human rights violations' in Eastern Europe while tolerating the same at home."[8] Horne's observation was as profound as it was disregarded.

A deeper look, however, reveals the two issues as integrally intertwined. On the one hand, U.S. authorities—claiming to be the land of freedom and against communism—were compelled to transform their treatment of Black people from second-class citizens to something approximating that of full Americans. As Mary Dudziak has written, "At a time when the U.S. hoped to reshape the world in its own image, the international attention given to racial segregation was troublesome and embarrassing. The focus of American foreign policy at this point was to promote democracy and to 'contain' communism. However, the international focus on U.S. racial problems meant that the image of American democracy was tarnished."[9]

At the same time, this highly contentious moment in the Cold War impelled the powers that be toward all-out suppression of domestic communism and the denigration of their vaunted freedoms in carrying this out. It was a paradoxical situation that few historians, aside from Horne, have acknowledged.

In Prison

Amid all this was the fact that the two Smith Act trials of 1949 and 1952 had seen the conviction and sentencing of twenty-eight communist leaders, most of whom were either in jail or on the run.

Those sentenced were not treated gently. Despite being seventy-four years old, Jacob Mindel, husband of CP leader Elizabeth Gurley Flynn, was refused parole. Alexander Bittelman, already in his mid-sixties, had to serve five years in the Atlanta federal prison. Betty Gannett, serving her sentence in the reformatory for women in Alderson West Virginia, was "twice assigned such heavy manual labor in storehouses as lifting hundred-pound sacks" despite suffering from arthritis and angina. Jack Stachel, who had heart disease, was incarcerated in Danbury Prison. West Indian communist Claudia Jones, who suffered from asthma and a heart condition, was forced to work at a loom in the Alderson reformatory—after ten months of this, she had to be admitted to a New York hospital.[10]

Even worse was the situation for Robert Thompson, who had been viciously beaten near his home in 1948. Thompson, who had become a fugitive after the Smith Act, had been arrested in California's High Sierra region by a raiding party of fifteen FBI agents who kept him chained to a tree under the blazing California sun for three hours. He was then sent to New York's Federal Detention Center in Manhattan to await trial for jumping bail. While there, he was attacked by a Yugoslav seaman and fascist named Alexander Pavlovich. Struck from behind with a metal bar, Thompson sustained serious injuries, having to have a metal plate implanted under his scalp. Pavlovich was being held for deportation to his home country. There he faced execution for having assassinated communists.[11]

As such, the authorities appeared to have been keen to mete out punitive incarceration and were less concerned with the health and safety of their communist prisoners. Further, such maltreatment and brutality telegraphed a message. Communists were as bad as, if not worse than, violent criminals—and should be treated as such. While the abuse may not have risen to the level of more authoritarian regimes, one could be forgiven for drawing parallels.

Khrushchev's Bomb

As daunting as prison and the wider repression were, they did not break the core spirit of the Communist Party—which had a vested interest in holding to its world view. The same cannot be said of the speech on February 25, 1956, by Soviet Premier Nikita Khrushchev. That speech would upend the world communist movement and plunge the U.S. party into crisis.

The target of the address was the previous leader of the Soviet party, Joseph Stalin. Framed as a polemic against the cult of the individual, it delivered a litany of charges that candidly spoke of the ruthless methodology of Stalin. According to Khrushchev, "Instead of proving his political correctness and mobilizing the masses, he [Stalin] often chose the path of repression and physical annihilation, not only against actual enemies but also against individuals who had not committed any crimes against the Party and the Soviet Government."[12] Stalin, in other words, *had* done the things the communists had long minimized or refused to acknowledge.

For the U.S. party, which had been able to survive the disorientation that accompanied the Soviet-German nonaggression pact, the congressional committees, federal indictments, and the treachery of turncoats and government spies, Khrushchev's speech was a weapon of far more lethality.

While standing strong against the U.S. power structure required courage of a kind, it also tended to reinforce their commitment; they were, after all, under attack by their capitalist enemy. But Khrushchev's revelations tore at the bedrock on which their ideals rested. The communist project in the Soviet Union, which was supposed to embody the quintessence of human liberation, had executed hundreds of thousands of its own under the murderously paranoid justification that they were political enemies of the first order. For many thousands of U.S. communists, this was the last straw. What followed would be a rancorous fracturing, accompanied by the exit of many thousands of former loyal members.

Raiding *The Daily Worker*

Khrushchev's broadside against Stalin notwithstanding, the U.S. government did not let up. Less than a month after the speech, U.S. authorities took the bold step of shutting down *The Daily Worker*. In the droll account of *Time* magazine, "Four nattily tailored men entered Party headquarters on 12th Street in Manhattan and took the elevator to the 8th floor where the *Daily Worker* was produced. On entering the office, they proclaimed the place shut down, and proceeded to paste-up notices, 'THIS PROPERTY SEIZED FOR NONPAYMENT OF INTERNAL REVENUE TAXES.'" It was signed. "U.S. Treasury Department, Internal Revenue Service."

The workers at the newspaper were able to relocate to a floor where another publication was produced and put the paper out on time. That same day, however, branch offices of the newspaper were padlocked in Chicago and Detroit. For its part, the government tried to minimize things. Alfred Fleming, the regional commissioner of the Internal Revenue Service, portrayed the raids as a simple manner of funds due—there was a dispute over whether the paper was tax-exempt or not—"All we are interested in is getting some money."[13] Given everything heaped on the CP up to that point, it was not a convincing argument. While the paper would continue publication, they did so with the government relentlessly looking over their shoulder, threatening them with financial sanctions and shuttering of their offices.[14]

Internal Struggle

Those challenges taken into account, Khrushchev's speech remained a far more formidable challenge. What ensued in its wake was a level of internal struggle previously unimaginable. It would come to manifest itself in the development of four distinct party factions. One, roughly aligned around Benjamin Davis and the ailing William Z. Foster, sought to toe the line of the Soviet party. Another, centered around Eugene Dennis, staked out a middle ground between reform and toeing the pro-Soviet line but in actuality sought no hard break with the USSR. A third, embodied in *The Daily Worker* editor John Gates, sought a greater independence and essentially argued for a return of Earl Browder's more open, rightest grouping.[15] And finally, there was a small, ultraleft trend that included Black communist Harry Haywood (Haywood Hall), who argued for resurrecting the group's discarded Black Belt South theory—a Comintern policy from the twenties that considered Black people in the United States as constituting an oppressed nation within the larger country entitled to constitute a country in several states in the South, separate from the larger United States of America.[16] That tendency, with minimal influence at the time, would gain currency in the following decade with the rise of revolutionary Black nationalism.

Meantime, the other trends would clash and resolve at the 1957 sixteenth party conference. It was there that Eugene Dennis was elected the nominal party head. His centrist position, while suggesting reform, actually served as a gateway toward the adoption of a lasting pro-Soviet position. As things developed, Dennis would only occupy the post for two years before being dislodged.

Dennis would die in January 1961. His passing was followed by that of Foster the same year, and then Davis in 1964. Given that, the road was open for Gus Hall to rise to the top. Hall would take the group deeper into the waters of reformism and electoral politics—he would also become a perennial presidential candidate. His primary conviction, however, was an abiding loyalty to the Communist Party of the Soviet Union. It was that latter aspect that ensured the group would remain a prime target of anticommunist forces within the United States, spearheaded by the FBI. In this, the FBI decided to go from aggressive intelligence gathering to an aggressive disruption campaign.

COINTELPRO-CPUSA

The FBI's Counterintelligence Program (COINTELPRO) aimed at the CPUSA, began amid the struggle following Khrushchev's speech. In 1956, they articulated the aims of the new program:

> Generally, the above action has constituted harassment rather than disruption, since, for the most part, the Bureau has set up particular incidents, and the attack has been from the outside. At the present time, however, there is existing within the CP a situation resulting from the developments of the 20th Congress of the CP of the Soviet Union and the Government's attack on the Party principally through prosecutions under the Smith Act of 1940 and the Internal Security Act of 1950 which is made to order for an all-out disruptive attack against the CP from within.[17]

In the context of the factional contention in the party, the FBI's efforts at disruption "from within" manifested itself in intervening in those quarrels. Specifically, they worked to support the more moderate John Gates group: "Since Foster's faction represents the extreme revolutionary element inside the CP, his faction is more dangerous than the Gates faction from an internal security standpoint at this time."[18] To that end, they crafted a five-page missive on Foster, giving it the rhetorical title "Has Foster Helped the Party?" That document included a litany of complaints about Foster, before concluding he "has not been an asset to the Party in this country." After the document was duly drafted, the FBI outlined how it was to be used. Writing to its New York office, it instructed them—unless they had strong objections—"to select a strong Gates faction personality who dislikes Foster intensely, one in each of the Boroughs of Manhattan, Brooklyn, and the Bronx and mail a copy" to each. This was not to be a mail canvas; rather, "each of the three individuals selected should be one who could be expected to instigate some action against Foster inside the Party." It also suggested that the envelopes be addressed individually and at the top of the first page a notation should be made in longhand. For example, "Al, for your consideration," using the name of the particular individual to whom it was to be sent.[19] It is not possible to assess the impact this undertaking had, but one can safely assume it did not help the CP at this vulnerable time.

The bureau continued in this vein amid another struggle. In 1959, when Eugene Dennis was being challenged by Gus Hall, they again sought to influence the leadership struggle.[20] In this instance, they once more supported the more moderate force—such as he was—this time Eugene Dennis: "NY would like to add that it believes much of the difficulty the Party finds itself in today can be traced to DENNIS' failure as a leader and, therefore, it would be to our advantage to keep an indecisive individual, such as DENNIS, in command of the Party rather than GUS HALL or BEN DAVIS."[21] Despite their efforts, Hall beat out Dennis and took command of the group's leadership.

There is quite a bit that is remarkable here, but one point worth highlighting is that the FBI, leveraging its extensive intelligence of the CPUSA, was able—regardless of the success or lack thereof of any given operation—to act as a sophisticated political police entity.

The Sino-Soviet Split

Khrushchev's speech had far-reaching implications. Arguably the most consequential was its effect in corroding the relationship between China and the Soviet Union. While in the United States the two countries were portrayed as a monolithic bloc, the reality was far more complex.

On the one hand, Mao Zedong had few illusions about Stalin. As he said, "You could only speak favorably, and not unfavorably; you could only sing praises to his successes and virtues but were not allowed to criticize; if you expressed any criticisms he suspected you of being an enemy, and you were in danger of being sent to a camp or executed."[22] On the other hand, the Chinese party felt Khrushchev, in criticizing Stalin, was undermining key tenets of revolutionary Marxism-Leninism. As such, they were not on board with his unilateral denunciations. As Mao said,

> I would like to say a few words about the Twentieth Congress of the Communist Party of the Soviet Union. I think there are two "swords": one is Lenin and the other Stalin. The sword of Stalin has now been discarded by the Russians. Gomulka [the Polish communist leader] and some people in Hungary have picked it up to stab at the Soviet Union and oppose so-called Stalinism. The Communist Parties of many European countries are also criticizing the Soviet Union, and their leader is Togliatti [the leader of the Italian party]. The imperialists also use this sword to slay people with. Dulles [U.S. secretary of state], for instance, has brandished it for some time. This sword has not been

> lent out, it has been thrown out. We Chinese have not thrown it away. First, we protect Stalin, and, second, we at the same time criticize his mistakes, and we have written the article "On the Historical Experience of the Dictatorship of the Proletariat." Unlike some people who have tried to defame and destroy Stalin, we are acting in accordance with objective reality.[23]

That Mao considered the execution of hundreds of thousands during the Great Purge as "mistakes," rather than crimes, is telling of the "ends justify the means" philosophy that infected too many twentieth-century communists.[24] Regardless, his remarks, made in November 1956, were the beginnings of what would become a full break with the Soviets. As matters developed, China would come to terms with the United States and reframe the global order. That would not happen for another fifteen years, but Khrushchev's speech had set things on a certain path.

Leveraging White Chauvinism

Mao and the Soviets' position aside, the FBI would come to utilize the fault lines of the Sino-Soviet split to further their own disruptive aims. That, however, was still a few years off. More immediately, they sought to play on vulnerabilities that had become apparent due to an internal campaign against racism within the group. The campaign, referred to as combating white chauvinism, began in 1949 and would last until 1953, though it would continue in a diminished form thereafter.

William Z. Foster, who would bring the campaign to a close, would both criticize its excesses—it was a highly destructive initiative—and claim it as necessary. As he said, "White workers are often deeply penetrated with the poisonous white chauvinism and even the Communist Party itself has to be on constant guard against its infection."[25] In reality, this was a runaway internal purge, one that saw hundreds of communists expelled for real and perceived abuses—all amid the repression coming down during the Smith Act trials.[26]

The FBI, via its informants, was well aware of the initiative. As such, they looked for opportunities to leverage any conflicts in Black-white relations that might be destructive to the group. One case in point was in Detroit, where a local CP leader, Phil Schatz—a defendant in a Smith Act prosecution there—was said to have sold a house in his neighborhood around the same time as a Black family moved in.[27] On learning this, the bureau proposed popularizing the incident among "all Negro members of the Michigan Communist Party (CP) District." They would do this via a bogus letter that read in part, "I learned recently . . . that because a family of my race moved in next door to Phil Schatz, he and Gert sold their house after just a short time there. The reason is obvious. They don't want to live near one of our race."[28] In that case, the FBI held off on the idea. This was not out of any moral qualms but because "anonymous letters are looked upon with a great deal of suspicion," and "it is doubtful that one individual would know the identities and residences of all the Negro members."[29] In other words, who but the FBI or some other anticommunist entity would be responsible for such a mailing?

In another instance, the FBI did pursue a disruptive mailing, as Dorothy Healey would discover in her own FBI file. In February 1961, the Los Angeles office mailed eighty-five copies of a "green sheet" (apparently the color of the paper used), which repeated chauvinism claims made against the white leadership in the Southern California district. The mailing, claiming to be from a small group of Black comrades, said that Black comrades in LA were relegated to certain isolated sections of the party, were not given positions of responsibility, and "must intermarry before they are fully accepted by the Party." As such, the "Negro Question" had "been given only lip service."[30] In a letter summarizing the results, the Los Angeles office happily reported that, because of the mailings, membership in the "Compton Section dropped to such a point where the section was disbanded and merged with Moranda Street Section." Further, as they reported, the Moranda section of the LA party "was once the largest and most active in the district," but because of the bureau's provocations, it now "spent so much time fighting the district leadership that recruiting and fund raising practically ceased."[31]

From TOPLEV to SOLO

Khrushchev's speech and the ensuing internal struggle led to the party bleeding members. In March 1952—despite the anticommunist laws, loyalty programs, HUAC and McCarthy hearings, and Smith Act trials—the party retained about 25,497 members.[32] By 1957, after Khrushchev's speech, the FBI estimated that membership had sunk to 11,504.[33] By 1965, the bureau was estimating the group had been reduced to 3,693 members.[34] These figures were arrived at in no small measure because of the FBI's network of informants.

While COINTELPRO may have inaugurated a new type of disruptive activity, the gold standard of intelligence, informant penetration, continued. In 1958, the FBI reported having 408 informants supplying intelligence on the CP.[35] By 1968—despite an exponential loss of members—the FBI still had 318 informants.[36] The full story of CP informants was, however, bigger than the absolute number of people reporting to the FBI.

An important element of informant recruitment was the continuation of the TOPLEV program, the effort to flip "top-level" communists to inform on their comrades. TOPLEV, begun in 1952, had by March 1954 netted thirty new informants and confidential sources.[37] The bureau, pleased with such successes and wanting to build on it, in July 1957 published an internal report that served as a primer on the program. As they outlined, they considered there being "two principal stages to communist informant development." The first was "the subject's break with communism"; the second, and more consequential, was "the subject's assumption of an active role in combating communism." To get from one point to the next was, in their view, a transitional phase—"a mid-point between allegiance to the communist movements and positive cooperation as an informant." In this, "agents [need] to recognize the transitional phase . . . and to bring the subject into it, or observe that he is in it, before placing too much emphasis on winning his positive cooperation as an active informant." One reads the report as akin to the process of how a therapist or counselor, working through phases with a patient, does not want to push too far too fast for fear of alienating the subject. The limits of that analogy, however, were that the FBI was not concerned with helping the former communist but was attempting to weaponize them against their former comrades.

That same report noted the specific particularities of Black members: "As a group, Negroes in the communist movement have excellent potential for informant development." It noted that they had entered the movement for "the betterment of the status of their races" and/or for "personal gain in the form of economic and social advantage." In the bureau's experience, "successful interviews with Negroes demonstrated that an initial approach developed around the topic of civil rights often succeeded in engaging the subject in conversation when a direct reference to communism might have caused him to end the interview abruptly." One cannot help but be struck by how the bureau—too often dismissed as a simple-minded racist organization—sought to use the white supremacist landscape to their advantage.

Along with such insights, they noted that "agents had to have a thorough knowledge of communist theory" and that "agents had to have the ability to listen" and should employ "subtle flattery." As for those who "had a religious temperament . . . agents found it helpful to contrast the outstanding religious freedom and opportunity in the United States with restrictions imposed on religion in Soviet satellite states."[38]

***

The most important recruitment under TOPLEV was that of Jack and Morris Childs, recruited in 1952. Work with the brothers was proceeding so well that in 1958, the FBI gave the pair the confidential moniker: Operation SOLO.

By 1959, Morris Childs was delivering stunning insights to the FBI of the CP's internal operations. Exemplary of this is a memo from June 1959, "Eugene Dennis, National Secretary, Communist Party (CP), USA desired that CG 5824-S [Morris Childs's FBI code name] make another trip to Russia and China in late July or early August 1959, for the purpose of presenting the line of the majority of the CP, USA to the communist parties of the Soviet Union and China. In connection with this proposed trip, we are presenting specific missions for the informant to accomplish while abroad."[39] This memo makes clear that Morris Childs was not a run-of-the-mill snitch, supplying routine intelligence. Rather, he was someone operating at the highest levels of the party, tasked with carrying out key responsibilities.

SOLO would be as much an implement for gathering information on the CP as it was for accumulating intelligence on the thinking of the Soviet party. Author John Barron writes that by the late 1950s, the FBI had redirected the SOLO operation to more specifically monitor the Soviet Union, though the Childs brothers "continued, passively and incidentally, to gather information about party activities, especially those that might illuminate secret Soviet actions and intentions."[40]

While Barron's description holds a lot of truth, it belies how integral the SOLO operation was to the continued viability of the U.S. party. This was most on display in the fact that the Soviets were underwriting the American party. In the fall of 1961, based on information from the Childs brothers, the FBI reported that the Soviets had supplied the CPUSA with $714,385 (about $7,000,000 today), while China had given only $50,000 ($500,000 today). The way the money was dispensed is instructive. Among other things, it paid the funeral expenses of William Z. Foster, $800 ($8,000); the college tuition of Eugene Dennis's son—the elder Dennis had died that January—$1,700 ($17,000); funds to Gus Hall for operational costs of the CP National Office, $5,000 ($51,000); and a stipend to Gus Hall of $5,000 ($51,000).[41]

The funds coming from the USSR were no small matter. The party had gone from a membership base of tens of thousands to a dwindling cohort of a few thousand. With that loss of membership came the loss of a larger financial base. For the Soviets, who were locked into a highly dangerous cold war, the CPUSA was a key resource for insights into the situation in the United States—as skewed as what that group could offer—and an organization that could promote Soviet interests in the United States. While the Soviets may have had an exaggerated sense of the influence of the American party, they had to work with what was available.

Leveraging Discontent

Beyond simple informant recruitment was an attempt to use disaffected members in service of the bureau's larger agenda. In this, their efforts involving two former high-profile communists are instructive.

The author Howard Fast joined the Communist Party in 1943. He was known worldwide, having written books such as *Freedom Road*, *Citizen Tom Paine*, and *Spartacus*. Fast had also confronted the reactionaries during the 1949 Peekskill Riot.[42] He also served three months in prison—where he began writing *Spartacus*—in June 1950 for his refusal to cooperate with the HUAC, which was investigating the Joint Anti-Fascist Committee. Fast was one of eleven professionals convicted for contempt, which included the committee's chairman, Dr. Edward K. Barsky.[43] As such, Howard Fast, who represented the Communist Party culturally not only in the United States but globally, was an important symbol legitimating the communist position.

The Khrushchev speech, however, had been devastating for him. In its aftermath, he penned an essay for the communist publication *Mainstream* titled "My Decision," where he explained why he had decided to disassociate from the party. As he wrote, "I feel that the Communist Party of the United States—mostly through events beyond its control—is compromised to a point it can no longer make any effective contribution to the continuing struggle for democracy and social justice." It was a full-on break, born out of no small amount of internal turmoil. Regardless, if not surprisingly, it was received poorly by his former comrades.[44]

For the FBI, however, this was an opportunity not to be missed. They proceeded to duplicate Fast's article and mail it to party members. In the memo explaining their reasoning, they said, "The CP would find it extremely difficult to find valid and convincing reasons to publicly criticize the FBI for mailing copies of CP articles to CP members who are supposed to read the CP press anyway." As such, the article had been "anonymously disseminated via sixteen offices to more than 200 communists throughout the country."[45] Again, the FBI was using the internal conflicts within the Communist Party against it.

The FBI, as things developed, was not done with Fast. In early 1961 they decided to approach him directly and ask that he become an informant. While Fast did not fully turn on his former comrades, he was not entirely unhelpful: "[Fast] was interviewed by Agents of this Bureau on several occasions and although he did not furnish information concerning individuals with whom he was associated in the Party, he did give a good account of his own Party history and a general account of the workings of the Communist Party. It is believed that his defection is complete and that he no longer presents a menace to the internal security of the country."[46] The bureau's conclusion was consistent with their litmus test for loyalty. For them, it was not enough to quit the party. One had to declare their break with communism. Only by doing so could they be excluded from the FBI's ongoing attention. In that respect, Fast had ticked all the necessary boxes.

Another target of FBI attention, someone who had held an even more prominent position in the CP, was Earl Browder. Browder, who had been driven out of the party in a most humiliating way in 1945, was more than happy to talk, if on his own terms.

In the early 1960s, FBI agents had a series of meetings with Browder. The agents hooked him by playing on his ego. As they described their first encounter, "After a brief exchange of pleasantries, the agents explained that they had called upon BROWDER for the purpose of soliciting his opinion and viewpoints on the theoretical aspects of the current split between the Communist Parties of the Soviet Union and China." Browder took the bait.

What followed was an ongoing exchange where Browder—no longer in a position of prestige and respect in his former party—held forth. He "gave his opinion on the Sino-Soviet rift: China will eventually be isolated and forced to accede to the wishes of the CPSU [Communist Party of the Soviet Union]." He also told the agents that Stalin was "an absolute leader and dictator" who dissolved the Comintern "to complete his dictatorship." Further, he offered that Khrushchev was "not a theoretician" but was rather "a politician." Beyond that, he said—not entirely incorrectly—"he [Browder] was purged from the CP for advocating the same principles that KHRUSHCHEV is espousing today."

The agents and FBI could not have been more pleased: "In view of BROWDER'S friendly, cordial manner he will be recontacted within a period of 45 days. The interview will be carefully planned and material will be brought to him for his analysis."[47] They would go on to speak with him seven more times between 1963 and 1964. Each time they escalated the questioning to try to get hard intelligence. To Browder's credit, those efforts were not fruitful. For example, when they asked him about espionage for the Soviets, he denied there was such a thing. While this was no doubt in his own interests, it also indicated a certain line he would not cross.[48]

Like Howard Fast, Browder too was rewarded for his cooperation by being taken off the bureau's more aggressive radar: "It is felt that the subject might not have been completely cooperative during the interviews, but in view of his health [he had recently suffered a stroke], and age, it is believed that he does not constitute a threat against the security of the United States at the present time." They moved him from the Security Index—which required frequent updates and consequent surveillance—to the more passive Reserve Index.[49]

A Changed Dynamic

While the CPUSA continued as a far smaller group, it was still pursued by the HUAC—though the HUAC itself was losing power. This was on full display when San Francisco police turned fire hoses on the mainly student demonstrators who were being kept from entering the hearing rooms when the committee met in that city.[50] The incident made national news and sparked a report by the FBI to the HUAC outlining the current state of the communist movement among youth. In it, Hoover noted the impact of events such as the Cuban revolution and offered to the committee that "a spokesman at one of the party's national executive committee meetings" had recently noticed "students want to know what socialism is."[51] Communism may have been changing, but it was not—for the moment—going away.

Similar concerns were expressed by the committee's chairman, Frances E. Walter: "It was with only a relative few that Lenin seized control of the Government of Soviet Russia. Only a few—some 3 or 4 percent—in Soviet Russia today are Communists. Only 1 or 2 percent of the captive nations are Communists. The Communist conspiracy operating on American soil—let it be emphasized and reemphasized—is part and parcel of the world conspiracy and the thousands of communists in the United States are for all intents and purposes foreign agents on American soil who are dedicated to our destruction."[52] All his hyperbole and concerns about the power of small numbers aside, Walter's statement went to the nub of the concern for the U.S. power structure. The Communist Party was not only anathema to the principles of Western capitalism, but it was a vehicle of the United States' chief global rival. As such, it could be nothing other than an enemy. This was how the CP was viewed as it entered what would be an unprecedented period of tumult in the 1960s.

10

Hounded (1964–1970)

> It is a rough, tough, dirty business, and dangerous . . . that is dangerous to the persons who are being affected, not to the Bureau.
>
> **WILLIAM SULLIVAN**, FBI

The Communist Party entered the tumultuous sixties as a weakened and diminished organization. Along with the massive number of members who had left was the death of a large percentage of its veteran leadership. Adding to this, the Sino-Soviet split was becoming far more pronounced—something the FBI worked to their advantage. The HUAC was still investigating communists, the courts were weighing whether to demand party members formally register, and the FBI intensified its Counterintelligence Program aimed at the group. By the early 1970s, most of this would be at an end. However, the party would first have to go through it.

COINTELPRO and the Sino-Soviet Schism

The FBI had been keenly following the Sino-Soviet split, assessing its impact on the CP, and planning accordingly. In 1960, the bureau reported on a document circulating within the party that "in essence supports the Soviet position in its current ideological dispute with the CP of China." It went on to note, "If our informants are carefully briefed and instructed, they should be able to raise doubts as to whether this NEC [National Executive Committee] resolution should be approved and inject other controversial issues related to this dispute." In the FBI's view, and as part of their COINTELPRO aimed at the CPUSA, this was "a golden opportunity to utilize [their] informants in an effort to revive the factionalist situation that formerly existed between the right-wing and left-wing elements inside the CP, USA."[1] In this way, the bureau was again intervening in a major controversy in the communist world to push their own agenda.

To that end, in 1965 they held a one-day conference focused on the Sino-Soviet split. While the document detailing the event is highly redacted, certain things come through. Specifically, the bureau wanted agents with a certain level of sophistication: "Personnel participating in this conference must be thoroughly briefed on all phases of Communist Party USA activity within their respective field office territory as well as factional communist activity including pro-Chinese Communist organization and intelligence matters." It then lists as references for background a pro-Chinese faction of Belgium, the publication *Hammer and Steel* of the New England Party of Labor, *The Far East Reporter*, *The China Daily News*, China Books and Periodicals, and the Progressive Labor Movement.[2] All these, in one way or another, were either open to or sympathetic to the Maoist position in the Sino-Soviet split. While the political sophistication of the FBI has generally been given short shrift, reports such as this show that they paid considerable attention to such matters, and they did so amid a shifting and complex situation in the global communist world.

Flowing from that political understanding, and also as part of their COINTELPRO-CPUSA, the FBI had a particular focus on the Progressive Labor Movement (PLM)—later to be the Progressive Labor Party (PLP or PL). That group emerged after the expulsion of two top communists: Milt Rosen, formerly of the CP's New York State Committee, and Mort Scheer, who headed the Buffalo party.[3] PL was of particular focus because of its sympathy to Maoist China and its adversarial relationship with the CP. As the FBI wrote, "It is known that the 'Progressive Labor' group is a thorn in the side of the CP and has been strongly denounced in 'The Worker' (1/7/63)"—the party's Sunday newspaper.[4]

Early on, it appeared the FBI was scrambling to infiltrate PL. One missive coming out of Buffalo in October 1964 pointed out, "We had already advised that we would attempt to switch [CP] informants, where possible, into PLM clubs."[5] That problem resolved itself with the disappearance of the Buffalo group. As they reported in January 1965, "The spotlighting of PLM in April 1964, HCUA Hearings [under the title, 'Communist Activities in the Buffalo'] virtually destroyed that group locally."[6]

Regardless, the bureau pursued a program of harassment that would negatively impact both the Communist Party and Progressive Labor Movement. One of the measures they employed was targeting Bill Epton—a Korean War veteran running for New York City council as the PLM candidate. In doing this, the aim was to "antagonize the CP into renouncing EPTON as a candidate."[7] To that end, one of the measures they employed was mailing the campaign literature of Epton to the CP in hopes it would provoke as much.

Not only did they wish to undermine Epton's political campaign, but they also sought to pit the CP against PL and other groups. For example, the New York office suggested reaching out to PL and the Young Americans for Freedom "to suggest these organizations conduct counter demonstrations and distribute their literature at the communist [CPUSA] May Day celebration." The New York office also offered a bit of snark: "The participants in the May Day celebration in New York are of an unkempt and motley appearance"; as such, they suggested "pertinent photographs of a participant be made available to cooperative news media sources."[8] While the suggestion seems petty, the FBI's influence among certain media figures meant it was no less serious.

The Ad Hoc Scheme

The bureau's attention to the Sino-Soviet split had led them to mount efforts to split PL and the CP as part of the bureau's COINTELPRO-CPUSA effort. Another initiative anchored in that schism, objectively a counterintelligence operation, existed as a program in its own right. This was the creation of a national organization that mimicked that of a pro-Chinese faction operating within the Communist Party.

The bureau, despite the avalanche of disclosures that followed the 1975 Church Committee hearings, and the revelations after the conclusion of Operation SOLO in the early 1980s, has never publicly commented on its scheme called the Ad Hoc Committee for a Scientific Socialist Line, later named the Ad Hoc Committee for a Marxist-Leninist Party (AHC). Details of the undertaking, however, are laid out in the personnel file of Carl Freyman—someone the bureau was eager to extol because he was the agent who recruited Morris Childs.

Freyman's file reveals, in meticulous detail, the AHC operation. This comes through by way of a description of the accomplishments of Freyman's subordinate and the architect of the AHC, Herbert K. Stallings:

> It will be recalled that in November 1962, this agent [Stallings] created from his own imagination based upon developments within the communist movement in the Chicago area a non-existent Ad Hoc Committee (AHC) for a Scientific Socialist Line as the publishers of an anonymously circulated "Ad Hoc Bulletin." This bulletin, in direct line with the Bureau's overall objective, is designed to disrupt and fragmentize the communist movement in the Chicago area, and nationally if possible. It has taken a pro-Chinese, Marxist-Leninist line, and the general overall purpose of the bulletin is to create in the eyes of the CP the existence of a factional grouping within the Illinois District and nationally if possible which adheres to the Chinese interpretation of Marxism-Leninism, as against the pro-Soviet line of the CPUSA and the Illinois District.[9]

The bureau was fabricating an organization in order to exacerbate the problems the Sino-Soviet split was causing for the U.S. Communist Party.

This undertaking was both well thought through and audacious. In a memo recommending a bonus for Stallings, the FBI noted, "During the pertinent period this agent successfully continued this fictitious committee through the publication of five separate original documents, each with a specific purpose in mind, but all with the general overall purpose of causing factionalism within the CP." The bureau credited Stallings's "extensive knowledge of Marxism-Leninism" along with his "creative research and writing" in authoring these newsletters. As they pointed out, "Through the careful preparation of these and other documents by this agent, there has been no tie by the Party of this counterintelligence program to the Bureau and the potentialities for the continuance of this fictitious committee in the future remain unlimited."[10]

The results for the CP were significantly disruptive, leading to numerous expulsions. Here is how the bureau described one case in early 1964:

> [REDACTED] has possibly been expelled secretly. She no longer submits her club dues to the Party office. Other Party members have resigned or stopped attending meetings or have joined left-wing caucuses. The number in this category is unknown; however, there are six in a caucus headed by [REDACTED] out of the Railroad Club alone. It has also been reported that other individuals have quit the Party over the expulsion. There were also a number of people in the Nationality Section of the Party who are sympathetic to [REDACTED] who are no longer attending meetings of the CP. We feel that the total loss to the CP in expulsions, resignations, and those boycotting meetings could number approximately 25.[11]

All this the result of a phony newsletter—though the initiative would evolve to include several informants and reach beyond the CP organization alone.

Targeting Leadership

The "false flag" operation of the AHC aside, the FBI, as had long been the case, had as its chief target the CP's leadership. In March 1964, bureau headquarters distributed a Counterintelligence-CPUSA memo "requesting counterintelligence be initiated against all active members of the National Committee, CP, USA."[12] What ensued was a flurry of attacks.

Among them was a campaign inspired by a column from Elizabeth Gurley Flynn, chair of the National Committee, in *The Worker*, urging readers to offer their criticisms. As such, the bureau suggested agents "responsible for communist-type investigation" be told of Flynn's column and "urged to prepare such letters exposing the antics of various comrades."[13] The hypocrisy here is that the bureau, which never failed to criticize the CP for its authoritarian nature, decided to use this measure of openness to disrupt it.

More ominously, they sought to divide two of the group's most prestigious leaders—Ben Davis and Gus Hall. As they noted, "in the past, GUS

HALL harbored ill feelings toward BEN DAVIS" and even had "expressed the suspicion that BEN DAVIS was an FBI informant." This was based on the fact that Hall had once "observed DAVIS going through desk drawers other than his own at CP headquarters."

More substantially, they noted that Davis was frustrated that the party did not seem to be playing as big a role in the civil rights movement as he thought it should be. As they wrote, "DAVIS' dissatisfaction is in the open, [and] it is believed that DAVIS serves counterintelligence by remaining in the leadership of the CPUSA and openly criticizing the CP's stand regarding Negro Matters." As such, they felt that "when DAVIS has run his full course of criticism, consideration should then be given to further antagonize HALL against DAVIS. As DAVIS becomes more bitter and HALL becomes more critical of DAVIS, HALL will be in a better frame of mind to believe anything concerning DAVIS."[14] Such was the disruptive—and unscrupulous—long game they were playing.

A year later, in May 1964, they entertained another scheme, this to get Davis to renounce the party in full. "There is a possibility Davis might be prompted by his current situation to repudiate the communists on the basis that the Party is insincere in regard to the plight of the American Negro. It is possible we could instigate or encourage such action by him through the use of a third party such as an eminent and respected Negro or political leader." To that end, they considered having an outsider work on him, "a noncommunist personal friend of Davis, such as several of the individuals he met in Atlanta."[15] How that might have played out is anyone's guess. By this point, Davis was in the process of dying.

In June 1964, the FBI reported, "Davis has developed cancer and is reported to have a minimum of 6 months to live. Although he is not aware his current illness is terminal, when he does realize this, he is likely to have sincere reflections relating to the years he has wasted as a communist leader which resulted in his completely ineffectual effort to benefit his race." They reiterated their idea from the previous year: "There is a possibility Davis might be prompted by his current situation to repudiate the communists on the basis that the Party is insincere in regard to the plight of the American Negro."[16] The matter was still in the discussion and consideration phase when Davis died on August 22, 1964. The FBI coldly noted his passing, writing, "The Security Index cards in the NYO [New York office] have been destroyed."[17]

The Case of William Albertson

While the idea of playing up Gus Hall's baseless suspicions that Ben Davis was an informant never came to fruition, such was not the case with the district leader of the New York Party, William Albertson. The impetus for the "snitch jacketing" of Albertson came as a means to protect the bureau's most important intelligence undertaking, Operation SOLO, and its key operative, informant Morris Childs.

The framing of Albertson came about after a news report by the reactionary syndicated columnist Victor Riesel. In a piece written on April 14, 1964, Riesel reported on details of a leadership meeting of the CPUSA—something Gus Hall understood could be known by only fourteen or fifteen people.[18] How Riesel obtained his information is unclear. He was, himself, a staunch anticommunist, a sometime bureau asset, and plugged into multiple sources.[19] However, his column on the meeting was problematic for the FBI. That was because Morris Childs was among the people Hall knew were at the meeting. If suspicion ended up focusing on Childs, it would be devastating for the FBI and Operation SOLO. As such, they enacted a scheme to misdirect attention. They did so by planting a forged letter in William Albertson's car, one that appeared to be a message for his (fictional) FBI handler. Hall fell for it. As a result, Albertson was expelled from the party as an informant.

What is striking here is the cluelessness of the party's leadership in being manipulated in this manner. In 1965, Gus Hall pontificated about the evidence against Albertson in a report to the party's National Board. As an FBI report noted, he told the assembled comrades, "Two handwriting experts from New York, two from Chicago, one from Los Angeles as well as some from the Soviet Union, have viewed the letter and the conclusion was that only a 5% possible error existed." As the bureau summed up, "HALL felt there was nothing to talk about although doubts existed in the minds of some."[20]

The Albertson case is exemplary of the group's exaggerated confidence in its own internal security methods and helps explain how Morris Childs was able to stay in place for as long as he did. Rather than do a review of every person who could have leaked the information to the press, the party leadership was content to put the matter to rest on a single piece of—conveniently discovered—falsifiable evidence. That was all it took to disgrace a loyal comrade.

Nonetheless, for the FBI, it meant their informant, Morris Childs, was able to continue as the bureau's most highly placed source. He would never be discovered.

***

The attacks on Gus Hall, Ben Davis, and William Albertson were full-on. In contrast, the tack on Henry Winston was cautious—if for legal, rather than ethical, reasons. As the bureau reported, "WINSTON has a suit of $1,000,000 pending against the U.S. for negligence on the part of the government in caring for him in prison when he had a brain tumor which has left him partially blind." Given that, and the fact he had just returned from the Soviet Union and his responsibilities had not yet been set, they felt that "no counterintelligence action against WINSTON should be instituted until a very opportune occasion."[21] The FBI, engaging in all manner of underhanded deeds, was ever wary of undertakings that might expose them.

Aptheker and Healey

Party theoretician and National Board member Herbert Aptheker was a particular target of the FBI's Communist Party COINTELPRO operations. In the context of the upheaval arising throughout the country, they were especially concerned with undermining Aptheker's effectiveness on college campuses.

On May 2, 1963, FBI headquarters requested "the views of the Seattle Office as to how this menace to college-level citizens can be combated." Agents in Seattle responded that the best method for curtailing Aptheker's "pyrotechnic oratory" was to try to stop the appearances before they happened: "Where there is no fire, there is no need for the services of a fire department."[22] An example of such prevention had taken place the previous year—this being an organized disruption of another appearance. As Seattle reported, "The anti-Communist element had no difficulty seating themselves in advantageous positions." Once in place, they began "heckling and booing," culminating when "the entire anti-Communist assembly, on a cue from one of its leaders, arose and started marching through the aisles of the hall singing patriotic songs." They "then marched out of the hall into the mezzanine where they continued their serenade despite threats from a hastily organized Communist Party 'security squad.'" In an after-report, they bragged that there was "no indication [of] FBI involvement in this matter."[23]

The bureau was also keen to undermine Aptheker's role in something called the American Institute for Marxist Studies (AIMS)—an entity set to propagate Marxism. In their view, the institute was "a Communist Party-inspired and controlled propaganda vehicle" that needed disrupting.[24] What followed was a concerted effort to disrupt the project. The New York office drafted a statement to "be given the widest possible circulation," reading, "The CPUSA, in its constant effort to woo adherents to its philosophy if not actually into its ranks, is again forming a propaganda organization, this time a very subtle one under the name of the American Institute of Marxist Studies."[25]

In doing this, they did not want to step on themselves. As such, they noted a column by Fulton Lewis Jr.—a bureau journalistic source—"Dateline 4-14-64 (scheduled for release 4-15-64), exposes the communist Party control of AIMS, therefore, it is not desired you make further release of the statement you have previously submitted for release to cooperative news sources at the Seat of Government [Washington, D.C.]."[26] While ultimately the bureau was unable to stop the AIMS, it was not for want of trying.

***

On the West Coast, the bureau set their sights on party leader Dorothy Healey. In October 1958, they wrote and distributed a fabricated "opposition" leaflet—in the emphatic uppercase—which called into question her leadership. It read, "COMRADES: REMOVE DOROTHY HEALY [*sic*] FROM LEADERSHIP BEFORE FURTHER DAMAGE IS DONE. DOROTHY HEALY HAS IN THE PAST AND NOW IS TRYING TO CAUSE FRICTION WITHIN THE NATIONAL COMMITTEE; Why has DOROTHY continued to confuse the issues? cause friction? and disunity in our Party?"

The leaflet also suggested Healey was working with the authorities: "REMEMBER THIS: The House Un-American Activities Committee receives information from those who talk before it in closed sessions as well as open sessions. DOROTHY HEALY [*sic*] TESTIFIED RECENTLY BEFORE THIS BODY IN LOS ANGELES, IN A CLOSED SESSION

FOR MORE THAN FOUR HOURS AND FORTY-FIVE MINUTES. She says she told them NOTHING. THE COMMITTEE DOES NOT KEEP PEOPLE ON THE STAND FOR SUCH A LONG PERIOD UNLESS THEY SAY SOMETHING. ARE WE TO BELIEVE DOROTHY'S WORDS ON THIS TO THE PARTY? WE DON'T BELIEVE HER STORY . . . DO You????"[27] That plan fell flat. Healey would remain in the California CP for another fifteen years before resigning in 1973.[28]

Other Targets

While zeroing in on the party's leadership was a priority, the bureau was also quick to pick up on any opportunities against regular members. One unfortunate was discovered to have been arrested for narcotics. The bureau sent out a news release in the spring of 1963: "REDACTED a former official in New York City of the REDACTED a communist front organization was arrested on REDACTED along with several other beatniks in his apartment on the Lower East Side in New York as a wholesaler of narcotics." The press release went on to report that "REDACTED was caught with 50 pounds of marijuana and the paraphernalia for weighing and straining the dope." It concluded by speculating on connections: "Police are now looking for Junior's [the redactions make it unclear why they use this name] pipeline to communist countries and the source of his narcotics traffic. The Red Chinese have long used narcotics to weaken the youth of target countries."[29] It is unclear if any press picked up on the report and its more fantastic assertions.

While the bureau's claims in that instance come across as clownish, such was not the case with what they did to Aaron Libson. Libson was a communist activist living in Philadelphia. In 1966, he was arrested by undercover police in a "tearoom"—a restroom in a public park used for gay hookups—on a sodomy charge. Unfortunately for Libson, the FBI, who knew he was a communist, learned of the arrest.

What followed was a COINTELPRO operation to "neutralize Libson with the party and embarrass the party generally." To achieve this, they anonymously called James Dolsen, the head of the Philadelphia CP, and they also contacted one of their press contacts "who has been used quite successfully in the Counterintelligence Program and has always protected the Bureau's interests."[30]

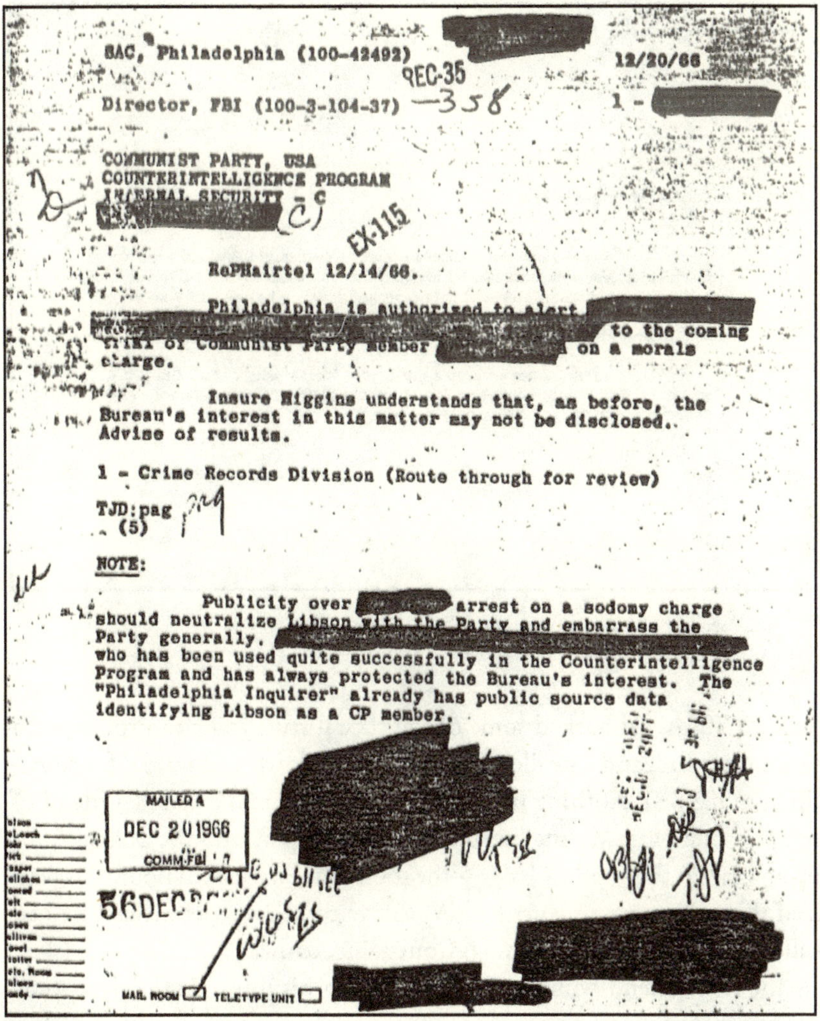

SAC, Philadelphia (100-42492) 12/20/66

REC-35

Director, FBI (100-3-104-37) —358 1 -

COMMUNIST PARTY, USA
COUNTERINTELLIGENCE PROGRAM
INTERNAL SECURITY - C
(C)

EX-115

RePHairtel 12/14/66.

Philadelphia is authorized to alert to the coming trial of Communist Party member on a morals charge.

Insure Higgins understands that, as before, the Bureau's interest in this matter may not be disclosed. Advise of results.

1 - Crime Records Division (Route through for review)

TJD:pag
(5)

NOTE:

Publicity over arrest on a sodomy charge should neutralize Libson with the Party and embarrass the Party generally. who has been used quite successfully in the Counterintelligence Program and has always protected the Bureau's interest. The "Philadelphia Inquirer" already has public source data identifying Libson as a CP member.

MAILED 4
DEC 20 1966
COMM-FBI

56DEC

MAIL ROOM TELETYPE UNIT

FIG. 10.1 FBI memo on Aaron Libson
FBI COINTELPRO memo

Libson would later describe what followed: “When I had the arrest, I pleaded nolo contendere—I do not wish to contend—on a Friday. The next day, Saturday, I woke up and got ready for work, and as I looked at the paper that morning, there was a small article saying, ‘Local Red arrested.’ I had a suicide plan ready just in case it came out, so I thought, OK, this is it and I carried out the plan.” As he recalled, “I wasn’t going to do anything at my house where my family would find me, so I rented a room at the Arch

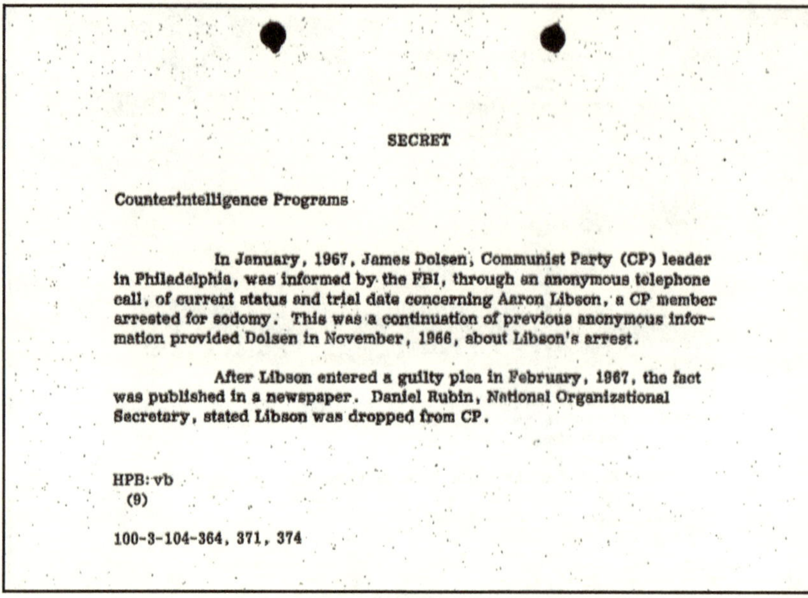

SECRET

Counterintelligence Programs

In January, 1967, James Dolsen, Communist Party (CP) leader in Philadelphia, was informed by the FBI, through an anonymous telephone call, of current status and trial date concerning Aaron Libson, a CP member arrested for sodomy. This was a continuation of previous anonymous information provided Dolsen in November, 1966, about Libson's arrest.

After Libson entered a guilty plea in February, 1967, the fact was published in a newspaper. Daniel Rubin, National Organizational Secretary, stated Libson was dropped from CP.

HPB:vb
(9)

100-3-104-364, 371, 374

FIG. 10.2 Second FBI memo on Aaron Libson
FBI COINTELPRO memo

Street YMCA. I'd packed some of the crystal stuff you clean toilets with in some tin foil, and I swallowed that and laid down and waited for something to happen. Nothing happened. In the interim, I'd called a friend of mine. While I was waiting for something to happen with the poison, I got up and sat on the window ledge—the room was on the fifth floor. . . . I realized the poison wasn't working." As things turned out, the friend he had called arrived and stopped things from going further.

The same friend would help Libson keep his job: "[He] called some people, including a lawyer, who called my job and talked to them. They said they had no problems with me coming back to work despite the arrest. From then on, I became known as the 'Gay Red' and people came to respect me to the point that I was elected union shop steward and then chief. People accepted me for who I was and how I presented myself."[31]

While all that was true, the bureau would nonetheless count it as a victory: "After Libson entered a guilty plea in February 1967, the fact was published in a newspaper, Daniel Rubin, National Organizational Secretary, stated Libson was dropped from the CP."[32]

COINTELPRO–Bob Dylan

One of the more outrageous—if peculiar—efforts by the bureau was a measure targeted at the Emergency Civil Liberties Committee (ECLC), a group with heavy CP participation aimed at asserting democratic rights. A few weeks after John F. Kennedy had been assassinated, the group held its annual awards dinner, where they presented the artist Bob Dylan with their Tom Paine Award. Unfortunately for the ECLC, Dylan had been drinking throughout the evening and was in a feisty mood. When he took the podium to accept the award, he gave a freely associating speech where he talked about youth, Cuba, and the Kennedy assassination: "I got to admit that the man who shot President Kennedy, Lee Oswald, I don't know exactly where—what he thought he was doing, but I got to admit honestly that I too—I saw some of myself in him. I don't think it would have gone—I don't think it could go that far. But I got to stand up and say I saw things that he felt, in me—not to go that far and shoot."[33] The audience responded to his remarks with boos and hisses. However, there were five FBI informants in the audience, and they reported back that Dylan had said, "I got to stand up and say I saw things that he felt, in me—not to go that far, *but he is not sure*" (emphasis added). The clause at the end, which Dylan did not say, cast the remarks far more provocatively, leading the FBI to report Dylan to the "Secret Service, Assistant Attorney General Yeagley, and to the intelligence agencies of the armed services."[34]

Dylan would offer a quasi-apology afterward, issuing a statement saying, "When I spoke of Lee Oswald, I was speakin of the times I was not speakin of his deed if it was his deed the deed speaks for itself." However, the FBI turned the incident into a COINTELPRO operation: "Under the Counterintelligence Program, it is urged that this statement of BOB DYLAN, made at this meeting, be brought to the attention of all the bureau's contacts in the mass media field so that proper publicity will be given to DYLAN, who by means of his folk singing, has the ability to have some communication with American youth. In addition, publicity of this sort will point up the type of organization the Emergency Civil Liberties Committee is to honor an individual of Dylan's mentality."[35] As a result, a journalistic source of the bureau, nationally syndicated columnist Fulton Lewis Jr., published a report that detailed the dinner, noting the attendance of Robert Thompson, a "top-ranking Communist official once convicted of violating the Smith Act, and Harvey O'Connor, the oft-identified Communist." It also slammed James Baldwin, who too was honored at the dinner, as a "liberal egghead." He then turned his pen on Dylan: "The [ECLC] Tom Paine Award went to folksinger Bob Dylan, who wore dirty chinos and a worn-out shirt. He accepted the award 'on behalf of all those who went to Cuba because they're young and I'm young and I'm proud of it.' He went on to say that he saw part of Lee Harvey Oswald 'in myself.' "[36] Lewis's ties to Hoover and thus the FBI can be seen in a letter Hoover wrote soon after the journalist's death, with a note on the bottom that read, "Fulton Lewis, Jr., was a good friend to the Bureau and the Director."[37]

How this impacted the ECLC is hard to say. However, the incident came at a time when Dylan's career was in transition, and he was already under attack from some in the liberal and left-wing folk music milieu. The publicity the FBI generated around this event could not but have added to his difficulties.

Antisemitism

A major focus of counterintelligence measures against the CP was the exploitation of the mistreatment of Jews in the Soviet Union, using it as a wedge within the CP—a group with a considerable number of members with Jewish heritage. In the view of the FBI, "The issue of anti-Semitism within the Soviet Union is extremely sensitive to the communists and no counterintelligence opportunities should be overlooked."[38]

As such, they enthusiastically reported in 1962, "During the past year, for example, out of 21 anonymous mailings of anti-communist literature to long time active communists, ten of these have involved the issue of anti-Semitism in the Soviet Union." While the agents did not claim to know "the full extent of [their] success under this phase of psychological warfare," they did "know that the receipt of this type of literature [had] raised doubts and concern on the part of the recipients and they [were] becoming more insistent that Party leaders answer questions regarding anti-Semitism in the Soviet Union."[39]

In this, they were not simply relying on their own efforts but using the media to do the work for them. As such, they documented a list of articles anonymously mailed. Among them were the following:

3/26/62 *NY Herald Tribune*, "Two Jews Executed in Russia."
3/15/62 *NY Herald Tribune*, "Fear for the Jews in Soviet."
4/10/62 *NY Herald Tribune*, "Red Firing Squads Kill Three Lithuanian Jews."
3/12/62 *New York Times*, "Change in Problems of Jews Is Cited."
3/13/62 *New York Times*, Letter to the Times: "Discrimination Against Judaism in the Soviet Union."[40]

The report went on to list several more articles that had been mailed.

Along with the mailings, the FBI worked with the American Jewish Committee (AJC): "The NYO has discreetly provided a contact at the AJC material regarding anti-Semitism in the USSR for use in the preparation of articles published by AJC." It continued, "The NYO has casually suggested to this contact that non-Jewish leaders in American business and art be requested to aid the cause of those Jews in the USSR who are being persecuted."[41]

It also reported on the efforts of the Workmen's Circle, a Jewish cultural organization: "[The Circle] has announced it will organize a 'National Indignation Week' to arouse American public opinion against the USSR because of the Soviet Union's anti-Semitism, picketing at the UN and Soviet Embassy are planned." As such, the New York FBI "suggested the Bureau, through its contacts in the mass media field, give as much publicity as possible to these activities."[42]

Such use of the matter of antisemitism would be something both the larger political and cultural apparatus would opportunistically use as the Cold War proceeded toward its final phase.

Ridicule, Etcetera

COINTELPRO operated on many levels, from the incendiary to the infantile. This comes through in various "ridicule" campaigns. In 1966, the bureau developed an anonymous mailing, listing sarcastically titled publications the party's Jefferson Book Store in New York was said to carry.[43] Among the items listed was "'Soviet Medical Progress Today,' by Wm. Z. Foster and Eliz. Gurley Flynn." Both Flynn and Foster had died while being treated in the Soviet Union. Another title, "How to Succeed in Real Estate by Claude Lightfoot," referred to the Black communist leader in Chicago who had been accused by the *Chicago Tribune* of being a slumlord, this because of a property

JEFFERSON BOOK STORE
100 East 16th Street
New York City

Announcement Announcement

The following books are also available at the
Modern Book Store in Chicago and Global Books in Detroit:

How to Live Like a Millionaire on $85 a week by Gus Hall.

Chaste Makes Waste by Dorothy Healy and a host of Co-Authors.

How to Succeed in Real Estate by Claude Lightfoot.

Soviet Medical Progress Today by Wm. Z. Foster and
Eliz. Gurley Flynn.

A Communist Youth's Guide to Good Grooming by [redacted]

How Political Indoctrination Almost Cured My Son From
Smoking Pot by Henry Winston.

Still Available: A History of Labor Unions in the USSR by
Joseph Stalin (A one page leaflet).

FREE

"Be Kind to Communists"
button with every purchase.

Other Buttons for Sale:

Alienation Can Be Fun
Stamp Out Reality
All for Hall
No Equal Rights for Birchites
Let the State Disintegrate

SOVIET UNION TRAVEL KITS

Kit includes:

1. Pair of rose colored glasses.
2. Secret list of synagogues in S.U. (showing all three locations).
3. "I Hate Khrushchev" button with removable name plate.
4. New Soviet regulations on Search and Seizure.

We change American money into Rubles at Official Exchange Rates.

Rubles changed to American money at unofficial rate.

To what do you attribute your child's membership in the Communist
Party?

Herbert Aptheker - "It was mainly proper parental guidance".

Why did your children never join the Communist Party?

Gus Hall - "They don't want a government which will make them
share the wealth they are going to inherit".

ENCLOSURE

FIG. 10.3 Circular developed to ridicule the CP's Jefferson Book Store
FBI COINTELPRO files

he had inherited from his parents.[44] Finally, the fake ad advertised free buttons reading "Alienation Can Be Fun" and "Let the State Disintegrate"—that is, LSD. The "inside baseball" content and outright weirdness of the ad were probably its most striking features.[45]

The bureau also had a penchant for doggerel. One of these involved mailing postcards with the following verse, claiming to be written by Gus Hall:

A Message From Our Leader:

Once we were many
But now we are few.
At the rate we are going,
We'll soon be just two . . .

Another project came in the form of a newsletter titled "Party Affairs," which they described as "a cross-section of humor; jokes and poems, tending to ridicule, discredit and show disrespect for current and deceased Party members." One exemplary "poem" targeted the recently deceased William Z. Foster, who had undergone treatment in the Soviet Union.

THE LATE WM. Z. FOSTER
To the Soviet Union went ill WM. Z.
To acquire a cure for his bad malady
But the Russian M.D.s with skill were not blessed
And poor WM. Z. became their bequest.[46]

It is difficult to fathom what the FBI thought this would accomplish, beyond letting the receiving communists know they knew how to contact them.

One last COINTELPRO measure is worth recapping here. In 1966, utilizing their "Crime Records Division"—the euphemistic title for the FBI section that organized sending material to friendly news sources—the bureau launched a COINTELPRO against a summer camp. The camp, called Webatuck, was also known as Camp Unity and was attended by Black and white youth.

The bureau initiated a scheme that involved sending information to the *New York Daily News*, which they "expected to fully develop this story so as to completely expose and disrupt this secret communist school." They were not wrong. What resulted was a full front-page story—in two-inch-high letters—"Inside a Secret Commie Camp." The account claimed, "Big name leaders of the Communist Party are instructing hand-picked youth from throughout the US on how to infiltrate the civil rights movement as professional agitators."[47]

While the article could be dismissed as sensational and hyperbolic, the fact that the FBI, in 1966, could manipulate a major paper into making an anticommunist story its front page—in the country's largest city—was no small accomplishment.

Hoodwink

Beyond COINTELPRO, one other FBI anticommunist undertaking is worth mentioning. In 1966, the bureau initiated something it called

Operation Hoodwink, aimed at creating dissension between La Cosa Nostra and the CP.

The effort, by any account, was playing with fire. It is difficult to imagine the bureau was not aware it could lead to people being killed—something they appear to have been all too comfortable with. One of the things they did to that end was send a fictitious letter to *The Daily Worker*—hoping it would be reprinted—from someone they named "I. Cohen." In it, they asked the paper to point out "the dangers of La Cosa [Nostra, or LCN]" and to have the paper "inform the working and oppressed classes" of the "nefarious practices" of "organized criminal elements." It does not appear the letter was published.

Another poison-pen letter was used in a mailing, came in the aftermath of someone throwing an explosive device into the basement of the party's headquarters on Twenty-Sixth Street. While no one was hurt, the bomb blew out windows and damaged the basement. In the aftermath of that incident, the FBI, using addresses recently printed in a story in *The New York Times* on the Mafia, sent a letter to the heads of the New York crime families. Addressed "Mr. Hoodlum Leader," it accused them of the bombing and threatened, "Someday through socialist reform, we Communists will take over this country and then we will be able to fight you people good with our own bombs and guns."[48]

Despite their best provocative efforts, the program failed to achieve the requisite "tangible results." As such, the New York office reported, "The NYO knows of no present issues which might precipitate a clash between the CP, USA, and LCN."[49] Here again, it was not for want of trying.

The Sixties' Impact

The efforts aimed at the CP came about at a time when the larger threats to the "internal security" of the United States lay elsewhere. While the CP retained a marginal political viability, it was increasingly challenged by the rise of the New Left—most prominently in the Students for a Democratic Society—and the Black freedom and Black liberation movements, with such groups as the Student Non-Violent Coordinating Committee, the Black Panther Party, and Revolutionary Action Movement, this along with the massive anti–Vietnam War movement, which operated through different organizational entities.

While the CP sought to work with and influence those movements, it was simply not capable of being as radical as what was going on. As Los Angeles communist leader Dorothy Healey noted, "In the 1960s the Soviet Union had little or no appeal to young people—Black or white—as a model of revolution or of a desirable socialist society. It seemed old, staid, repressive, and even counter-revolutionary to young activists."[50]

That last point was on display when Soviet tanks rolled into Czechoslovakia in August 1968 to squelch the reform movement led by Alexander Dubcek. For the rebellious youth and others, this was anathema to everything they were undertaking. For their part, the CP leadership was more than a little uncomfortable with these new radicals. As Daniel Rosenberg, citing one member, writes, "Many in leadership hated the 1960s. And were unable to deal with young people coming in who reflected those experiences."[51]

***

Paradoxically, it was at this time of great social and political upheaval that major elements of governmental repressive control were undone—largely in the interests of calming the social tumult and retaining legitimacy. This had begun in 1957, when the Supreme Court reversed its earlier upholding of the Smith Act, this in response to a challenge by the California communists who had been convicted under the act in 1951. Though the Smith Act would stay on the books, it would now draw a distinction between abstract advocacy and advocacy as a prelude to or initiation of violent action—the latter being criminal, the former not.[52] The decision essentially led the way to ending the Smith Act as an instrument to imprison communists.

Matters did not stop there. In 1964, the court issued a ruling in the case of *Aptheker v. Secretary of State*, named after party theoretician Herbert Aptheker. The case successfully challenged the provision of the McCarran Act (the Subversive Control Act of 1950), which prohibited a communist from obtaining a passport.[53] That decision was followed in 1965 by the ruling in *Albertson v. Subversive Activities Control Board* (SACB)—Albertson being the same person as the victim of FBI snitch jacketing. The ruling struck down the provision mandating communist registration. It did so based on the Fifth Amendment protection against self-incrimination.[54] The SACB would take a further blow in 1967 when the Supreme Court eliminated the proscription of communists working for the federal government.[55]

Finally, in 1969 the Supreme Court issued a decision in *Brandenburg v. Ohio*, which overturned a criminal syndicalism conviction against a leader of the Ku Klux Klan. The ruling held, "A state may not forbid speech advocating the use of force or unlawful conduct unless this advocacy is directed to inciting or producing imminent lawless action and is likely to incite or produce such action."[56] This effectively nullified the multitude of criminal syndicalism and criminal anarchy laws that had made it a crime to teach and advocate the principles of revolution.

***

The reversing of these laws happened at a time when the CP was arguably the weakest it had ever been. They had lost tens of thousands of members; the majority of their veteran leaders were aged, dead, or dying; and the Soviet Union held little appeal for those inspired by things such as the revolution in Cuba or the radicalism of the Chinese communists.

Had it not been for the CP's ongoing relationship with the CPSU, it is conceivable they would have garnered only minimal attention from the U.S. government. That, however, was not the case. What this meant is they would continue to be a target of congressional investigators, FBI special agents, and others throughout the seventies and eighties, up until the collapse of the Soviet Union in 1991.

11

Final Conflicts (1971–1991)

> My fellow Americans, I am pleased to tell you today that I've signed legislation that will outlaw Russia forever. We begin bombing in five minutes.
>
> **RONALD REAGAN**, "joking" in 1983

The Communist Party entered the seventies bruised, battered, and decimated. It remained, nonetheless, a coherent organization with the abilities that come from years of experience and the mere fact of not having been obliterated. However, just as the group's origins were integrally tethered to the creation of the Soviet Union, their raison d'être in their later years was firmly linked to the fragile empire, which had become their key benefactor. As such, its implosion would mean a decimation beyond anything it had encountered up to that point.

The Watergate Era

In 1975, the Senate convened its Select Committee to Study Governmental Operations with Respect to Intelligence Activities—popularly known as the Church Committee, after its chairman, Idaho Senator Frank Church. The committee—charged with investigating the malfeasance of the Central Intelligence Agency, the National Security Agency, the Internal Revenue Service, and the FBI—unearthed a treasure chest of secrets on the part of these agencies, including significant details on the FBI's Counterintelligence Program.

The Church Committee affirmed the extensive reach of the bureau and the presidential decisions that drove them. As they reported, not only did FDR empower the agency to take charge of domestic intelligence in the run-up to World War II: "Two public presidential statements on FBI domestic intelligence authority by President Truman in 1950 and by President Eisenhower in 1953 specifically declared that the FBI was authorized to investigate 'subversive activity,' electing the broader interpretation of the conflicting Roosevelt directives." Despite the Church Committee's language suggesting the FBI wantonly pushed the limits—"electing the broader interpretation" of directives—the overarching fact was that the bureau was but one element in a systemic drive against U.S. communism, a drive that would continue.

One of the more sensational elements the committee revealed was the specifics of the Counterintelligence Program (COINTELPRO). COINTELPRO had come to light inadvertently, after a group of peace activists conducted a break-in at an FBI regional office in Media, Pennsylvania, a suburb of Philadelphia. Among the thousands of pages of documents the group seized was a reprint of a *Barron's* article discussing how college protests should be handled more forcefully. Attached to the article was a routing slip dated August 9, 1968, with the subject "COINTELPRO-New Left." The stolen material was in turn mailed to the press, most of whom ignored it. One journalist, however, Betty Medsger at *The Washington Post*, did not. As a result, news of the Counterintelligence Program, which had been a closely held secret for the past fifteen years, ever so tentatively made its way into the public.[1]

As a consequence of the seized material, when Congress dug into the mandate and actions of the FBI, COINTELPRO became a focus. They then demanded and began to receive an avalanche of documents detailing the particular programs: against white hate groups, Black hate groups, the Socialist Workers Party, the New Left, and the largest of all, "Counterintelligence Program: Communist Party."

Problematizing this for the authorities was that Operation SOLO, while not a COINTELPRO undertaking, was integrally related to it. As such, the Church Committee, which was digging into the efforts aimed at Martin Luther King Jr., had to be briefed on the FBI's intelligence on a King adviser named Stanley Levinson, someone Morris and Jack Childs claimed was a secret communist. As such, when the matter of efforts the bureau leveled at King came up, things became tricky. This comes through in an exchange between Senator Church and the FBI's Deputy Director, James B. Adams:

> THE CHAIRMAN: Why did the FBI do it? [pursue King]
>
> MR. ADAMS: Well, we have to approach two parts, in my estimation, Senator Church. One, the basis for our investigation of Martin Luther King, which was to determine Communist influence on him, my hands are tied in discussing that, somewhat on the basis that there is certain information which today, from an ongoing operation is sensitive and which, of course, we have made known to you and certain staff members. I would like to say on the basis that from our review we feel that we initially had a basis for investigating Martin Luther King.[2]

Adams's "hands were tied" because Jack Childs—one-half of Operation SOLO—was the person who had told the FBI that Levinson was a communist. It would take the work of historian David Garrow to finally bring to light the fact that the Childs brothers were high-level informants. In researching his book on King and the FBI, Garrow shows how he had to fight for disclosure of SOLO—an effort that was only successful *after* that program was shut down.[3] The reason for keeping it secret was simple enough. In 1975, the Soviet Union still existed—and would continue to do so for the next fifteen years. As such, the bureau and the government they served were not going to expose such a precious stream of information, just as they were not going to relent in their unwelcome attentions to the CP.

That helps explain why Attorney General Edward Levi's April 1976 restrictions on domestic security investigations carried certain exceptions. While those rules dictated that mere advocacy of violence was not sufficient for the FBI to initiate an investigation, it included the caveat that any group deemed to be working to advance the interest of a foreign power *could* be scrutinized.[4] As such, the CPUSA would remain a focus. Not only that, but Congress in 1978 enacted the Foreign Intelligence Surveillance Act (FISA), which established the Foreign Intelligence Surveillance Court (FISC). The law and the court were measures that created a wholly legal mechanism for the surveillance of groups such as the CPUSA.

The court itself was made up of eleven federal judges picked by the chief justice of the United States. The court worked via nonpublic—secret—sessions. In these, the only people present were one judge and a government representative. The court's authority allowed it to issue orders for electronic surveillance, monitoring phone calls, physical searches, and combing through business records.[5] The bar for approval required only showing the "target of the surveillance is a foreign power or agent of a foreign power" or that a foreign political organization or group was suspected of being engaged in international terrorism.[6]

In 1979, of the 199 applications put before the court for orders and extensions of surveillance, all were approved.[7] While the exact nature of the cases is not known, what is known is that Operation SOLO continued, and the government kept an open investigation of the CPUSA going throughout the decade of the 1980s.

More Open

The tumult of the sixties had upended a solid chunk of the anticommunist consensus that had been in effect since the darkest days of the Second Red Scare. The country had seen riots of unprecedented ferocity in nearly every major city, its campuses had been racked by demonstrations and confrontations that had spiraled into open street fighting, and the military had come through the loss of the Vietnam War battered and fractured. Given that, the ability of the powers that be to implement and enforce the types of laws they had brought down in the twenties and forties was seriously constrained—and counterproductive to reasserting the legitimacy of those responsible for governing. It was in such a situation that some of the limits on radical and revolutionary organizing—including the freedom to openly advocate violent revolution—were removed. In their place, the main limits were reserved for those who planned, or had undertaken, violent action.

In this situation, the CPUSA could now operate in ways previously unimaginable. They even publicly heralded that they had reintroduced membership cards, the former smoking gun of proof used by Congress and the FBI to pursue and indict party members. According to Gus Hall, "The younger people wanted them. They're proud to be Communists." As he explained, "It's a pleasure to present the party's position now. What's interesting is that you very seldom meet someone who is purposefully nasty. People disagree, but they are respectful."[8]

Unfortunately, this newfound freedom coincided with the party now being but one of many small and marginal entities in U.S. society. Even more problematically, it occurred at a time when the FBI had achieved the pinnacle of its infiltration of the group.

A Compromised Vehicle

In 1968, the bureau reported having 318 informants in the CP.[9] By 1975, that number had dropped to 203.[10] However, given the bureau had calculated the group's membership at just shy of 3,700 in the mid-1960s, and the likelihood is that it had diminished in the 1970s, it is reasonable to assume the per capita ratio of informants to members continued to be alarmingly high (*if* the group had four thousand members at that time, about one of every twenty would have been an informant).[11]

Even were that not the case, the CP had a far bigger problem. While they claimed Henry Winston held the spot of second in command after Gus Hall, the FBI saw things differently. For them, the "number two man in the American party" was their informant, Morris Childs.[12] Childs had thoroughly ingratiated himself with Hall, in no small part because he was the conduit for major funding from the Soviet Union. By 1977, he had made fifty-two missions to Moscow on behalf of Hall and the U.S. party. These visits, among other things, involved Childs lobbying for and collecting funds from the Soviets. This went from $1,066,742 in 1970 ($8.6M today) to $1,792,676 in 1975 ($10.4M), to $2,775,000 in 1980 ($10.6M).[13] These were staggering sums.

Money of that caliber could not but have a qualitative impact on the group. Despite the best intentions and progressive activity of rank and file members, who were unaware of the transfer of funds, the efforts of the CPUSA were largely underwritten by the Soviets. Worse—and this was a mighty paradox—that underwriting was facilitated in large part by the efforts of two disaffected comrades working intimately with the U.S. government as spies against the Soviets. Put starkly, throughout the 1960s into the 1980s, the FBI was instrumental in facilitating the considerable funding—and, by extension, the operation—of the CPUSA.

All this was in line with the transformation of the CP from a domestic radical force to a well-funded instrument to promulgate Soviet interests inside the United States. While the reasons for the U.S. government pursuing the group had fundamentally changed, from combating their radical influence to countering their efforts on behalf of a foreign power, the necessity to suppress them had not.

***

The work of Jack and Morris Childs also made the bureau privy to the most nuanced problems of the party. With the rise of revolutionary Black nationalism, represented by people such as Eldridge Cleaver, Stokely Carmichael (Kwame Ture), and Huey Newton, the CP was increasingly having internal tensions with Black communists. This can be seen in the following from Jack Childs:

> HALL stated that in addition to HENRY WINSTON, others who are causing him problems are REDACTED and the attitude of ANGELA DAVIS in regard to the CP defense efforts in her behalf, Furthermore, HALL is not at all happy with JAMES JACKSON, HALL could be satisfied with JACKSON'S activities if JACKSON would settle down to work; however, JACKSON always seems to get lost somewhere. This is true to such an extent that when JACKSON returned from Venezuela recently, HALL had to press JACKSON very hard to get him to give a report to the Political Committee, CPUSA, When JACKSON gave his report, the report was so vague and general that it was worth nothing.[14]

The reference to Angela Davis revolved around one of the rare bright spots, fraught as it was, for the CP in the early 1970s. Davis, a communist professor from Southern California, had been targeted by the government because guns registered in her name were used by the Black revolutionary Jonathan Jackson at the Marin County Courthouse, where he took hostages—and was later killed along with two prisoners and a judge—in a failed effort to free his brother George Jackson. While there was no evidence Davis supported the action, the fact that her weapons were used allowed the government to pursue her as an accessory. The international campaign to free her buoyed the CP's radical credibility at a time when they had largely been relegated to the background.[15]

In another entry in Jack Childs's file, Hall appears to have been especially frustrated with his fellow Smith Act defendant Henry Winston: "HALL stated that HENRY WINSTON is obviously being consumed by his black nationalism. He noted that [NY communist] TED BASSETT wrote an excellent reply to the attack on the CPUSA by ELDRIDGE CLEAVER of the Black Panther Party (BPP). Yet, WINSTON attacked BASSETT for writing that article, The fact of the matter is that WINSTON condemns the Panthers privately but never moves a finger to condemn by name either the Panthers or the other revolutionaries. According to HALL, WINSTON encourages these black militants and their nationalism."[16] This was meaty stuff. Aside from highlighting the challenges the CP confronted vis-à-vis the revolutionary Black nationalist movement is the fact that there was very little that went on within the CP throughout the 1960s and 1970s that the FBI did not know about.

Into the Eighties

The 1970s, as it would turn out, were only a brief interlude between the Vietnam Era and the final phase of the Cold War. The era of "Détente" was quickly replaced by heightened tensions, which reached a tipping point in December 1979 with the Soviet invasion of Afghanistan.

As the new decade began, Gus Hall and his party promoted themselves with high-profile, but overwhelmingly symbolic, runs for the U.S. presidency in 1972 and 1976 with Black comrade Jarvis Tyner as the vice-presidential candidate. In 1980, Hall would again run, this time with Angela Davis.

Profiling the group, *The New York Times* underscored the official conservatism of the CP: "The Communist Party considers itself very respectable." Notably, the group was able to gain rights to appear on the ballot in twenty-four states and in the District of Columbia—"the most since the 1930s." In Hall's view, "We are the only responsible left party. The other left, the ultraleft, the TV radicals, I call them, they just leech onto our meetings. One so-called party disappears, another comes. Everyone wants to

FIG. 11.1 Vote Communist: Gus Hall for president, Jarvis Tyner for vice president, 1975 or 1976 Communist Party of the United States of America, https://www.loc.gov/pictures/item/2016648826/

know what happened to the New Left? They're in the Communist Party U.S.A."[17] That assessment, though hyperbolic, bore elements of truth. Having a strong financial base—if because of Soviet support—and a seasoned cadre who had confronted, and largely withstood, the extreme repression meted out to them was no mean feat.

That said, the electoral runs for president were depressing affairs. The best showing they had was in 1976—the pinnacle of disarray for the U.S. ruling apparatus—with the Hall ticket garnering all of 58,709 votes, or .07 percent. In this, they were far behind the Trotskyist Socialist Workers Party's candidate, Peter Camejo, who garnered 90,986. Worse, white supremacist Lester Maddox garnered considerably more than either leftist with 170,373 votes.[18]

As such, the CP was hardly a political threat in any meaningful way. The reason for the FBI's and the United States national security apparatus's continued concern with them was the position they occupied in what was to become the final phase of the Cold War.

The Reagan Years

The CP received renewed repressive attention with the ascent of Ronald Reagan to the presidency in 1981. While Reagan pushed for new and more deadly weapons for the United States' contention with the Soviet Union—the fantastical Star Wars scheme among them—the CP countered by taking an active role in the disarmament and anti–nuclear weapons movement.

The FBI, of course, was monitoring this. In 1982, Edward J. O'Malley, the bureau's assistant director for intelligence, testified before Congress. He noted that the CP was "outside the mainstream of American political life" and that while it lacked "organizational strength and a large membership," it nonetheless had "responded to Soviet requests for assistance with fervor." Further, he outlined what he saw as the group's problematic activity: "The organization has initiated letter-writing campaigns, sponsored and participated in demonstrations and rallies, formed coalitions with other organizations, and sponsored seminars and workshops to promote Soviet views on arms control and disarmament matters to spur the American peace movement."[19]

Given the world had entered a period of danger not seen since the Cuban Missile Crisis or the Korean War, it is difficult to fathom activity in the pursuit of lessening the possibility of a nuclear exchange as threatening or dangerous. Yet given what the Reagan administration was undertaking against the Soviets, it was.

***

Congress also turned its attention to another matter regarding the CP. In hearings, Alabama Senator Jeremiah Denton brought up "another issue; namely, the registration of CP, Communist Party of U.S.A., as foreign agents." Referencing earlier testimony from the FBI, he noted that "the KGB has clandestinely transferred funds to the CPUSA" and that Soviet officials working through their embassy in Washington and the Soviet Mission in the United Nations were "in regular contact with CPUSA members and officials of CPUSA front groups." As such, he asked FBI Director William Webster, "Why was the Communist Party not required to register?" Webster responded, "I believe we are now in the area of discussing an investigative technique and an investigative strategy in the area of foreign counterintelligence, and for that reason, I would like to answer that question in the closed session."[20]

Webster's response was a result of the need to hide the fact that Operation SOLO had been the key instrument in those funds having made their way to the CPUSA. The exchange with Denton, which took place in February 1983, occurred after word of Operation SOLO had become public. However, while *The Washington Post* had broken the story of Professor David Garrow's discovery in September 1981, the details were minimal.[21] The SOLO files themselves, which held information of the money flowing to the CPUSA, would not be released for another twenty years.[22]

Regardless, when initial news of Operation SOLO broke, the reaction from the Communist Party was denial. *The Washington Post* reached out to Lem Harris, a party member from Connecticut who had known the Childs brothers—Jack by then was dead and Morris in secret retirement. As they reported, Harris "thought it unlikely that they were FBI informants. 'If the FBI discovered the Soviets funding the American Communist Party,' he said, 'I'm sure they would have trumpeted the news because that's just what Hoover would have wanted.'" It was a response consistent with a view on the part of many communists that they were more clever than the bureau. Gus Hall's reaction was more telling. According to a friend with him at the time, on learning of the informants, he "became ashen."[23]

That SOLO lasted as long as it did was not a matter of naivete, stupidity, or laziness. As historian Daniel Rosenberg notes, there had, in fact, been suspicions. However, "Despite queries from Commission members, the NRC [National Review Commission] did not consider the possibility that Morris Childs was an FBI asset."[24] This is not particularly surprising. The reality was that the party had a vested interest in such a thing *not* being true.

***

SOLO or not, Ronald Reagan's CIA Director William Casey was keeping the spotlight on communism and the CP. In a 1985 speech to the Dallas Council on World Affairs, he noted, "The Soviet Communist Party's International Information Department is responsible for developing and overseeing the implementation of Soviet media campaigns. Another organ of the Communist Party, the International Department of the Communist Party, coordinates the activities of the various front groups and friendship societies, as well as the role of foreign communist parties."[25] The party may not have been garnering the repressive attention it had merited in earlier years, but it was hardly out of the headlights.

A sense of the attention being levied came by way of a scandal of the bureau's operations against a coalition supporting the left-wing forces then fighting a civil war in El Salvador. The coalition went by the acronym CISPES, standing for Committee in Solidarity with the People of El Salvador. According to Reagan's press secretary, Marlin Fitzwater, the government had "reason to believe that CISPES was engaged in international terrorism or supported known terrorist elements"; Fitzwater also told the press that as a result of FBI reports, the administration believed CISPES "was established with the assistance of the Communist Party U.S.A. and the Communist Party of El Salvador."[26] It was a broad and specious allegation, categorically denied by the group.

In the mid-1980s, the Church Committee hearings and the Levy guidelines on domestic security investigation were still fresh. As such, any revelation that the FBI was returning to earlier behavior was controversial and newsworthy. As a result, Congress held hearings to investigate the matter. During the hearings, Wisconsin Representative James Sensenbrenner raised the idea of a wider communist conspiracy: "It must also be made clear that CISPES is not the Boy Scouts. According to available information, CISPES was established with the assistance of the American Communist Party, the U.S. Peace Council, and the Salvadoran Communist Party."[27] The spotlight shone on the FBI's activity nonetheless put the brakes on things, at least to a degree. Compared to earlier bureau scandals, this was a lesser one. It was, nonetheless, indicative that sixty years on, the bureau was still prioritizing the CP as a target.

The Late Years of the USSR

The revelations on SOLO came late in the game, at a time when the Soviet Union was slowly but surely unraveling. In 1986, Reagan met in Reykjavík, Iceland, with the new Soviet Premier Mikhail Gorbachev. Gorbachev, who came to power in 1985, assumed the post of general secretary of the CPSU after a prolonged succession crisis. Leonid Brezhnev had died in 1982, followed by Yuri Andropov, who died in office less than two years later, only to be followed by Konstantin Chernenko, who lasted a little over a year.

While Gorbachev's time in office would be longer and would seriously turn down the temperature of the Cold War through his policy of openness (Glasnost) and reform (Perestroika), he did so as the United States was making a major push against the USSR—deploying missiles in Europe, funding mercenary armies against procommunist forces in Nicaragua, invading the Caribbean country of Grenada, bombing Libya, and appropriating billions of dollars for weapons programs such as the Star Wars initiative, aimed at eliminating any advantage the Soviets would have in a nuclear strike. Amid all this, the Soviets faced a huge domestic crisis in the Soviet Republic of Ukraine, with the explosion of the nuclear plant and extensive radioactive fallout at Chernobyl.

In hindsight, the writing was on the wall—though few saw as much at the time. Unfortunately for the CPUSA, it was the Soviet Union on which their fortunes rose or fell. Their future was not to be a bright one.

Stumbling Toward a Finish

What is striking in all this is that despite the dramatic changes underway in the Soviet Union, the FBI—which had been targeting U.S. communism since its days when it was the Bureau of Investigation in 1919—continued an open investigation on the CP. Here is what they wrote in September 1990: "Inasmuch as current defector information has confirmed that the CP, and thus its front groups are still funded and controlled by the International Department, Central Committee, Communist Party, Soviet Union (ID/CC/CPSU) which is an integral Soviet active measures organ that is used to promote Soviet policy objectives worldwide, the NYO opines that analysis of the information provided by assets who are reporting on CPUSA activities can provide the US intelligence community with useful positive intelligence regarding (1) Current Soviet Active measures; and (2) Soviet foreign policy objectives."[28] Fifteen months later, the Soviet Union would collapse.

For their part, the Communist Party acted as though time and history were on its side. On August 4, 1990, Gus Hall delivered a report to the CP's National Committee. In it, he offered a rather sunny assessment: "The Party has also been involved in some important election campaigns, such as the electoral races in New York, New Haven, Hartford, Seattle, Pennsylvania, Ohio, Michigan, and California"—noting that this included "progressive and especially African-American candidates." He further highlighted the party's role in "initiating groups, coalitions, and organizing united front actions in response to the intensified racist violence around the country" and that "Communists are also working in the environmental movements." Finally, he reported that the group had "Party commissions in auto, steel, teachers, and hospital and health care" and noted, "Our members are activists and leaders in the struggle for women's equality," working in organizations such as the Coalition of Labor Union Women, Women for Racial and Economic Equality, and the National Organization for Women.

Hall's assessment belied the reality of an aging—he, personally, was eighty years old at the time—and dwindling organization on the brink of obscurity. As the FBI noted, "As of early 1990, the ICP [Illinois Communist Party] was continuing its practice of encouraging party members, particularly the elderly, to donate a portion of their assets to the CP. It was being suggested that party members so inclined put such assets in a trust for the benefit of the Party now (rather than after their demise)"—the initiative garnered about $9,000.[29]

***

All this came to an abrupt halt at the end of 1991. With the collapse of the Soviet Union, the CPUSA underwent a major split in which around one-third of its membership exited to form the Committee of Correspondence. Joe Sims, who became editor of the party journal *Political Affairs*, told historian Daniel Rosenberg that the party "barely survived." In a telling description, Rosenberg writes of how six months after the group's Twentieth-Fifth National Convention—which ended in a schism—"a [Gus] Hall visitor discovered the once bustling headquarters nearly empty: 'We found ourselves on what seemed like an entirely deserted floor: a huge floor with many rooms. I couldn't find him and started to yell for him, and when he answered finally, and I followed his voice, it led me straight into an office where Gus was sitting at a desk.'"[30]

The Communist Party would continue—Hall himself would be ninety years old when he passed away in October 2000. Without the Soviet Union, however, it was of little consequence. The contestation between the guardians of U.S. society and the American communists, a conflict that had occupied so much of the twentieth century, was, for all intents and purposes, over.

Conclusion

●●●●●●●●●●●●●

Communism didn't just fall. It was pushed.

GEORGE H. W. BUSH, 1993

To read the history of the efforts against the U.S. Communist Party in the last century, one would likely conclude that the response by the powers that be was one that was by and large an overreaction. The communists, after all, never came close to laying hold to any significant political power. While that conclusion holds some truth, it obscures something fundamental. Exaggeration of the threat or not, U.S. communism was an instrument of an ideology anathema to everything American—God, family, and private property. Or, in the understated hostility of Dean Acheson, "We are interested in stopping the spread of communism because communism is a doctrine that we don't happen to like."[1] As such, the U.S. government and the various social and cultural institutions that reinforced it were never going to passively countenance an ideology or organization—whatever its faults—that challenged the core of its being, let alone one that held allegiance to something other than the national interests of the United States. That was true in 1920. It was true in 1946. And it was true in 1991.

This explains why before they had even organized into a fully coherent organization, the communists were under fire by the ruling elements of an ascendant and expanding U.S. empire. Beginning with laws aimed at the disruptive tactics of anarchists, the U.S. power structure criminalized revolutionary advocacy. The government, in the words of the Supreme Court, upheld its right to "extinguish the spark without waiting until it has enkindled the flame."[2] As such, they proscribed any speech that argued for revolution, regardless of whether it was actionable, gaining currency, or otherwise.

While the pushback in response to the Draconian measures of rounding up mainly radical immigrants in the Palmer and Lusk raids meant that most of those detained were not deported—though hundreds were—the leadership of the emergent party was not so lucky. Charles Ruthenberg, Benjamin Gitlow, Harry Winitsky, James Larkin, and Isaac E. Ferguson were imprisoned for the high crime of distributing a manifesto that called for, but made no moves toward, a Bolshevik-style revolution.

This would become a pattern in the ensuing decades—particularly for the leadership of what would become the CPUSA. The group and its leaders were systematically targeted by an aggressive Department of Justice, with J. Edgar Hoover leading the charge. Ruthenberg and William Z. Foster would be brought up on charges of criminal syndicalism. Later, Foster would be jailed for leading a demonstration of the unemployed, before again being jailed when he ran for president. Such election undermining, it should be noted, would continue when Earl Browder was arrested during his 1936 presidential campaign. Meantime, rank and file communists and their supporters were pursued on strike lines, at unemployed demonstrations, and when advocating for the end of the Jim Crow system—this at a particularly vulnerable time for U.S. capitalism, which was struggling through the depths of the Great Depression.

Matters would only escalate as the country approached World War II. Seeing the communist line as one that undermined their support of England against Nazi Germany, the government lashed out. It imprisoned Browder—again striking at the group's leadership—for traveling to the Soviet Union under an assumed name. At the same time, they passed laws targeting communists: the Voorhis Act, the Hatch Act, and the Smith Act. It was here too that the president conferred extraordinary power onto the FBI, allowing it to operate as a political police agency, one befitting of the soon-to-be preeminent global empire. While the CP whipsawed positions from that of an antiwar stance during the Soviet-German nonaggression pact to being all in on the war when the Soviet Union was invaded, the FBI did not relent. Their CPUSA files stayed open, leaders' phone lines were tapped, and new investigations were initiated.

As the Second World War transformed into the Cold War, the alliance between the United States and the USSR was ruptured. In its place was the most aggressive repression ever launched against the CPUSA. While stopping just shy of fully criminalizing the group, the government systematically imprisoned, or held under indictment, its leadership. It also passed new and onerous laws targeting the organization. And through hearings, political demagoguery, and a reactionary media juggernaut, it created a social climate in which communism became a social pariah, disparaged as a disease—antithetical to everything the country was said to stand for.

While there was a measure of sanity that returned with the end of the Korean War, the death of Stalin, and Khrushchev's rightward swing—it was not the end of the repression. The height of the anticommunist fever may have peaked, but the Cold War continued. Because of this, attacks on the communists persisted—though with a different impetus.

The United States may no longer have been threatened by the communists on domestic security grounds, but they were wholly intolerant of its role as an agent of their chief global rival. What followed was a mind-boggling campaign of disruption, running parallel with a high-stakes espionage effort operating at the top reaches of the party. Paradoxically, at the same time as they attacked the group, they facilitated its funding through the work of their spies, Morris and Jack Childs. It was only with the collapse of the USSR that this ended.

While the magnitude of attacks varied between 1917 and 1991, there was never a time when U.S. communism was not a high-priority target of the U.S. political and law enforcement apparatus. The repressive attention leveled at the CPUSA was unprecedented. Put simply, there has never been anything on this scale toward a domestic political organization before or since.

As for the communists, the historical picture projected of them has largely been informed by the fact that they were on the losing side. As such, there is a dearth of disinterested assessments. In the United States, it is the default that not only is communism bad, but the CPUSA was for all intents and purposes an abomination. This is hardly fair.

For all its ills, as a vehicle for social justice—especially in its middle years—the CPUSA contributed to moving things ahead, and its cadres and supporters paid a steep price for doing so. Not only did they—Black, white, and otherwise—join with the masses of Black people in their struggle against the American apartheid system; they were among the bravest fighters for union rights, the rights of the unemployed, the rights of tenants, and all those inhabiting the bottom layers of U.S. society. Tellingly, the scant attention paid to this is inverse to the attention to the multitude of things they did wrong.

That is not to dismiss the universe of faults of this group; they were as manifold as they were intractable. Though here another point should be made. While there is no shortage of critiques of U.S. communism, there is a glaring absence of work analyzing the scope and impact of repression on it. As such, one might conclude that the problems of the CPUSA were wholly their own. With all that is presented here, it ought to be obvious that was not the case. How things might have been different were the repression not as furious as it was is a valid, if academic, question—things developed as they did, not as they might have.

That said, the aim of this book was not to offer yet another judgment on a group that no longer occupies a space of much influence. Rather, it was to shine a light on an extraordinary, intensive, and unrelenting repressive project. In doing so, it is the hope that we can gain a clearer understanding of the not-far past and, perhaps, be better suited to confront an uncertain future.

Appendix 1
CPUSA Leaders Imprisoned

(Under Smith Act unless noted otherwise)

Last	First	Position/Notes	Trial	Served
Bittelman	Alexander	Theoretician	1952	3 years
Browder	Earl	General secretary: Espionage Act	1917	1 year
		Passport violation	1943	14 months
Charney	George	Trade union director	1952	3 months
Davis	Benjamin	NYC councilman	1949	3.4 years
Dennis	Eugene	General secretary	1949	3.8 years
Flynn	Elizabeth Gurley	Head of Women's Commission	1952	2.4 years
Foster	William Z.	General secretary: Unemployment demonstration	1930	6 months
Gannett	Betty	National education director	1952	2 years
Gates	John	Editor, *Daily Worker*	1949	4 years
Gitlow	Benjamin	Founder and early leader: criminal syndicalism (NY)	1919	2 years
Green	Gil	Member National Board	1949	5 years
Hall	Gus	Member National Board	1949	8 years
Jerome	Victor Jeremy (V. J.)	Head of Cultural Commission	1952	3 years

(continued)

Last	First	Position/Notes	Trial	Served
Jones	Claudia	Women's Commission secretary	1952	1 year
Perry	Pettis	Head of Farm and Negro Commission	1952	28 months
Potash	Irving	Head of Furriers Union	1949	4 years
Ruthenberg	Charles	Early leader: criminal anarchy (NY)	1917	2 years
		Criminal syndicalism (MI)	1919	2 years
Stachel	Jacob (Jack)	Editor, *Daily Worker*	1949	4 years
Thompson	Robert	New York Party Head	1949	7 years
Trachtenberg	Alexander	Head of International Publishers	1952	3 months
Williamson	John	Member National Board	1949	4 years
Winston	Henry	Member National Board	1949	5 years
Winter	Carl	Member National Board	1949	4 years

SOURCES: Alexander Bittelman, Tamiment finding aid; Earl Browder, obituary, *New York Times*, June 28, 1973; George Charney, obituary, *New York Times*, December 14, 1975; Benjamin Davis, obituary, *New York Times*, August 24, 1965; Eugene Dennis, obituary, *New York Times*, February 1, 1961; Elizabeth Gurley Flynn, obituary, *New York Times*, September 6, 1964; William Z. Foster, obituary, *New York Times*, September 2, 1961; Jack Stachel and John Williamson, "Greetings to Communist Leaders," *Daily Worker*, March 3, 1955; Betty Gannett, obituary, *New York Times*, March 5, 1970; John Gates, obituary, *New York Times*, May 24, 1992; Gil Green, Mari Jo Buhle, Paul Buhle, and Dan Georgakas, eds., *Encyclopedia of the American Left* (Garland, 1990), 279; Benjamin Gitlow, Gitlow Papers finding aid, UNC Charlotte; John Williamson, Marx Memorial Collection, John Williamson Collection; Gus Hall, *Elliot Robert Barkan, Making It in America: A Sourcebook on Eminent Ethnic Americans* (ABC-CLIO, 2001), 147; V. J. Jerome, Jerome Yale papers finding aid; Claudia Jones, "Claudia Jones Loses," *New York Times*, November 10, 1955; Pettis Perry, New York Public Library, Perry Papers finding aid; Irving Potash, "Returning Red Seized by FBI," *New York Times*, January 5, 1957; Charles Ruthenberg, obituary, *Washington Post*, March 3, 1937; Robert Thompson, obituary, *New York Times*, October 17, 1965; Alexander Trachtenberg, obituary, *New York Times*, December 17, 1966; Henry Winston, obituary, *New York Times*, December 16, 1986; Carl Winter, obituary, *New York Times*, November 20, 1991.

Appendix 2
FBI Files Referenced

Name	FBI Reference	Pages	Source
Browder, Earl	100-25693 & 40-3798	1206	Internet Archive (archive.org) and author FOIA
Budenz, Louis	Louis Budenz Part 01	102	FBI Vault
Childs, Jack	100-32992	560	Internet Archive
COINTELPRO-CPUSA	100-3-104, Sections 7, 18, 30, 40, 47, & 61	1224	Gale Archives Unbound
	100-3-104-3, BA [Baltimore]	44	"
	100-3-104-9 [Chicago] Sections 1–9	1418	"
	100-3-104-12, DL [Dallas]	6	"
	100-3-104-18, HN [Honolulu]	13	"
	100-3-104-21, IP [Indianapolis]	5	"
	100-3-104-26, LA [Los Angeles] Section 3	277	"
	100-3-104-31, NK [Newark] Section 6	23	"
	100-3-104-34, [New York] Sections 1–21	5291	"
	100-3-104-37, PH [Philadelphia] Section 6	185	"

(*continued*)

Name	FBI Reference	Pages	Source
	00-3-104-40, PD [Portland] Section 2	53	"
Davis, Benjamin, Jr.	100-23825, 1B2, Sub 6	332	Gale Archives Unbound / Gerald Horne Collection
	100-23825, 1B2	72	"
	Headquarters 100-149163 Section 1	177	"
	Headquarters 100-149163 Section 21	187	"
	Headquarters 100-149163 Section 25	374	"
	NY 100-23825, 4	515	"
Compic	100-138754 Enclosures (E.B.F.'s) [Enclosure Behind Files] Serial 250	73	Gale Archives Unbound
Cunningham, Agnes, and Gordon Friesen	100-HQ-30231	134	Author FOIA
Freyman, Carl	FBI Personnel File	283	Internet Archive
Fast, Howard	100-327116	1427	Gale Archives Unbound
Foster, William Z.	61-330	42	Internet Archive
Green, Aaron "Archie"	121-1646-1	111	Author FOIA
Hammond, John	100-12265	184	Author FOIA
Hoodwink	100-446533	62	FBI Vault (vault.fbi.gov)
Jones, Claudia	Claudia Jones Part 1 of 10	67	FBI Vault
Lautner, Jonathan	100-16177, NY 66-3901	690	Internet Archive
Lomax, Allan	101-HQ-899	202	Author FOIA
Robbin, Ed	100-530-LA	435	Author FOIA
Scott, Adrian	100-20655	334	Gale Archives Unbound
Silber, Irwin	100-404340	608	Author FOIA
SOLO	Solo-6	222	FBI Vault
Seeger, Peter	100-HQ-200845	162	Author FOIA
Spiegel, Jack	122-WF-361 & 158-CG-21	211	Author FOIA
TOPLEV	CPUSA-TOPLEV-HQ-67, CPUSA-TOPLEV-HQ-68	729	Internet Archive
Wood, Hallie	100-181329, 100-SA-3754 v.1, 100-WFO-27987 v.1	463	Author FOIA
		18,503	

Chronology

1901 William McKinley assassinated

1902 New York State Criminal Anarchy Law enacted

1917 Lenin's Bolshevik Party seizes power in Russia

1919 Bomb explodes at Attorney General A. Mitchell Palmer's home, beginning of the first Red Scare
Communist International (Comintern) created

1923 Workers (Communist) Party, later named the Communist Party USA, formed

1928 Comintern declares a Third Period, predicting a new revolutionary upsurge

1930 International Unemployment Day demonstrations

1931 Scottsboro Boys arrested in Alabama

1933 Hitler comes to power in Germany
The Third Period gives way to the Popular Front

1936 CPUSA General Secretary Earl Browder arrested in Indiana while campaigning for president

1938 FDR increases the FBI's power in combating espionage and domestic subversion

1939 The Soviet Union and Nazi Germany sign a nonaggression pact
Earl Browder is sent to prison for passport fraud

1940 The Voorhis Act mandating registration of organizations working for foreign powers, adopted

1941 Nazi Germany invades the Soviet Union
The Smith Act is passed, making it federal a crime to teach and advocate revolution

1944 The CPUSA dissolves to form the short-lived Communist Political Association

1945 Atomic bombs are dropped on Hiroshima and Nagasaki

1947 The Truman Doctrine is declared, initiating the Cold War
The Taft-Hartley bill is adopted, prohibiting communists from serving as union officers
Truman institutes Loyalty Oaths for federal employees
The Hollywood Ten are charged with contempt of Congress

1949 The leaders of the Communist Party are convicted under the Smith Act
Rioters attack communists and their supporters in Peekskill, New York

1950 The Korean War breaks out
Congress passes the anticommunist McCarran Act

1952 Former communist Morris Childs is recruited as an FBI informant. Julius and Ethel Rosenberg are executed as atomic spies

1954 Joe McCarthy is censured in the Senate
The Communist Control Act is passed, nominally making the CPUSA illegal
Joseph Stalin dies

1956 Nikita Khrushchev denounces Stalin, prompting massive defections from the CPUSA
The FBI launches its Counterintelligence Program (COINTELPRO) against the CPUSA

1957 Supreme Court decides *Yates v. United States*, curtailing the Smith Act

1960 As part of the deepening Sino-Soviet schism, the Soviet Union removes advisers from China

1961 FBI informant, Morris Childs, funnels $714,385 (about $7M today) from the Soviets to the U.S. party

1962 Cuban Missile Crisis

1968 The USSR invades Czechoslovakia

1969 Supreme Court issues *Brandenburg v. Ohio* removing prohibitions on advocacy speech that did not directly call for violence

1971 Activists steal records exposing COINTELPRO, the FBI discontinues the program

1975 Senate Church Committee Hearings investigate domestic intelligence operations

1982 Informant Morris Childs, Gus Hall's money conduit to the USSR, retires, ending Operation SOLO

1991 The Soviet Union Collapses
One-third of the remaining CPUSA leave to form the Committee of Correspondence

Acknowledgments

I want to thank the following people who helped me navigate this process in myriad—sometimes direct, sometimes subtle—ways: Terry Leonard and Emily Paige, who took the time to read the manuscript and offer their thoughts, fixes, and insights. Chip Gibbons, for sharing the file on the CPUSA the bureau kept during the 1980s. Conor Gallagher, my go-to person to figure out if I am making any sense whatsoever. Nicole Solano and the folks at Rutgers University Press. To the group of friends who sat and listened to me present on the topic and offered their kind and thoughtful feedback, including Page Dougherty, Hillary Postman, Glenn Robb, Henry Valenti, and Danielle Zora. Despite such crucial help, this work, its outlook, its orientation, and any errors are all mine.

Notes

Introduction

Epigraph: J. Edgar Hoover, *Masters of Deceit: The Story of Communism in America and How to Fight It* (Henry Holt, 1957).

1 "48 Hurt in Clashes at Robeson Rally," *New York Times*, September 5, 1949; Joseph North, "25,000 Hear Robeson at Peekskill," *Daily Worker*, September 5, 1949; and Scott Martelle, *The Fear Within: Spies, Commies, and American Democracy on Trial* (Rutgers University Press, 2011), 203.
2 I. A. "World Communism in Figures," *World Today* 14, no. 5 (1958): 212–216, http://www.jstor.org/stable/40393877.
3 Robert Justin Goldstein's compilation, *Little "Red Scares": Anti-Communism and Political Repression in the United States, 1921–1946* (Routledge, 2016), goes a long way toward correcting the fragmented view too often put forward. Also see David Caute, *The Great Fear: The Anti-Communist Purge Under Truman and Eisenhower* (Simon and Schuster, 1978); Beverly Gage, *G-Man: J. Edgar Hoover and the Making of the American Century* (Viking, 2022); Robert Murray, *Red Scare: A Study in National Hysteria, 1918–1920* (McGraw Hill, 1964); and Ellen Schrecker, *Many Are the Crimes: McCarthyism in America* (Little, Brown, 1998).

Chapter 1 Opening Salvos (1901–1920)

Epigraph: "35 Taken in Raid Held for Anarchy," *New York Times*, November 10, 1919.

1 Evan Andrews, "The Assassination of President William McKinley," History.com, September 6, 2016, https://www.history.com/news/the-assassination-of-president-william-mckinley.
2 Wyatt Kingseed, "The Assassination of William McKinley," *American History* 36, no. 4 (October 2001), 22; "Czolgosz Guilty, Jury Takes 35 Minutes to Find Its Verdict," *New York Times*, September 25, 1901.

3 Kingseed, 22.
4 "Stone Not an Anarchist," *New York Times*, September 12, 1901.
5 "Stamp Out Anarchy," *New York Times*, September 11, 1901.
6 Clarence F. Birdseye, Robert C. Cumming, and Frank B. Gilbert, *Annotated Consolidated Laws of the State of New York, as Amended, January 1, 1918*, vol. 5 (Matthew Bender, 1918), 5611.
7 "Espionage Act of 1917 and Sedition Act of 1918," National Constitution Center, accessed August 5, 2023, https://constitutioncenter.org/the-constitution/historic-document-library/detail/espionage-act-of-1917-and-sedition-act-of-1918-1917-1918.
8 "Officers Investigate 'Bible Students' Here," *Los Angeles Times*, March 1, 1918; Charles Taze Russell, *The Finished Mystery* (New York: International Bible Students Association, 1917), 247.
9 "20 Years in Prison for 7 Russellites," *New York Times*, June 22, 1918.
10 Erick Trickey, "When America's Most Prominent Socialist Was Jailed for Speaking Out Against World War I," *Smithsonian Magazine*, June 15, 2018, https://www.smithsonianmag.com/history/fiery-socialist-challenged-nations-role-wwi-180969386/.
11 Eugene V. Debs, "The Canton, Ohio Speech, Anti-War Speech," June 16, 1918, Marxists.org, accessed August 5, 2023, https://www.marxists.org/archive/debs/works/1918/canton.htm.
12 "The United States of America v. Eugene V. Debs," National Archives Catalog, accessed August 5, 2023, https://catalog.archives.gov/id/2765897.
13 Justin Peters, "The Bomb-Throwing Anarchists Who Terrorized Boston 100 Years Before the Tsarnaevs," *Slate*, April 26, 2013, https://slate.com/news-and-politics/2013/04/luigi-galleani-palmer-raids-the-bomb-throwing-anarchists-who-terrorized-boston-100-years-before-the-tsarnaevs.html.
14 "Palmer and Family Safe on Second Floor When Explosion Wrecked Lower Part of House," *New York Times*, June 3, 1919.
15 Paul Avrich, *Sacco and Vanzetti: The Anarchist Background* (Princeton University Press, 1991), 137–148, https://www.jstor.org/stable/j.ctv131bwkz.14.
16 Avrich, 149–162.
17 "Palmer & Family Safe," *New York Times*, June 3, 1919.
18 "New York Office of the Bolsheviki Raided by State," *New York Times*, June 13, 1919.
19 "2,000 'Reds on Lists' Flynn Tells Palmer of Plans to Finally Crush Anarchy," *Washington Post*, June 19, 1919.
20 "200 Caught in New York," *New York Times*, November 8, 1919.
21 Beverly Gage, *G-Man: J. Edgar Hoover and the Making of the American Century* (Viking, 2022), 69–70.
22 Seventeen of those arrested would eventually be indicted for criminal anarchy but would have their charges dismissed in 1925. William H. Siener, "The Red Scare Revisited: Radicals and the Anti-Radical Movement in Buffalo, 1919–1920," *New York History* 79, no. 1 (1998): 23–54, http://www.jstor.org/stable/23182288.
23 "Raid from Coast to Coast," *New York Times*, January 3, 1920.
24 William Z. Foster, *History of the Communist Party of the United States* (International Publishers, 1952), 174–175.
25 "Way Opened to Deport 3,000 Secretary Wilson's Decision Declared," *Baltimore Sun*, January 27, 1920.

26 "The Left Wing Manifesto," *Revolutionary Age*, July 5, 1919, Marxisthistory.org, accessed August 22, 2023, http://www.marxisthistory.org/history/usa/parties/spusa/1919/0705-lwnc-leftwingmanifesto.pdf.
27 U.S. Supreme Court, Gitlow v. New York (1925), National Constitution Center, accessed August 22, 2023, https://constitutioncenter.org/the-constitution/supreme-court-case-library/gitlow-v-new-york.
28 "Dissenting Opinion in Gitlow v. New York," Teaching American History, accessed August 22, 2023, https://teachingamericanhistory.org/document/dissenting-opinion-in-gitlow-v-new-york/.
29 The *Brandenburg v. Ohio* decision adopted the spirit of the dissent criteria for allowable speech. See "Brandenburg v. Ohio (1969)," First Amendment Encyclopedia, accessed August 22, 2023, https://www.mtsu.edu/first-amendment/article/189/brandenburg-v-ohio.
30 "The Gitlow Case (1920)," Clarence Darrow Digital Collection, University of Minnesota Law Library, accessed May 9, 2024, https://librarycollections.law.umn.edu/darrow/trials_details.php?id=14.
31 "Winitsky Hears of Pardon Action Two Days Later: Gets Copy of *Freiheit* by Accident," *Daily Worker* (Chicago), January 16, 1924, Marxisthistory.org, accessed August 21, 2023, http://www.marxisthistory.org/history/usa/parties/cpusa/1924/0116-dw-winitskypardon.pdf.
32 "Irish Agitator Is Deported," *Washington Post*, April 22, 1923.
33 "People v. Ferguson," Casetext, argued June 7, 1922, decided July 12, 1922, accessed August 22, 2023, https://casetext.com/case/people-v-ferguson-101.
34 Mark Lendler, *Gitlow v. New York: Every Idea an Incitement* (University Press of Kansas, 2012), 15.
35 "Will Seek Repeal of Anti-Red Statues," *Baltimore Sun*, February 18, 1924.
36 "249 Reds Sail, Exiled to Soviet Russia," *New York Times*, December 22, 1919.
37 Boris Egorov, "How the U.S. Deported Its Radicals to Soviet Russia," *Russia Beyond*, September 27, 2019, https://www.rbth.com/history/331044-how-us-deported-its-radicals.
38 "Assail Louis Post for Releasing Reds," *New York Times*, May 1, 1920.

Chapter 2 Underground and Above (1921–1927)

Epigraph: "Gitlow v. State of New York," June 1925, Justia U.S. Supreme Court, accessed July 26, 2024, https://supreme.justia.com/cases/federal/us/268/652/.

1 "History of the Comintern. Sections: Communist Party, USA," Marxists.org, accessed September 5, 2023, https://www.marxists.org/history/usa/parties/cpusa/encyclopedia-american-left.htm.
2 Theodore Draper, *The Roots of American Communism* (Viking, 1957), 366.
3 Draper, 371.
4 Draper, 372; "'K-97' Quit Job in Shipyards to Unmask Reds," *New York Times*, April 8, 1923.
5 "Hunt 40 Radicals Who Escaped Raid," *New York Times*, August 26, 1922; "Ruthenberg Is Convicted of Syndicalism," *New York Times*, May 3, 1923.
6 "C.E. Ruthenberg, Head of Communists, Dead," *Washington Post*, March 3, 1927.

7 Max Bedacht, *Underground and Above: A Memoir of American Communism in the 1920s*, Marxists.org, accessed August 8, 2023, 1, https://www.marxists.org/history/usa/parties/cpusa/1967/nomonth/0000-bedacht-underground.pdf.
8 Benjamin Gitlow, *I Confess: The Truth About American Communism* (E. P. Dutton), 1939, 65.
9 Daeha Ko, "Rough Beginnings," Communism in Washington State History and Memory Project, accessed August 8, 2023, https://depts.washington.edu/labhist/cpproject/ko.shtml.
10 Gitlow, *I Confess*, 66.
11 Gitlow, 67.
12 Bedacht, *Underground and Above*, 1.
13 Communist Party of America, "Rules for Underground Party Work" (leaflet), 1920, Marxists.org, accessed July 26, 2024, https://www.marxists.org/history/usa/parties/cpusa/1920/03/0300-cpa-undergroundrules.pdf.
14 "New Raid on Reds Discloses 'Rules for Fight on U.S.,'" *New York Times*, May 1, 1922.
15 Edward Anderson, "Department of Justice Surveillance Report of the Activities of Edward Lindgren, Abram Jakira, and Israel Amter, April 29–30, 1921," Marxists.org, accessed January 22, 2025, https://www.marxists.org/history/usa/government/fbi/1921/0506-anderson-surveillance.pdf.
16 Draper, *Roots of American Communism*, 227–229; Beverly Gage, *The Day Wall Street Exploded: A Story of America in Its First Age of Terror* (Oxford University Press, 2010), 275.
17 Draper, *Roots of American Communism*, 228.
18 *Stenographic Report of the "Trial" of L. C. Fraina* (Central Executive Committee of the Communist Party of America, 1920), 5, https://archive.org/details/fraina-trial-1bitBW.
19 Draper, *Roots of American Communism*, 235.
20 William Z. Foster, *History of the Communist Party of the United States* (International Publishers, 1952), 175.
21 Foster, 176.
22 "The Open Communist Party—the Task of the Hour," *Workers' Council* (New York) 1, no. 8 (October 15, 1921), 120–121, Marxists.org, accessed August 28, 2023. https://www.marxists.org/history/usa/pubs/workers-council/08-workers-council-1921.pdf.
23 Bedacht, *Underground and Above*, 2.
24 "Open Communist Party," 122.
25 Foster, *History of the Communist Party*, 180–182; H. J. Lenon, "Bureau of Investigation Confidential Surveillance Report of the Unity Convention of the Communist Party of America: Woodstock, NY—May 15–28, 1921," Marxists.org, accessed August 28, 2023, https://www.marxists.org/history/usa/parties/cpusa/1921/05/0528-ryan-unityconvention.pdf.
26 Beverly Gage, *G-Man: J. Edgar Hoover and the Making of the American Century* (Viking, 2022), 107; Select Committee to Study Governmental Operations with Respect to Intelligence Activities, United States Senate, *Intelligence Activities and the Rights of Americans, Book II* (U.S. Government Printing Office, 1976), 30–31 (hereafter Church, *Book II*).
27 Edward J. Brennan to J. Edgar Hoover, May 7, 1925, "Re: Workers Party of America: N.Y. File 61-4," William Z. Foster FBI file, FBI Reference, 61-330, 4 (hereafter, Foster FBI file).

28 John L. Hass, "In Re: Communist Activities: (List of Names and Addresses of Communists in Buffalo)," June 21, 1926, Foster FBI file, 26.
29 M. F. Burger, "Title: James B. Cannon and Lista M. Cannon (Rose Karsner)," July 6, 1925, Foster FBI file, 10–11.
30 Foster, *History of the Communist Party*, 175.
31 Draper, *Roots of American Communism*, 280.
32 Draper, 389–390.
33 Foster, *History of the Communist Party*, 195.

Chapter 3 The Third Period (1928–1933)

Epigraph: Statement of Hon. Hamilton Fish Jr., a representative in Congress from the State of New York, April 17, 1930, *Investigation Into Activities of Communists in the United States*, Hearings Before the Committee on Rules, House of Representatives, Seventy-First Congress, Second Session, on H. Res. 180, 1930, 6.

1 J. Louis Engdahl, "C.E. Ruthenberg Hurried From Canton Workhouse to Testify in Debs' Free Speech Trial," *The Milwaukee Leader*, September 11, 1919, Marxists.org, accessed January 22, 2025, https://www.marxists.org/history/usa/parties/spusa/1918/0911-engdahl-ruthfromcanton.pdf.
2 "Ruthenberg Is Convicted of Syndicalism," *New York Times*, May 3, 1923; Jim Dubelko, with research support from Raymond L. Pianka, "Charles E. Ruthenberg: America's Most Arrested Man," Cleveland Historical, accessed September 10, 2023, https://clevelandhistorical.org/items/show/722; "C.E. Ruthenberg, Head of Communists, Dead," *Washington Post*, March 3, 1927; "Communists Will Put Ashes of Ruthenberg Among Their Heroes Buried in the Kremlin," *New York Times*, March 5, 1927.
3 Comintern Sixth Congress, 1929, *The Programme of the Communist International*, Marxists.org, accessed September 13, 2023, https://www.marxists.org/history/international/comintern/6th-congress/ch01.htm.
4 A sense of the Third Period bravado and sectarianism on the part of the communists comes through in a news report from November 1928: "Bloodless war was waged yesterday at a peace meeting in Union Square. One thousand amused passers-by stood silently while 200 Communists tried unsuccessfully for two hours by impromptu parades, heckling, and singing, to break up an anti-war meeting sponsored by the Youth's Peace Committee, including Socialists and the Women's Peace League." "Reds and Pacifists Clash in Union Sq," *New York Times*, November 11, 1928.
5 "The Cases of Sacco & Vanzetti," Law Library, Mass.gov, April 30, 2018, https://www.mass.gov/law-library/the-case-of-sacco-vanzetti.
6 "Due Process of Law," *New York Times*, December 26, 1921.
7 Felix Frankfurter, "The Case of Sacco and Vanzetti," *The Atlantic*, March 1927.
8 Mike Gold, "Strike! Picket! Protest! Until the Last Minute," *Daily Worker*, August 22, 1927.
9 Gold.
10 Norman Markowitz, "The Communist Party in the '30s: The Depression and the Great Upsurge," *People's World*, May 14, 2019, https://www.peoplesworld.org/article/the-communist-party-in-the-30s-the-depression-and-the-great-upsurge/.

11 Fraser Ottanelli, *The Communist Party of the United States: From the Depression to World War II* (Rutgers University Press, 1989), 21.
12 Markowitz, "Communist Party in the '30s."
13 Brent D. Glass and Michael H, "Gastonia Strike," NCPedia, 2006, https://www.ncpedia.org/gastonia-strike; "All 7 Convicted at Gastonia Trial," *New York Times*, October 22, 1929. "Jury Acquits Four in Strike Flogging," *New York Times*, October 20, 1929.
14 Glass, "Gastonia Strike."
15 Ron Soodalter, "The Price of Coal," *Kentucky Monthly*, September 30, 2016, http://www.kentuckymonthly.com/culture/history/the-price-of-coal/; Tony Bubka, "The Harlan County Coal Strike of 1931," *Labor History* 11, no. 1 (July 3, 2008): 41–57, https://doi.org/10.1080/00236567008584106.
16 Bubka, "Harlan County Coal Strike," 41.
17 Bubka, 52.
18 Bubka, 55–56.
19 Robert W. Cherny, *San Francisco Reds: Communists in the Bay Area 1919–1958* (University of Illinois Press, 2024), 36.
20 "Red March on City Hall Made Fiasco by Police," *Los Angeles Times*, March 7, 1930.
21 Peggy Dennis, *The Autobiography of an American Communist* (Lawrence Hill, 1977), 48; "Communists Suspect Convicted," *Los Angeles Times*, April 13, 1930.
22 "Hunt Launched for Red Leader," *Los Angeles Times*, July 19, 1930.
23 "Newark Court Bars Unbelievers at Trials," *New York Times*, June 11, 1930.
24 "Women Convicted as Reds," *New York Times*, April 1, 1930.
25 "Red's Freed on Bond," *New York Times*, July 9, 1930.
26 "Jail 13 in Mine Strike," *New York Times*, June 26, 1931.
27 "Dreiser Indicted for Syndicalism," *New York Times*, November 17, 1931.
28 Dave Tabler, "Criminal Syndicalism Comes to Harlan, KY," *Appalachian History*, November 15, 2017, https://www.appalachianhistory.net/2017/11/criminal-syndicalism-comes-to-harlan-ky.html; "Theodore Dreiser," *Discover Indiana*, accessed February 5, 2024, https://publichistory.iupui.edu/items/show/133.
29 "Great Depression Facts," Franklin D. Roosevelt Library and Museum, accessed February 5, 2024, https://www.fdrlibrary.org/great-depression-facts.
30 "35,000 Jammed in Square: Views of the Red Rioting," *New York Times*, March 7, 1930.
31 "35,000 Jammed in Square."
32 "35,000 Jammed in Square."
33 "11 Parents Fined in Red Riot Case," *New York Times*, March 20, 1930.
34 "Four Killed in Riot at Main Ford Plant," *New York Times*, March 8, 1932; Ken Coleman, "On This Day in 1932: 4 Killed During Ford Hunger March," *Michigan Advance*, March 2019, https://michiganadvance.com/briefs/on-this-day-in-1932-4-killed-during-ford-hunger-march/.
35 "Red Leaders Jailed 6 Months to 3 Years," *New York Times*, April 22, 1930; Edward P. Johanningsmeier, *Forging American Communism: The Life of William Z. Foster* (Princeton University Press, 1994), 254.
36 Johanningsmeier, *Forging American Communism*, 262.
37 "Los Angeles Police Seize W.Z. Foster," *Los Angeles Times*, June 29, 1932.
38 Johanningsmeier, *Forging American Communism*, 266–267.

39 Frank Donner, *Protectors of Privilege: Red Squads and Police Repression in Urban America* (University of California Press, 1990), 47–64; *Encyclopedia of Chicago*, "Red Squad," accessed March 20, 2025, http://www.encyclopedia.chicagohistory.org/pages/1049.html.

40 Donner, *Protectors of Privilege*, 48.

41 Thomas Aiello, *The Routledge History of Police Brutality in America* (Routledge, 2023), 201.

42 "Woman Gets 15 Years for Poisoning Husband," *The Washington Post*, December 28, 1929.

43 "14 Demonstrators Guilty at Capital," *New York Times*, December 2, 1931.

44 "Reds on Trial Up-State," *New York Times*, February 9, 1932.

45 "8 Rioters Seized at Relief Bureau," *New York Times*, April 16, 1932.

46 "Communists Find City Jail Fertile Place for Recruits," *The Washington Post*, December 7, 1928.

47 Schomburg Center for Research in Black Culture, "International Labor Defense," NYPL.org record group summary, https://nyplorg-data-archives.s3.amazonaws.com/uploads/collection/pdf_finding_aid/Sc_Micro_R-980.pdf.

48 Harry McDevitt, "Few Would Be Fools Enough to Support Communists If They Knew About Them," *Philadelphia Tribune*, March 16, 1933.

Chapter 4 Marginalized in the Mainstream (1934–1939)

Epigraph: Franklin Roosevelt, "Address at the Democratic State Convention," Syracuse, N.Y., September 29, 1936, The American Presidency Project, accessed January 14, 2023, https://www.presidency.ucsb.edu/documents/address-the-democratic-state-convention-syracuse-ny. The full quote is "Communism is a manifestation of the social unrest which always comes with widespread economic maladjustment. We in the Democratic Party have not been content merely to denounce this menace. We have been realistic enough to face it. We have been intelligent enough to do something about it."

1 "Flashes of Red in the German Picture: Thälmann Leader of the Communists Says His Party Is Equipped for Revolution, but Awaits the Right Moment," *New York Times*, April 3, 1932.

2 "Republican Review Banned," *New York Times*, February 19, 1933.

3 Richard J. Evans, *The Coming of the Third Reich* (Penguin, 2005), 314.

4 "Ernst Thälmann—Shot to Death in the Crematorium," Buchenwald Memorial, accessed March 24, 2024, https://www.buchenwald.de/en/geschichte/biografien/bag-ausstellung/ernst-thaelmann.

5 "COMMUNISTS: Hero," *Time*, July 11, 1949, https://content.time.com/time/subscriber/article/0,33009,853784,00.html.

6 Emphasis in original. Georgi Dimitrov, "The Fascist Offensive and the Tasks of the Communist International in the Struggle of the Working Class Against Fascism," Main Report delivered at the Seventh World Congress of the Communist International, August 2, 1935, Marxists.org, accessed September 26, 2023, https://www.marxists.org/reference/archive/dimitrov/works/1935/08_02.htm#s6.

7 Earl Browder, "What Is Communism?," *New Masses*, June 25, 1935, Marxists.org, accessed January 23, 2025, https://www.marxists.org/archive/browder/what-is-8.pdf.

8 "The History of the 1934 General Strike," May 23, 2019, Tenderloin Museum, accessed September 29, 2023, http://www.tenderloinmuseum.org/public-programs-2019-1/2019/5/23/the-history-of-the-1934-general-strike.

9 Chris Carlsson, "The General Strike of 1934," FoundSF, accessed March 24, 2024, https://www.foundsf.org/index.php?title=The_General_Strike_of_1934.

10 "Eight Coast Reds Convicted, Six Freed," *New York Times*, April 2, 1935; People v. Chambers (Crim. No. 1533. Third Appellate District. September 28, 1937), Justia U.S. Law, accessed September 29, 2023, https://law.justia.com/cases/california/court-of-appeal/2d/22/687.html.

11 "Trial Shows Red Menace Grips State," *Los Angeles Times*, February 28, 1935.

12 "Scottsboro Boys," History.com, February 22, 2018, https://www.history.com/topics/great-depression/scottsboro-boys; Douglas O. Linder, "The First Scottsboro Trials (April, 1931)," Famous Trials, University of Missouri–Kansas City Law, accessed January 15, 2024, https://www.famous-trials.com/scottsboroboys/1563-firsttrial.

13 "5,000 Fight Police in Harlem Streets," *New York Times*, March 19, 1934.

14 Mark Naison, *Communists in Harlem During the Great Depression* (University of Illinois Press, 1985), 141.

15 Naison, 142.

16 Naison, 142.

17 "12 Indicted in Riot," *New York Times*, March 22, 1935.

18 Peter T. Alter, "Remember the Memorial Day Massacre," Chicago History Museum, May 30, 2021, https://www.chicagohistory.org/remembering-the-memorial-day-massacre/.

19 "Gus Hall Is Ousted in 'Purge' of C.I.O.," *New York Times*, July 4, 1937.

20 Sam Tannenhaus, "Gus Hall, Unreconstructed American Communist of 7 Decades, Dies at 90," *New York Times*, October 17, 2000.

21 "Anti-Gerson Drive Pressed by Legion," *New York Times*, February 14, 1938.

22 "First Gerson Job Voided by Court," *New York Times*, May 8, 1938.

23 "Subversives Views Defined by Isaacs," *New York Times*, July 31, 1941; "Simon Gerson Snubs Senator's Questions," *New York Times*, August 6, 1954.

24 "State Acts to Ban Reds in Public Jobs," *New York Times*, March 20, 1938.

25 "Lehman Defends Veto," *New York Times*, April 16, 1938.

26 Maria Cristina Fava, "The Composers' Collective of New York, 1932–1936: Bourgeois Modernism for the Proletariat," *American Music* 34, no. 3 (Fall 2016): 301–343, https://doi.org/10.5406/americanmusic.34.3.0301; Taylor Dorrell, "An American Communist Classical Playlist," *People's World*, March 15, 2024, https://peoplesworld.org/article/an-american-communist-classical-playlist-the-composers-collective-on-spotify/.

27 SAC [Special Agent in Charge] New York to Director, FBI, "Re: Aaron Copland, Security Matter–C," August 8, 1950, Aaron Copland FBI file 100-HQ-370562, 24 (hereafter Copland HQ file). In 1957, when Copland was up for an appointment as a professor at the University of Buffalo, *Hearst* magazine attempted, unsuccessfully, to sabotage things by supplying the bureau with background of Copland's leftism: "Copland may have not been a dues-paying member of the Party, but he was a campaign committee for the election of Browder and Ford in the presidential election of 1936, known as the Committee of Professional Groups for Browder and Ford. The espousal of the presidential and vice-presidential candidates of the Communist

Party surely means some degree of Communist sympathy." For his part, Copland claimed in affidavits and under oath that he was not a communist but had only been aligned with various progressive causes. Despite what the FBI suspected, they had no evidence to prove it. Copland HQ file, 228–241; Darlene Superville, "Noted Composer's FBI File is Both Sharp, Flat," *Los Angeles Times*, May 11, 2003.

28 J. Edgar Hoover to SAC New York, "Re: John Henry Hammond, Jr., Internal Security-C," June 1, 1942. Hammond FBI file, NY-100-12265, 10 (hereafter FBI Hammond).

29 Russell S. Garner Report, "John Henry Hammond, Jr. with aliases: John Hammond, Henry Hammond, Henry Johnson," February 15, 1943, Character of Case, Internal Security-Custodial Detention, FBI Hammond, 22 (hereafter Garner Report).

30 Garner Report, 22.

31 For more, see Aaron J. Leonard, *The Folk Singers and the Bureau: The FBI, the Folk Artists and the Suppression of the Communist Party, USA, 1939–1956* (Repeater Books, 2020).

32 James G. Ryan, *Earl Browder: The Failure of American Communism* (University of Alabama Press, 1997), 108.

33 Communist Party of the United States of America, *The Election Platform of the Communist Party* (Workers Library Publishers, 1936).

34 Ryan, *Earl Browder*, 112.

35 "Reports Browder Barred," *New York Times*, September 13, 1936.

36 "Browder Is Jailed in Terre Haute," *New York Times*, October 1, 1936.

37 Ryan, *Earl Browder*, 118.

38 Ryan, 114.

39 Ryan, 117.

40 Ryan, 114–115; "Tampa Gang Attacks Browder Rally," *Daily Worker*, October 26, 1936.

41 William E. Leuchtenburg, "Franklin D. Roosevelt: Foreign Affairs," UVA Miller Center, accessed August 31, 2024, https://millercenter.org/president/fdroosevelt/foreign-affairs.

42 "Radicals Stage Anti-Nazi Demonstration In Capital," *Baltimore Sun*, July 29, 1934.

43 "Police Quell Riot over Fascist Band," *New York Times*, October 1, 1934.

44 For more, see ¡ALBA!: The Abraham Lincoln Brigade Archives, accessed June 3, 2024, https://alba-valb.org/.

45 "U.S. Bans Service in Spanish Forces," *New York Times*, January 14, 1937.

46 "29 American Volunteers Arrested in Muret," *Le Journal*, April 5, 1937, translation from *The Volunteer*, ALBAvolunteer.org, June 1, 2024, https://albavolunteer.org/2024/06/twenty-nine-american-volunteers-arrested-in-muret/.

47 Peter N. Carroll and David Christiano, "Online Lesson: The Spanish Civil War: U.S. Foreign Policy Between the World Wars," ¡ALBA!, April 1995, https://alba-valb.org/online-lesson-plan-the-spanish-civil-war-u-s-foreign-policy-between-the-world-wars/.

48 "Rumrich Nazi Spy Case," FBI, accessed August 3, 2024, https://www.fbi.gov/history/famous-cases/rumrich-nazi-spy-case; "Seven Injured at Nazi Rally Here," *New York Times*, April 21, 1938.

49 D. A. Saunders, "The Dies Committee: First Phase," *Public Opinion Quarterly* 3, no. 2 (April 1939): 223–238, https://doi.org/10.1086/265286.

50 Robert Justin Goldstein, *Little "Red Scares": Anti-Communism and Political Repression in the United States, 1921–1946* (Routledge, 2016), 243.
51 "An Analysis of FBI Domestic Security Intelligence Investigations: Authority, Official Attitudes, and Activities in Historic Perspective," Select Committee to Study Governmental Operations with Respect to Intelligence Activities of the United States Senate, *Intelligence Activities: Senate Resolution 21*, vol. 6 (U.S. Government Printing Office, 1976), 560.
52 "August 24, 1936: FDR Authorizes FBI to Resume Political Spying," Today in Civil Liberties History, ACLU, accessed March 26, 2024, http://todayinclh.com/?event=fdr-authorizes-fbi-to-resume-spying.
53 Church, *Book II*, 393.
54 Church, *Book II*, 393–394.
55 Beverly Gage, *G-Man: J. Edgar Hoover and the Making of the American Century* (Viking, 2022), 216.

Chapter 5 To War (1939–1945)

Epigraph: Franklin Roosevelt, Address to the Delegates of the American Youth Congress, Washington, D.C., February 10, 1940, American Presidency Project, accessed August 4, 2024, https://www.presidency.ucsb.edu/documents/address-the-delegates-the-american-youth-congress-washington-dc.

1 Martin Halpern, "What We Can Learn on the 80th Anniversary of the San Antonio 1939 Municipal Auditorium Riot," History News Network, August 25, 2019, https://historynewsnetwork.org/article/what-we-can-learn-on-the-80th-anniversary-of-the-s.
2 "Emma Tenayuca," National Park Service, accessed April 1, 2024, https://www.nps.gov/people/emma-tenayuca.htm.
3 "A Communist rally in San Antonio turns into a riot back in 1939," News4San Antonio, August 25, 2020, https://news4sanantonio.com/news/local/a-communist-rally-in-san-antonio-turns-into-a-riot-on-aug-25-1939.
4 For a fuller account of the German campaign against the Soviet Union see Geoffrey P. Megargee, *War of Annihilation: Combat and Genocide on the Eastern Front, 1941* (Rowman and Littlefield, 2007).
5 "Franklin Roosevelt's Fireside Chat After Germany's Invasion of Poland 9/3/1939," https://www.docsteach.org/documents/document/fireside-chat-german-invasion-poland; Turner Catledge, "Roosevelt in Plea: President, on Air, Asks the Nation to Observer True Neutrality," *New York Times*, September 4, 1939.
6 "'War Industries' Buoy the Markets Here," *New York Times*, September 2, 1939.
7 "Lend-Lease Act (1941)," Milestone Documents, National Archives, accessed February 9, 2024, https://www.archives.gov/milestone-documents/lend-lease-act.
8 "War in the Pacific," National Historic Park: Guam, National Park Service, accessed February 9, 2024, https://www.nps.gov/parkhistory/online_books/npswapa/Pearl%20Harbor/pearlharbor.htm.
9 Church, *Book II*, 30–31.
10 Church, *Book II*, 34.
11 James G. Ryan, *Earl Browder: The Failure of American Communism* (University of Alabama Press, 1997), 13–14.

12 Committee on Un-American Activities, House of Representatives, *Investigation of Un-American Propaganda Activities in the United States, Appendix, Parts I* (U.S. Government Printing Office, 1940), 812.

13 "Browder Admits False Passports," *New York Times*, September 6, 1939.

14 "Handwriting Used to Link Browder to Passport Fraud," *New York Times*, January 20, 1940.

15 Browder v. United States, 312 U.S. 335 (61 S. Ct. 599, 85 L. Ed. 862), no. 287, 1941, https://www.law.cornell.edu/supremecourt/text/312/335.

16 "Roosevelt Responds to Being Called a Communist," History.com, May 30, 2012, https://www.history.com/topics/us-presidents/presidents-fdr-denies-communist-agenda-video.

17 "Franklin Roosevelt, Address to the Delegates of the American Youth Congress," Washington, D.C., February 10, 1940, American Presidency Project, accessed January 26, 2025, https://www.presidency.ucsb.edu/documents/address-the-delegates-the-american-youth-congress-washington-dc.

18 U.S. Congress, "An Act to Prevent Pernicious Political Activities," Pub. L. No. 252, Document Cloud, accessed January 30, 2024, https://s3.documentcloud.org/documents/22987378/public-no252-76th-congress-chapter-410-1st-session-s1871-an-act-to-prevent-pernicious-political-activities.pdf.

19 "The Alien Registration Act, 1940," Citizen Source, accessed January 27, 2024, https://www.citizensource.com/History/20thCen/Smith.htm.

20 U.S. Congress, "Voorhis Act—18 U.S.C. § 2386," Justice.gov, accessed January 26, 2025, https://www.justice.gov/archives/jm/criminal-resource-manual-2067-voorhis-act-18-usc-2386.

21 Shirley A. Wiegand, *Books on Trial: Red Scare in the Heartland* (University of Oklahoma Press, 2007), 4–5.

22 "Censorship," Oklahoma Historical Society, accessed January 29, 2024, https://www.okhistory.org/publications/enc/entry?entry=CE003.

23 "Censorship."

24 Aaron J. Leonard, *The Folk Singers and the Bureau: The FBI, the Folk Artists and the Suppression of the Communist Party, USA, 1939–1956* (Repeater Books, 2020), 56.

25 *Daily Worker*, January 23, 1940; *The Worker*, May 17, 1942.

26 See, for example, Nick Lloyd, "The Story of Ramón Mercader, Trotsky's Assassin," Metropolitan Barcelona, October 28, 2010, https://www.barcelona-metropolitan.com/features/history/the-story-of-ramon-mercader/.

27 David North, "The Heritage We Defend," *The Militant*, February 7, 1942, https://www.wsws.org/en/special/library/heritage/06.html.

28 Donna T. Haverty-Stacke, *Trotskyists on Trial: Free Speech and Political Persecution Since the Age of FDR* (New York University Press, 2017), 1.

29 Carl Winter, "Minneapolis Trial Shows Labor Wary of Trotskyites," *Daily Worker*, December 17, 1941.

30 Church, *Book II*, 34.

31 J. Edgar Hoover to Mr. Lawrence W. C. Smith, January 12, 1942, Benjamin Davis FBI file, Headquarters 100-149163, section 1, 16.

32 SAC New York, July 26, 1943, "Re: Custodial Detention, Claudia Jones," FBI file 100-72390, part 1, 34.

33 FBI Los Angeles to Director, FBI, "Re: Edward Isidore Robbins, Supplemental Custodial Detention Memorandum," October 23, 1941, Ed Robbin FBI file, 100-530-LA, 19–21.

34 SAC Washington, D.C., February 5, 1943, "Re: Allan Lomax, Internal Security-Hatch Act," Alan Lomax FBI file 101-HQ-899 7; Report by REDACTED, "Re: Mrs. Gordon Friesen, w Aliases; Agnes Cunningham," January 29, 1943, Cunningham/Friesen FBI file 101-HQ-899, 3; Russell S. Garner, "Re: John Henry Hammond, Jr.," February 15, 1943, John Hammond FBI file 100-12265, 3.

35 According to the Church Committee, by the end of 1954 there were 26,174 names on the Security Index—the revised name of the custodial detention list. Of those, 11,033 were high-priority targets, categorized as COMSAB (Communist Sabotage) or DETCOM (Detain Communist). Select Committee to Study Governmental Operations with Respect to Intelligence Activities, United States Senate, *Detailed Staff Reports on Intelligence Activities and the Rights of Americans, Book III* (U.S. Government Printing Office, 1976), 446 (hereafter Church, *Book III*).

36 Robert Justin Goldstein, *Little "Red Scares": Anti-Communism and Political Repression in the United States, 1921–1946* (Routledge, 2016), 289–314.

37 "12 More Dropped at City College," *New York Times*, May 20, 1941.

38 "Schappes Guilty of Perjury Charges," *New York Times*, June 29, 1941; "Schappes to Start to Prison Tomorrow," *New York Times*, December 14, 1943.

39 "Browder Is Free as Presidents Cites Need for War Unity," *New York Times*, May 17, 1942.

40 Frederick W. Post, "Title: Howard Melvin Fast," June 27, 1944, Howard Fast FBI file 100-327116, Howard Fast 1, 291.

41 See Leonard, *Folk Singers*, 85; SAC Detroit to Director, FBI, "Subject: Gordon Friesen, Office of War Information, Internal Security Hatch Act," December 11, 1944, 100-HQ-30231, 53.

42 Memorandum for the Officer in Charge, "Subject Peter Seeger, Pvt.," June 18, 1943, FBI file 100-HQ-200845, Section 1, 39.

43 Memorandum for the Officer in Charge, "Subject Peter Seeger, Pvt.," March 20, 1943, FBI file 100-HQ-200845, Section 1, 124.

44 P.I.O. Kessler Field, MI, "Peter Seeger, Pvt.," March 25, 1943, FBI file 100-HQ-200845, section 1, 116.

45 Memorandum for the Officer in Charge, "Subject Peter Seeger, Pvt., Governors Island, N.Y.," 5 March 1943, FBI file 100-HQ-200845, Section 1, 84.

46 See FBI file 100-HQ-200845, Section 1, 140, 147, 149.

47 Church, *Book III*, 421.

48 Earl Browder, *Moscow, Cairo, Tehran* (Workers Library Publishers, January 1944), 11.

49 Louis F. Budenz, "Communist Assn. Born; Constitution Adopted," *Daily Worker*, May 22, 1944.

50 Conversation between Ben Davis and Gene Dennis, May 8, 1945, 10:30 a.m., FBI file NY 100-23825, Volume 2, 3.

51 "On the Dissolution of the Communist Party of the U.S.A.," *Cahiers du Communisme*, April 1945, Marxists.org, https://www.marxists.org/history/international/comintern/sections/france/1945/dissolution-communist-party-usa.htm.

Chapter 6 Clampdown (1946–1947)

Epigraph: "Affidavit of Noncommunist Union Officer," National Labor Relations Board, Form NLRB 1081 (6-51).

1 Martin Dies to Harry S. Truman, July 16, 1946, in Peter Steinberg, *The Great Red Menace: US Prosecution of American Communists, 1947–1952* (Greenwood Press, 1984), x.
2 Harry S. Truman, "Address of the President: Recommendation for Assistance to Greece and Turkey," March 12, 1947, National Archives, accessed January 27, 2025, https://www.archives.gov/milestone-documents/truman-doctrine; "Text of President Truman's Speech on New Foreign Policy," *New York Times*, March 13, 1947.
3 "Marshall Plan: (1948)," National Archives, accessed September 12, 2024, https://www.archives.gov/milestone-documents/marshall-plan.
4 "Text of President Truman's Speech in Reply to Republican Charges on 'the Communist Issue,'" *New York Times*, September 29, 1948.
5 "Executive Order 9835," Harry S. Truman Library and Museum, accessed September 24, 2024, https://www.trumanlibrary.gov/library/executive-orders/9835/executive-order-9835.
6 Glen A. Harter, "San Francisco Field Office Report on Aaron Green," April 1, 1948, FBI file 121-1646-1, 14 (hereafter Harter to SFO).
7 Harter to SFO, 18–19.
8 Anthony Leviero, "883 Federal Employees Resign Jobs Rather Than Face Loyalty Trials," *New York Times*, September 23, 1948. David Caute writes that on the whole, "under Truman 1,210 were dismissed and about 6,000 resigned." Overall in the 1947–1956 period, "there were 2,700 civilian dismissals and 12,000 resignations." David Caute, *The Great Fear: The Anti-Communist Purge Under Truman and Eisenhower* (Simon and Schuster, 1978), 274.
9 Harry S. Truman, "On the Veto of the Taft-Hartley Bill," June 20, 1947, UVA Miller Center, https://millercenter.org/the-presidency/presidential-speeches/june-20-1947-veto-taft-hartley-bill.
10 H.R. 3020, Pub. L. No. 101, "Labor Management Relations Act, 1947," GovInfo, accessed January 29, 2025, https://www.govinfo.gov/content/pkg/COMPS-8190/pdf/COMPS-8190.pdf.
11 Joseph Starobin, *American Communism in Crisis* (University of California Press, 1975), 158.
12 Starobin, 168–169.
13 Jack D. Spiegel, "Affidavit of Noncommunist Union Officer," June 9, 1953, FBI file 122-HQ-1781, section 1, 4.
14 SA [Special Agent] Robert F. Barry, "Title Jack Drobny Spiegel," April 14, 1965, FBI file 158-65, 74.
15 Jay Schaffner, "Jewish Communists and Other Radicals in Chicago," January 1, 1970, JewishCurrents, accessed January 29, 2025, https://jewishcurrents.org/jewish-communists-and-other-radicals-in-chicago.
16 Joseph A. Loftus, "C.I.O. Expels Three More Unions," *New York Times*, February 16, 1950.
17 Subcommittee to Investigate the Administration of the Internal Security Act and Other Internal Security Laws of the Committee on the Judiciary, United

States Senate, *Communist Domination of Union Officials in Vital Defense Industry-International Union Mine, Mill, and Smelter Workers* (U.S. Government Printing Office, 1952), x (hereafter *Communist Domination of Union Officials*).

18 *Communist Domination of Union Officials*, x.

19 Christine Marin, "The Union, Community Organizing, and Civil Liberties: Clinton Jencks, Salt of the Earth, and Arizona Copper," Biblioteca Virtual Miguel Cervantes, accessed January 29, 1925, https://www.cervantesvirtual.com/obra-visor/the-union-community-organizing-and-civil-liberties-clinton-jencks-salt-of-the-earth-and-arizona-copper-in-the-1950s-0/html/d8810290-dff6-4857-885e-f369eb544b0d_3.html; Clinton Jenks, obituary, *Los Angeles Times*, December 23, 2005.

20 "Clinton Jenks," Wrongfully Convicted Database record, ForeJustice.org, accessed August 9, 2024, http://forejustice.org/db/Jencks--Clinton-.html.

21 "An Act to Regulate Immigration of Aliens to, and the Residence of Aliens in, the United States," Pub. L. No. 301, February 5, 1917.

22 Thomas Sakmyster, *Red Conspirator: J. Peters and the American Communist Underground* (University of Illinois Press, 2011), 149.

23 Sakmyster, 151–152.

24 "Alien Communist Deports Himself," *New York Times*, May 9, 1949.

25 "Eisler Held Here as Enemy Alien; Once Called 'Brains' of Communists," *New York Times*, February 5, 1947.

26 "Hann's Eisler Ordered Deported," *New York Times*, February 13, 1948; "Hanns Eisler, 64, Composer, Dead," *New York Times*, September 7, 1962.

27 *Annual Report of the Immigration and Naturalization Service: For the Fiscal Year Ended June 30, 1953* (U.S. Department of Justice, Immigration and Naturalization Service, 1953), 58, Google Books, accessed January 31, 2025, https://www.google.com/books/edition/Annual_Report_of_the_Immigration_and_Nat/BokUAQAAMAAJ?hl=en&gbpv=1f.

28 Caute, *Great Fear*, 235–236; "Ferdinand Smith Freed," *New York Times*, August 12, 1949; "Witness, Called 'Liar' by Doyle," *New York Herald Tribune*, March 26, 1948; "Hearing Finds Barrager Red; Deportation Ordered," *Newsday*, April 10, 1953.

29 Caute, *Great Fear*, 238; "America: Harry Bridges Convicted of Perjury," Britishpathe.com, accessed August 9, 2024, https://www.britishpathe.com/asset/186657/.

30 Church, *Book III*, 436.

31 "Internal Security Act of 1950 (McCarran Act)," Brian Loveman, accessed August 9, 2024, https://loveman.sdsu.edu/docs/1950InternalSecurityAct.pdf.

32 Church, *Book III*, 441.

33 Peter Bowen, "The Hollywood Ten: And Then There Were Ten," Bleeker Street, accessed June 14, 2024, https://bleeckerstreetmedia.com/editorial/hollywood-ten.

34 Committee on Un-American Activities, House of Representatives, *Hearings Regarding the Communist Infiltration of the Motion Picture Industry* (U.S. Government Printing Office, 1947), 72; "'Hollywood Ten' cited for contempt of Congress," This Day in History, November 24, 1947, History.com, accessed June 14, 2024, https://www.history.com/this-day-in-history/hollywood-10-cited-for-contempt-of-congress.

35 FBI Los Angeles report, "Title: Robert Adrian Scott," June 24, 1946, FBI file 100-287200, 15.

36 Becky Little, "Who Were the Hollywood 10?" History.com, March 24, 2023, https://www.history.com/news/hollywood-10-biographies.

37 FBI Report, *Communist Infiltration of the Motion Picture Industry*, July 8, 1947, FBI file 100-138754, 63.

38 Amanda Vaill, "Jerome Robbins: About the Artist," PBS, American Masters, January 27, 2009, https://www.pbs.org/wnet/americanmasters/jerome-robbins-about-the-artist/1099/; "All-Time 'Namer of Names,' Martin Berkely," Today in Civil Rights History, September 19, 1951, website accessed August 9, 2024, https://todayinclh.com/?event=screenwriter-martin-berkeley-names-100-to-huac-all-time-top-namer.

39 Caute, *Great Fear*, 506–508; "On the Waterfront," Oscars, accessed March 23, 2025, https://www.oscars.org/events/waterfront; Norman Markowitz, "Budd Schulberg: Screenwriter Who Named Names," *People's World*, August 7, 2009, https://www.peoplesworld.org/article/budd-schulberg-screenwriter-who-named-names-could-have-been-a-contender/. The controversy of the film persists. In 2010 *The New York Times*, highlighted a discovery by historian James T. Fisher revealing the script for the film was written six weeks before Schulberg's HUAC testimony—thus, in his view, nullifying or at least diminishing it as a procooperation polemic. Joseph Berger, "A New Look at an Old Quarrel Over 'On the Waterfront,'" *New York Times*, January 7, 2010.

40 "Louis Francis Budenz," Catholicauthors.com, accessed January 30, 2025, http://www.catholicauthors.com/budenz.html.

41 "Budenz Papers," Providence College, accessed January 30, 2025, https://www.riamco.org/render?eadid=US-RPPC-budenz&view=biography.

42 "Budenz to Lecture on Communist Peril," *New York Times*, October 13, 1945.

43 Samuel A. Tower, "All Communists Here Are Spies, Budenz," *New York Times*, November 23, 1946.

44 J. Edgar Hoover, "Memorandum, Mr. L.M.C. Smith, Chief, Special Defense Unit," April 18, 1941, FBI file 1506904-0, section 01, 37.

45 C. P. Trussell, "Red 'Underground' in Federal Posts Alleged by Editor," *New York Times*, August 4, 1948.

46 "Miss Bentley Testifies," *New York Times*, July 30, 1948.

Chapter 7 Decapitation and Violence (1948–1949)

Epigraph: Howard Fast *Being Red* (Houghton-Mifflin, 1990), 231.

1 "Dennis Concedes He Changed Name," *New York Times*, March 31, 1947; Peggy Dennis, *The Autobiography of an American Communist: A Personal View of a Political Life 1925–1975* (Lawrence Hill, Creative Arts Book Co., 1977), 53–54.

2 "Communist Eugene Dennis Testifies Himself During His Trial in United States," HD stock footage, Critical Past, YouTube, accessed April 7, 2024, https://www.youtube.com/watch?v=P52ReRM6nWc.

3 Samuel A. Towers, "FBI Head Brands Communist Party a 'Fifth Column,'" *New York Times*, March 27, 1947; Mary Spargo, "FBI Director Warns of Red Fifth Column," *Washington Post*, March 27, 1947.

4 "Dennis, Communist Aide, Guilty of Contempt Over House Inquiry," *New York Times*, June 27, 1947.

5 "Communist Leaders Indicted by Federal Grand Jury in Anti-U.S. Plot," *New York Times*, July 21, 1948.

6 Scott Martelle, *The Fear Within: Spies, Commies, and American Democracy on Trial* (Rutgers University Press, 2011), 35–40.
7 See Robert M. Lichtman and Ronald D. Cohen, *Deadly Farce: Harvey Matusow and the Informer System in the McCarthy Era* (University of Illinois Press, 2008), 44.
8 "Text of Indictment of 12 Communists," *New York Times*, January 17, 1949.
9 *Constitution of the Communist Party of the United States of America*, article 9, section 2 (Communist Party USA, September 1945), 20.
10 Russell Porter, "Law Changed Cited: Medina Limits Sentence to Intent of Congress," *New York Times*, October 22, 1949.
11 "'Kill the Lawyers:' Smith Act Trial Attorneys Contempt Convictions Upheld," Today In Civil Liberties History, accessed January 26, 2025, https://todayinclh.com/?event=kill-the-lawyers-smith-act-trial-attorneys-convicted-of-contempt; Martelle, *Fear Within*, 229–230; "Top Court Uphold Contempt Jailing," *New York Times*, March 12, 1952.
12 Joseph Starobin, *American Communism in Crisis* (University of California Press, 1975), 4–5.
13 See Martelle, *Fear Within*, 105–106; Gerald Horne, *Black Liberation / Red Scare: Ben Davis and the Communist Party* (International Publishers, 2016), 35–43.
14 "Earl Brown Wins Over Communist," International News Service, *New Journal and Guide*, November 12, 1949.
15 M. Jay Racusin, "Court Denies Davis and Gates Right to Vote in Election Today," *New York Herald Tribune*, November 8, 1949.
16 "Davis Expelled; from Council by 15-to-0 Vote," *New York Herald Tribune*, November 29, 1949.
17 Memo, "Re: Benjamin J. Davis, Internal Security-C," April 28, 1949, Benjamin J. Davis Jr., FBI file 100-23825, section 6, serial 860-970, 159. For a synopsis of Davis testimony, see Martelle, *Fear Within*, 182–185.
18 "Attempt to Assassinate Bob Thompson," *Daily Worker*, September 28, 1948.
19 "'Detective' Is Arrested," *New York Times*, November 21, 1948.
20 "Progressive Party Platform of 1948," American Presidency Project, accessed April 7, 2024, https://www.presidency.ucsb.edu/documents/progressive-party-platform-1948.
21 Harry S. Truman, "Address at the Gilmore Stadium in Los Angeles," Harry S. Truman Library and Museum, September 23, 1948, accessed January 31, 2025, https://www.trumanlibrary.gov/library/public-papers/205/address-gilmore-stadium-los-angeles.
22 "Communists and Pro-Communists for Wallace," Harry S. Truman Library and Museum, accessed January 31, 2025, https://www.trumanlibrary.gov/library/research-files/report-communists-and-pro-communists-wallace?documentid=NA&pagenumber=2.
23 John N. Popham, "Wallace Pelted with Eggs," *New York Times*, August 31, 1948.
24 "Wallace and the Egg Throwers," *Los Angeles Times*, September 1, 1948.
25 "Postpone Louisville Interracial Picnic," *The Call* (Louisville, Ky.), October 8, 1948.
26 "Vignettes from the Life of Paul Robeson," Paul Robeson House and Museum, accessed January 27, 2024, https://www.paulrobesonhouse.org/vignettes-from-the-life-of-paul-robeson/.
27 Reprinted in Stuart Svonkin, *Jews Against Prejudice: American Jews and the Fight for Civil Liberties* (Columbia University Press, 1997), 137.

28 Aaron J. Leonard, *The Folk Singers and the Bureau: The FBI, the Folk Artists and the Suppression of the Communist Party, USA, 1939–1956* (Repeater Books, 2020), 129–134.
29 Martelle, *Fear Within*, 202.
30 Martelle, 202–203.
31 Roger M. Williams, "A Rough Sunday in Peekskill," *Smithsonian Magazine*, April 1976.
32 Ronnie Gilbert, *Ronnie Gilbert: Radical Life in Song* (University of California Press, 2015), 59.

Chapter 8 Prison and Pursuit (1950–1953)

Epigraph: J. Edgar Hoover, "Let's Keep America Healthy," *Journal of the American Medical Association*, November 25, 1950, https://jamanetwork.com/journals/jama/article-abstract/298100.

1 Memo to Director, FBI, "Title: John Lautner, with alias: John Lottner," 1950 (full date obscured by FBI stamp), John-HQ-1, 89, accessed August 10, 2024, https://archive.org/details/JohnLautner/Lautner%2C%20John-HQ-1/ (hereafter Lautner HQ-1).
2 Jack King, *Where the Action Is: Memoirs of a U.S. Communist* (New Outlook Publishers, 1985), 46.
3 Thomas Sakmyster, "The 'Lautner Affair' and the American Communist Party," *American Communist History* 9, no. 3 (2010): 257–291.
4 Edward Scheidt, SAC [NY] to Director, FBI, "Re: Information Received From Confidential Informant ND-588," September 28, 1950, Lautner HQ-1, 120–121.
5 Lautner HQ-1, 121. For CP member Joe Brandt, see ¡ALBA!, The Abraham Lincoln Brigade Archives, accessed September 3, 2024, https://alba-valb.org/volunteers/joseph-brandt/.
6 "John Lautner Expelled from CP as a Traitor," *Daily Worker*, January 17, 1950.
7 F. J. Baumgardner to Mr. Fletcher, "Subject: John Lautner Was, Internal Security-C, Bureau file #100-16177," January 30, 1950, Lautner HQ-1, 7, 66–67.
8 New York FBI telex to Director, FBI, marked Urgent, stamped September 25, 1950, Lautner HQ-1, 88.
9 New York FBI to Director, FBI, Re: John Lautner, September 25, 1950, Lautner HQ-1, 94.
10 New York FBI to Director, FBI, September 25, 1950, Lautner HQ-1, 95.
11 Series of memos dated April 9, 1951, with subject lines identifying prominent individuals, Lautner FBI file, Lautner HQ-2a, accessed August 10, 2024, https://archive.org/details/JohnLautner/Lautner%2C%20John-NYC-2a/.
12 Mao Zedong, *Quotations of Mao Zedong*, chap. 6, Marxists.org, accessed April 8, 2024, https://www.marxists.org/reference/archive/mao/works/red-book/ch06.htm.
13 See Sam Roberts, *The Brother: The Untold Story of the Rosenberg Case* (Random House, 2003), 238–241; and "The Manhattan Project: An Interactive History," U.S. Department of Energy, accessed January 22, 2024, https://www.osti.gov/opennet/manhattan-project-history/Events/1942-1945/espionage.htm.
14 John Seven, "Why Were the Rosenbergs Executed?," History.com, September 19, 2018, https://www.history.com/news/rosenbergs-executed-spies-cold-war.

15 "Secrets, Lies, and Atomic Spies," Nova Online, accessed August 10, 2024, https://www.pbs.org/wgbh/nova/venona/inte_19440921.html.
16 "Fourth American Held as Atom Spy," *New York Times*, July 18, 1950; Sam Roberts, "The Rosenbergs, 50 Years Later; Yes, They Were Guilty. But of What Exactly?," *New York Times*, June 15, 2003.
17 "Secrets, Lies."
18 Germany abandoned any attempt to build an atomic weapon in 1942. Fred Schwaller, "Why Didn't the Nazis Beat Oppenheimer, to the Nuclear Bomb?," August 15, 2023, *DW* (*Deutsche Welle*), https://www.dw.com/en/why-didnt-the-nazis-beat-oppenheimer-to-the-nuclear-bomb/a-66540463.
19 "President Truman Announces Soviets Have Exploded a Nuclear Device," This Day in History, September 23, 1949, History.com, accessed February 7, 2024, https://www.history.com/this-day-in-history/truman-announces-soviets-have-exploded-a-nuclear-device.
20 "Internal Security Act of 1950 (McCarran Act)," Brian Loveman, accessed August 9, 2024, https://loveman.sdsu.edu/docs/1950InternalSecurityAct.pdf (hereafter "Internal Security Act of 1950").
21 Martin Gruberg, "McCarran Internal Security Bill of 1950," Free Speech Center, Middle Tennessee State University, August 8, 2023, https://firstamendment.mtsu.edu/article/mccarran-internal-security-act-of-1950/#.
22 "Internal Security Act of 1950."
23 C. P. Trussell, "Congress Passes Bill to Curb Reds by Heavy Margins," *New York Times*, September 21. 1950; "HR 9490, Passage over Presidential Veto," Govtrack.us, accessed January 26, 2025, https://www.govtrack.us/congress/votes/81-1950/s444.
24 "Text of President's Message Vetoing the Communist-Control Bill," *New York Times*, September 23, 1950.
25 "The Anti-Communist Law," *New York Times*, September 25, 1950.
26 "21 U.S. Red Leaders Indicted on Charges of Conspiracy; 17 Arrested, 4 Still Sought," *New York Times*, June 21, 1951; "F.B.I. Seizes 17; Roundup Aimed at Peace Movement," *Daily Worker*, June 21, 1951.
27 Russell Porter, "12 Key Reds Seized Here and on Coast in Plot on Nation," *New York Times*, July 27, 1951.
28 Gus Hall, "Warmakers Plan a Fascist America," *Daily Worker*, July 31, 1950.
29 Max Gordon, "The Witchunters Want York Bread and Butter," *Daily Worker*, October 12, 1950.
30 Joseph Starobin, *American Communism in Crisis* (University of California Press, 1975), 241; "Hall, Fugitive Red Taken in Mexico," *New York Times*, October 11, 1951; "Gus Hall, Unreconstructed American Communist of 7 Decades, Dies at 90," *New York Times*, October 17, 2000.
31 "Communists: Reds in the Sierras," *Time*, September 7, 1953.
32 "Communists: Reds in the Sierras"; Gil Green, *Cold War Fugitive: A Personal Story of the McCarthy Years* (International Publishers, 1984), 132–133.
33 "Thompson, War Hero, Seized as Political Refugee," *The Worker*, September 6, 1953.
34 Memo to Director, FBI, September 28, 1950, Lautner HQ-1, 125.
35 Memo to Director, FBI, September 28, 1950.
36 Starobin, *American Communism in Crisis*, 220–221.
37 Starobin, 221.
38 Starobin, 3.

39 Green, *Cold War Fugitive*, 88.
40 Albert E. Kahn, *The Game of Death: Effects of the Cold War on Children* (Cameron & Kahn, 1953), 156.
41 Kahn, *Game of Death*, 157.
42 Green, *Cold War Fugitive*, 97; David Caute, *The Great Fear: The Anti-Communist Purge Under Truman and Eisenhower* (Simon and Schuster, 1978), 179; "Dashiell Hammett and Hunton Jailed in Red Bail Inquiry," *New York Times*, July 10, 1951.
43 SAC Detroit to Director, FBI, "Subject: Delinquency in Security Investigations," January 15, 1952, FBI file 100-358086, section 19, 93, FBI Vault, accessed January 31, 2025, https://vault.fbi.gov/custodial-detention-security-index/Part%2013/view.
44 John Thurber, "Carl N. Freyman: FBI Spy Recruiter, Handler," *Los Angeles Times*, June 11, 2001.
45 S. A. W. Rulon Paxman to SAC H. T. O'Connor, "CP, USA-TOPLEV, Internal Security-C, Morris Childs w.a.s., Security Matter-C," April 16, 1952, FOIA, 4, accessed January 31, 2025, https://archive.org/details/foia_Childs_Morris-Chicago-1/page/n3/mode/2up.
46 Green, *Cold War Fugitive*, 114.
47 J. Edgar Hoover, "Let's Keep America Healthy," *Journal of the American Medical Association*, November 25, 1950, https://jamanetwork.com/journals/jama/article-abstract/298100.
48 Federal Bureau of Investigation, *Stool Pigeon or Loyal Citizen*, August 1952, Government Attic, accessed January 26, 2025, https://www.governmentattic.org/docs/FBI_Monographs_Stool-Pigeon-Loyal-Citizen_1952-55.pdf.
49 Elizabeth Gurley Flynn, *Stool Pigeon* (New Century Publishers, 1949).
50 "Excerpts from Editorials on the Death of Joseph Stalin," *New York Times*, March 7, 1953 (hereafter Stalin editorials)
51 "Joseph Stalin," *New York Times*, March 5, 1953.
52 Stalin editorials.

Chapter 9 Disruption (1954–1963)

Epigraph: Mr. A. H. Belmont to Mr. L. V. Boardman, August 28, 1956, Mary Ferrell Foundation, accessed September 3, 2024, https://www.maryferrell.org/showDoc.html?docId=217414#relPageId=50&search=keeping_the%20pot%20boiling%20and%201956.

1 C. P. Trussell, "Congress Passes Softened Version of Communist Ban, Strips Party of Legal Rights," *New York Times*, August 20, 1954.
2 "Statement by the President upon Signing the Communist Control Act of 1954," August 24, 1954, American Presidency Project, accessed January 6, 2024, https://www.presidency.ucsb.edu/documents/statement-the-president-upon-signing-the-communist-control-act-1954.
3 Richard M. Fried, *Nightmare in Red: The McCarthy Era in Perspective* (Oxford University Press, 1990), 123.
4 "Joseph McCarthy," History.com, October 29, 2009, https://www.history.com/topics/cold-war/joseph-mccarthy.
5 Edward R. Murrow, "Editorial on Joseph McCarthy," Alphahistory, accessed January 6, 2024, https://alphahistory.com/coldwar/edward-r-murrow-on-mccarthy-1954/.

6 David Caute, *The Great Fear: The Anti-Communist Purge Under Truman and Eisenhower* (Simon and Schuster, 1978), 70.
7 "The Year Was . . . 1954," Roper Center, Cornell University, accessed March 8, 2024, https://ropercenter.cornell.edu/sites/default/files/2018-07/123048.pdf.
8 Gerald Horne, *Black Liberation / Red Scare: Ben Davis and the Communist Party* (International Publishers, 2016), 9.
9 Mary L. Dudziak, "Desegregation as a Cold War Imperative," *Stanford Law Review* 41, no. 1 (1988): 61–120, https://www.jstor.org/stable/1228836.
10 Caute, *Great Fear*, 209–210.
11 Caute, 209–210; Gil Green, *Cold War Fugitive: A Personal Story of the McCarthy Years* (International Publishers, 1984), 133.
12 Nikita Khrushchev, "On the Cult of Personality and Its Consequences," Wilson Center Digital Archive, accessed January 5, 2024, https://digitalarchive.wilsoncenter.org/document/khrushchevs-secret-speech-cult-personality-and-its-consequences-delivered-twentieth-party.
13 "The Press: Raid on the Worker," *Time*, April 9, 1956, "Gov't Plot to Gag 'Worker' Boomerangs," *The Worker*, April 1, 1956; Harrison Salisbury, "U.S. Seizes Offices of Daily Worker, Communist Party," *New York Times*, March 28, 1956; "Communist Plan Court Battle on Income Taxes," *New York Times*, April 1, 1957.
14 Committee for a Free Press, "Tax Aide Continues to Strangle Worker," *The Worker*, April 11, 1956.
15 Horne, *Black Liberation / Red Scare*, 271–284; John Gates, *The Story of an American Communist* (Thomas Nelson & Sons, 1958), 157–159.
16 Hannah Foster, "Black Belt Republic (1928–1934)," *Black Past*, March 9, 2014, https://www.blackpast.org/african-american-history/black-belt-republic-1928-1934/.
17 Director, FBI, to SAC New York, "Subject: CP, USA, Counterintelligence Program, IS-C," August 28, 1956, Mary Ferrell Foundation, accessed January 5, 2024, https://www.maryferrell.org/showDoc.html?docId=217414#relPageId=57&search=%22is_made%20to%20order%20for%20an%20all-out%20disruptive%20attack%20%22 2.
18 A. H. Belmont to L. V. Boardman, "CPUSA-Counterintelligence Program, Internal Security-C, Bufile No 100-3-104," July 8, 1957, FBI file CPUSA, 100-3-104, section 7, 115.
19 Director, FBI, to SAC New York, "Subject: Communist Party USA, Counterintelligence Program, Internal Security-C," July 9, 1957, FBI file CPUSA, 100-3-104, section 7, 106.
20 This tactic was used again by the bureau in the following decade, when the radical Students for a Democratic Society met in June 1969. At the time, the FBI instructed its considerable informant base to vote against the ascent of the Progressive Labor Party for leadership and in favor of the National Office, which would become the Weathermen—a group that embraced political violence. Aaron J. Leonard, "The FBI and the Shattering of the Students for a Democratic Society," *Truthout*, October 2, 2014, https://truthout.org/articles/the-fbi-and-the-shattering-of-students-for-a-democratic-society/.
21 SAC New York to Director, FBI, "Subject: Communist Party, USA, Counterintelligence Program, IS-C," November 19, 1959, FBI file 100-3-104, section 30, 16.
22 Stuart Schram, *The Thought of Mao Tse-tung* (Cambridge University Press, 1989), 122.
23 Mao Zedong, "Speech at the Second Plenary Session of the Eighth Central Committee of the Communist Party of China," November 15, 1956, Marxists.org, accessed

January 5, 2024, https://www.marxists.org/reference/archive/mao/selected-works/volume-5/mswv5_56.htm.

24 For more see Aaron J. Leonard, "Frank Dikötter, Mao's Great Famine," *Logos Journal* 10, no. 4 (2013), accessed January 30, 2025, https://logosjournal.com/article/frank-dikotter-maos-great-famine/.

25 William Z. Foster, *History of the Communist Party of the United States* (International Publishers, 1952), 478.

26 Aaron J. Leonard, *The Folk Singers and the Bureau: The FBI, the Folk Artists and the Suppression of the Communist Party, USA, 1939–1956* (Repeater Books, 2020), 171–172; Edward P. Johanningsmeier, *Forging American Communism: The Life of William Z. Foster* (Princeton University Press, 1994), 328–329.

27 E. Clemens, "Michigan Six, Smith Act Trial, 1953," Walter P. Reuther Library, Wayne State University, June 11, 2013, https://reuther.wayne.edu/node/10493.

28 SAC Detroit to Director, FBI, "Communist Party, USA, Counterintelligence Program, Internal Security-C," September 24, 1958, FBI file CPUSA, 100-3-104, section 18, 51.

29 Director, FBI, to SAC Detroit, "Communist Party, USA, Counterintelligence Program, Internal Security-C," September 30, 1958, FBI file CPUSA, 100-3-104, section 18, 46.

30 SAC Los Angeles to Director, FBI, "Subject CP, USA Counterintelligence Program, IS-C," August 30, 1960, FBI file CPUSA, 100-3-104, section 39, 4–6.

31 J. Edgar Hoover to New York FBI, September 8, 1961, in Dorothy Healey and Morris Isserman, *California Red: A Life in the American Communist Party* (University of Chicago Press, 1993), 128–129.

32 "Communist Party Membership Stats 1947, 1952," Archive.org, accessed August 11, 2024, https://ia804604.us.archive.org/30/items/communist-party-membership-stats-1947-1952/Communist%20Party%20Membership%20Stats,%201947,%201952.pdf.

33 "Estimated Communist Party Membership, as of June 30, 1957," author copy of FBI document.

34 "FOIA: CPUSA MEMBERS-NY 100-80638-41," Archive.org, accessed January 31, 2025, 132, https://archive.org/details/foia_CPUSA_MEMBERS-NY_100-80638-41.PDF/page/n131/mode/2up?q=3%2C693.

35 Harvey Klehr and John Earl Haynes, "Informants by the Hundreds: FBI Penetration of the CPUSA," *American Communist History* 21, nos. 1–2 (2022): 1–24, https://doi.org/10.1080/14743892.2022.2049668.

36 W. M. Felt to Mr. Tolson, "Subject: Inspection: Domestic Intelligence Division, Inspector Donald W. Morley, 2/12/68–2/28/68," March 6, 1968, FOIA: FBI Domestic Intelligence Division HQ 1, accessed March 3, 2024, 2, https://archive.org/details/foia_FBI_Domestic_Intelligence_Division-HQ-1/page/n1/mode/2up.

37 Mr. F. J. Baumgardner to Mr. A. H. Belmont, "Subject: Communist Party, USA Development of Top Level Security Informants (TOPLEV)," March 15, 1954, CPUSA-TOPLEV-HQ-68, 80.

38 Federal Bureau of Investigation, *Analysis of Successful Communist Informant Interviews*, Cryptome, July 1957, accessed January 5, 2024, https://cryptome.org/2016/04/fbi-snitches.pdf.

39 F. J. Baumgardner to A. H. Belmont, "Subject: SOLO, Internal Security–C," June 26, 1959, FBI Vault, SOLO-13, 10, accessed January 31, 2025, https://vault.fbi.gov/solo/solo-part-13-14-of/view.

40 John Barron, *Operation SOLO: The FBI's Man in the Kremlin* (Regnery, 1996), 262.
41 F. J. Baumgardner to W. C. Sullivan, "Subject: SOLO, Internal Security Communist," October 9, 1961, FBI Vault file SOLO-34, 8, accessed January 31, 2025, https://vault.fbi.gov/solo/SOLO%20Part%2034/view.
42 Scott Martelle, *The Fear Within: Spies, Commies, and American Democracy on Trial* (Rutgers University Press, 2011), 198–199.
43 "Passport Denied to Fast, Novelist," *New York Times*, June 8, 1950; Curator, "Former Voice of America Chief News Writer Howard Fast Sent to Prison for Contempt of Congress," Cold War Radio Museum, April 6, 2024, https://www.coldwarradiomuseum.com/timeline/former-voice-of-america-chief-news-writer-howard-fast-sent-to-prison-for-contempt-of-congress/.
44 Howard Fast, "My Decision," *Mainstream*, March 1957, 29–47; repr. in FBI file CPUSA, 100-3-104, section 7, 18–28.
45 Mr. A. H. Belmont to Mr. L. V. Boardman, "Subject: Communist Party, USA, Counterintelligence Program, Internal Security-C," July 17, 1957, FB file CPUSA, 100-3-104, section 7, 17.
46 Director, FBI, to SAC New York, "Re: Howard Melvin Fast, Security Matter-C," March 20, 1961, FBI file 100-327116 Howard Fast 2, 506.
47 SAC New York to Director, FBI, "Subject CPUSA–TOPLEV, Earl Russell Browder Security Matter C (Internal Security)," July 25, 1963, Earl Russell Browder FBI file D165101189, 134–139.
48 Report of James E. Gordon, "Earl Russell Browder, SM-C," February 3, 1965, Earl Russell Browder FBI file, D165101189, 210.
49 SAC New York to Director, FBI, "Earl Russell Browder aka, SM-C," January 5, 1966, Earl Russell Browder FBI file D165101189, 222.
50 Chris Carlson, "The House Un-American Activities Committee (HUAC) Hearing and Riot of 1960," FoundSF, accessed July 29, 2016, https://www.foundsf.org/index.php?title=The_House_Un-American_Activities_Committee_(HUAC)_Hearing_and_Riot_of_1960.
51 J. Edgar Hoover, *Communists Target—Youth: Communist Infiltration and Agitation Tactics* (House Committee on Un-American Activities, U.S. Government Printing Office, 1960), 2.
52 Hoover, vii.

Chapter 10 Hounded (1964–1970)

Epigraph: "Church Committee: Volume 6—Hearings on the Federal Bureau of Investigation," Mary Ferrell Foundation, accessed March 3, 2024, https://www.maryferrell.org/showDoc.html?docId=1168#relPageId=34&search=%22rough,_tough%22.

1 Director, FBI, to SAC New York, "Subject: Communist Party, USA, Counterintelligence Program Internal Security-C," September 21, 1960, FBI file CPUSA, 100-3-104, section 40, 68.
2 Director, FBI, to Boston, Chicago, New York, San Francisco, and Seattle, "Subject: Communist Party, USA, Counterintelligence Program," February 19, 1965, FBI file CPUSA, 100-3-104-9, CG [Chicago], section 7, 83–86.
3 Rosen and Scheer would be joined for a short while by a group of West Coast communists: Leibel Bergman, Larry Harris, Gert Alexander, Dick Alexander (her husband;

the couple had formerly been in Buffalo and expelled at the same time), and FBI informant Darrell Grover. Their stay in the group was short lived, as they left in 1968 to form the Bay Area Revolutionary Union along with other Bay Area activists. Aaron J. Leonard and Conor A. Gallagher, *A Threat of the First Magnitude: FBI Counterintelligence & Infiltration from the Communist Party to the Revolutionary Union—1962–1974* (Zero Books, 2015), 57–58; Committee on Un-American Activities, House of Representatives, *Communist Activities in the Buffalo, N.Y. Area* (U.S. Government Printing Office, 1964), 1523.

4 SAC New York to Director, FBI, "Subject: CPUSA, Counterintelligence Program, IS-C (00:NY)," August 13, 1963, FBI file CPUSA, 100-3-104-34, NY [New York], section 6, 68–69.

5 SAC Buffalo to Director, FBI, "Subject: Communist Party, USA, New York District, Buffalo Division," 20 October 1964, FBI file CPUSA 100-3-104-6, BU [Buffalo], section 2, 45.

6 SAC Buffalo to Director, FBI, "Subject: Communist Party, USA, Counterintelligence Program, IS-C, ReBulet to New York, dated 11/6/64," January 11, 1965, FBI file CPUSA, 100-3-104-6, BU [Buffalo], section 2, 37.

7 SAC New York to Director, FBI, "CPUSA, Counterintelligence Program, IS-C (00:NY)," August 23, 1963, FBI file CPUSA, 100-3-104-34, NY [New York], section 6, 78.

8 Mr. F. J. Baumgardner to Mr. W. C. Sullivan, "Subject: Communist Party, USA, Counterintelligence Program, Internal Security-C (May Day 1964)," April 16, 1964, FBI file CPUSA, 100-3-104-34, NY [New York], section 9, 9.

9 Chicago SAC to Director, FBI, "Subject: Recommendation for Incentive Award," January 22, 1964, FBI file, Carl N. Freyman Employee file, 130 (hereafter Freyman file).

10 Freyman file, 131.

11 Freyman file, 141.

12 SAC New York to Director, FBI, "Subject: CP, USA-Counterintelligence Program, IS-C, REDACTED (00: New York)," April 14, 1964, CPUSA, 100-3-104-34, NY [New York], section 8, 93.

13 SAC New York to Director, FBI, "Subject: CPUSA, Counterintelligence Program, IS-C (Elizabeth Gurley Flynn)," May 1, 1964, FBI file CPUSA, 100-3-104-34, NY [New York], section 8, 15.

14 SAC New York to Director, FBI, "Subject: CPUSA, Counterintelligence Program, IS-C (00:NY)," June 14, 1963, FBI file CPUSA, 100-3-104-34, NY [New York], section 6, 6.

15 SAC New York to Director, FBI, "Subject: Communist Party, USA, Counterintelligence Program, Internal Security-C (Benjamin J. Davis)," May 5, 1964, FBI file 100-3-104-34, NY [New York], section 8, 61.

16 Mr. F. J. Baumgardner to Mr. W. C. Sullivan, "Communist Party, USA, Counterintelligence Program, Internal Security-Communist (Benjamin J. Davis)," June 19, 1964, FBI file Benjamin J. Davis Jr., Headquarters 100-149163, section 25, 85.

17 SAC New York to Director, FBI, "Subject: Benjamin Jefferson Davis, Jr. IS-C (00:NY)," August 24, 1964, FBI file, Headquarters 100-149163, section 25, 123.

18 John Earl Haynes and Harvey Klehr, "Framing William Albertson: The FBI's 'Solo' Operation and the Cold War," *Journal of Cold War Studies* 22, no. 3 (2020): 63–85, https://muse.jhu.edu/article/762892.

19 Aaron J. Leonard, "The Bureau and the Journalist: Victor Riesel's Secret Relationship with the FBI," *Truthout*, February 14, 2013, https://truthout.org/articles/the-bureau-and-the-journalist-victor-riesels-secret-relationship-with-the-fbi/.

20 SAC New York to SAC Baltimore, "Subject: CP, USA Organization, IS-C," CPUSA_Members-NY_100-80638-41, 122, https://archive.org/details/CPUSAMembers/CPUSA%20MEMBERS-NY%20100-80638-41/page/n7/mode/2up; Haynes and Klehr, "Framing William Albertson," 63–85.

21 SAC New York to Director, FBI, "CPUSA-Counterintelligence Program, IS-C; ISA-50 (Re Henry Winston)," April 23, 1964, FBI file CPUSA, 100-3-104-34, NY [New York], section 8, 58.

22 Gary Murrell, *The Most Dangerous Communist in the United States: A Biography of Herbert Aptheker* (University of Massachusetts Press, 2015), 156–157.

23 Murrell, 156.

24 F. J. Baumgardner to Mr. Sullivan, "Subject: Communist Party, USA, Counterintelligence Program, Internal Security-C" (American Institute for Marxists Studies), February 17, 1965, FBI file CPUSA, 100-3-104-34, NY [New York], section 12, 31.

25 Mr. F. J. Baumgardner to Mr. W. C. Sullivan, "Subject: Communist Party, USA, Counterintelligence Program, Internal Security-C" (American Institute for Marxists Studies), March 30, 1964, FBI file CPUSA, 100-3-104-34, NY [New York], section 8, 104.

26 Director, FBI, to SAC New York, "Subject: Communist Party, USA, Counterintelligence Program, Internal Security-C" (American Institute for Marxists Studies), April 22, 1964, FBI file CPUSA, 100-3-104-34, NY [New York], section 8, 35.

27 Dorothy Ray Healey and Maurice Isserman, *California Red: A Life in the American Communist Party* (University of Illinois Press, 1993), 167–168.

28 Healey and Isserman, 244.

29 SAC New York to Director, FBI, "Subject: CPUSA, Counterintelligence Program, IS-C (OO-NY)," June 14, 1963, FBI file CPUSA, 100-3-104-34, NY [New York], section 6, 2–3.

30 Director, FBI, to SAC Philadelphia, "Communist Party, USA, Counterintelligence Program, Internal Security–C (REDACTED)," December 20, 1966, FBI file CPUSA, 100-3-104-37, PH [Philadelphia], section 6, 4; Director, FBI, to U.S. Attorney General, "Subject: Counterintelligence Programs," August 18, 1975 (hereafter Director to AG, August 18, 1975), Mary Ferrell Foundation, https://www.maryferrell.org/showDoc.html?docId=216856#relPageId=35&search=aaron_libson%20and%20sodomy.

31 Suzi Nash, "Aaron Libson: Decades of Activism, from Civil Rights to Union Rights," *Philadelphia Gay News*, August 29, 2013, https://epgn.com/2013/08/29/23475021-aaron-libson-decades-of-activism-from-civil-rights-to-union-rights/.

32 Director to AG, August 18, 1975.

33 "Bob Dylan: 'You Can Boo, but Booing's Got Nothing to Do with It,' Bill of Rights Dinner—1963," Speakola.com, accessed January 28, 2025, https://speakola.com/arts/bob-dylan-tom-paine-acceptance-1963.

34 F. J. Baumgardner to Mr. W. C. Sullivan, "Emergency Civil Liberties Committee, Internal Security—C, Internal Security Act of 1950," December 23, 1963; for full document, see Aaron J. Leonard, "Newly Uncovered Documents Reveal the FBI's Campaign Against Bob Dylan," *Truthout*, December 30, 2023, https://truthout.org/app/uploads/2023/12/FBI-Memo-2.pdf.

35 SAC New York to Director, FBI, Emergency Civil Liberties Committee, December 16, 1963, Leonard, "Newly Uncovered Documents," https://truthout.org/app/uploads/2023/12/FBI-Memo-1.pdf.

36 Fulton Lewis Jr., "Emergency Civil Liberties Committee Holds Annual Dinner in New York," December 1963, Leonard, "Newly Uncovered Documents," https://truthout.org/app/uploads/2023/12/Lewis-Column.pdf.

37 Hoover to REDACTED, August 29, 1966, Leonard, "Newly Uncovered Documents," https://truthout.org/app/uploads/2023/12/Hoover-Fulton-Lewis-copy.pdf.

38 Director, FBI, to SAC New York, "Communist Party, USA, Counterintelligence Program, Internal Security-C (Jewish Question)," March 30, 1964, FBI file CPUSA, 100-3-104-34, NY [New York], section 8, 190.

39 F. G. Baumgardner to W. C. Sullivan, "Subject: Communist Party, USA, Counterintelligence Program, Internal Security-C," January 12, 1962, FBI file CPUSA, 100-3-104, section 61, 2.

40 SAC New York to Director, FBI, "Subject: CPUSA, Counterintelligence Program, IS-C (00: NY)," May 11, 1962, FBI file, 100-3-104-34, NY [New York], section 3, 17 (hereafter SAC New York, May 11, 1962).

41 SAC New York, May 11, 1962, 19.

42 SAC New York, May 11, 1962, 20.

43 SAC New York to Director, FBI, "Subject: Communist Party, USA Counterintelligence Program, Internal Security-C Advertisement for Jefferson Book Store," August 29, 1966, FBI file CPUSA, 100-3-104-34, NY [New York], section 17, 118 (hereafter "Advertisement Jefferson Book Store").

44 "U.S. Communists Angry About Lightfoot's 'Slum,'" *Chicago Daily Defender*, May 3, 1966.

45 "Advertisement Jefferson Book Store."

46 SAC New York to Director, FBI, "Subject: CP, USA Counter Intelligence Program, IS-C (Ridicule Operation)," February 14, 1967, FBI file CPUSA, 100-3-104-34, NY [New York], section 18, 30.

47 F. G. Baumgardner to W. C. Sullivan, "Subject: Communist Party, USA Counterintelligence Program, Internal Security-C (Camp Webatuck)," August 19, 1966, FBI file 100-3-104-34, NY [New York], section 17, 241.

48 "Bomb Thrown in Window Damages Communist Offices," *New York Times*, May 3, 1966; SAC New York to Director, FBI, "Subject: Hoodwink (IS)," December 6, 1966, FBI Hoodwink file, 53.

49 SAC New York to Director, FBI, "Subject: Hoodwink," July 31, 1968, FBI Hoodwink file, 3.

50 Healey, *California Red*, 213.

51 Daniel Rosenberg, "From Crisis to Split: The Communist Party USA, 1989–1991," *American Communist History* 18, nos. 1–2 (2019): 1–55, https://doi.org/10.1080/14743892.2019.1599627.

52 Yates v. United States, 354 U.S. 298 (1957), Justia U.S. Supreme Court, https://supreme.justia.com/cases/federal/us/354/298/.

53 Aptheker v. Secretary of State, 378 U.S. 500 (1964), Justia U.S. Supreme Court, accessed March 3, 2024, https://supreme.justia.com/cases/federal/us/378/500/.

54 Albertson v. SACB, 382 U.S. 70 (1965), Justia U.S. Supreme Court, accessed March 3, 2024, https://supreme.justia.com/cases/federal/us/382/70/.

55 United States v. Robel, 389 U.S. 258 (1967), Justia U.S. Supreme Court, accessed March 3, 2024, https://supreme.justia.com/cases/federal/us/389/258/.

56 Brandenburg v. Ohio, 395 U.S. 444 (1969), Justia U.S. Supreme Court, accessed March 3, 2024, https://supreme.justia.com/cases/federal/us/395/444/.

Chapter 11 Final Conflicts (1971–1991)

Epigraph: "Reagan 'Jokes' About Bombing Soviet Union, Aug. 11, 1984," Politico, August 11, 2017, https://www.politico.com/story/2017/08/11/this-day-in-politics-aug-11-1984-241413.

1 Betty Medsger, *The Burglary: The Discovery of J. Edgar Hoover's Secret FBI* (Knopf, 2014), 271–272.

2 Select Committee to Study Governmental Operation With Respect to Intelligence Activities of the United States Senate, *Intelligence Activities*, vol. 6 (U.S. Government Printing Office, 1976), 66.

3 David Garrow, "The FBI and Martin Luther King," *The Atlantic*, July/August 2002.

4 "The Federal Bureau of Investigation's Compliance with the Attorney General's Investigative Guidelines (Redacted)," Special Report, September 2005, Office of the Inspector General, Justice.gov, accessed October 23, 2022, https://oig.justice.gov/sites/default/files/archive/special/0509/chapter2.htm.

5 "About the Foreign Intelligence Surveillance Court," U.S. Foreign Intelligence Surveillance Court, accessed October 5, 2022, https://www.fisc.uscourts.gov/about-foreign-intelligence-surveillance-court; David Kris, "How the FISA Court Really Works," Lawfare.com, September 2, 2018, accessed October 5, 2022, https://www.lawfareblog.com/how-fisa-court-really-works.

6 "The Foreign Intelligence Surveillance Act of 1978 (FISA)" Bureau of Justice Assistance, Department of Justice, accessed October 5, 2022, https://bja.ojp.gov/program/it/privacy-civil-liberties/authorities/statutes/1286.

7 Select Committee on Intelligence, United States Senate, "Implementation of the Foreign Intelligence Surveillance Act of 1978–1979–80," October 30, 1980, 2, Intelligence.senate.gov, accessed September 12, 2024, https://www.intelligence.senate.gov/sites/default/files/publications/961017.pdf.

8 "U.S. Communists: Now Out in Open," *New York Times*, August 12, 1973.

9 W. M. Felt to Mr. Tolson, "Inspection, Domestic Intelligence Division: Inspector Donald W. Morley, 2/12/68–2/28/68," Archive.org, accessed February 16, 2024, https://archive.org/details/foia_FBI_Domestic_Intelligence_Division-HQ-1, 2.

10 "Addendum: Inspector H.E. Helgeson (F.B. Griffith: wmj 3/27/75)," Archive.org, accessed August 15, 2024, 162, https://archive.org/details/foia_FBI_Domestic_Intelligence_Division-HQ-6.

11 "Estimated Communist Party Membership as of September 30, 1964," Archive.org, accessed March 25, 2025, 4, https://archive.org/details/foia_CPUSA_MEMBERS-NY_100-80638-41.PDF/page/n3/mode/2up.

12 John Barron, *Operation SOLO: The FBI's Man in the Kremlin* (Regnery, 1996), 297.

13 Barron, 340.

14 SAC Chicago to Director, FBI, "Subject: CPUSA Cover Companies," February 26, 1971, from Jack Childs FBI file, 91, https://archive.org/details/foia_Childs_Jack-NYC-16a-18a (hereafter Childs, February 26, 1971).

15 Antonio Mejías-Rentas, "How Angela Davis Ended Up on the FBI Most Wanted List," History.com, January 25, 2023, https://www.history.com/news/angela-davis-fbi-most-wanted-list.

16 Childs, February 26, 1971, 91.

17 David A. Andelman, "Communists Rally in City and Recall Past Causes: Favors Arms Treaty Tass Covers Campaign," *New York Times*, October 20, 1980.

18 "1976 Presidential Election Results," Dave Leip's Atlas of U.S. Presidential Elections, accessed February 16, 2024, https://uselectionatlas.org/RESULTS/national.php?year=1976&minper=0&f=0&off=0&elect=0.

19 Permanent Select Committee on Intelligence, House of Representatives, *Soviet Active Measures* (U.S. Government Printing Office, 1982), 203.

20 Subcommittee on Security and Terrorism, of the Committee on the Judiciary United States Senate, *FBI Oversight and Authorization Hearings* (U.S. Government Printing Office, 1983), 36–37.

21 Charles R. Babcock, "Soviet Secrets Fed to FBI for More Than 25 Years," *Washington Post*, September 17, 1981.

22 "The SOLO File," National Security Archive, George Washington University, accessed April 19, 2024, https://nsarchive2.gwu.edu/NSAEBB/NSAEBB375/; David J. Garrow, *The FBI and Martin Luther King, Jr.: From "SOLO" to Memphis* (W. W. Norton, 1981), 35–38.

23 "Running SOLO: FBI's Case of Morris and Jack Childs, 1952–77," Harvey Klehr and John Earl Haynes, *Studies in Intelligence* 66, no. 1 (March 2022), CIA.gov, https://www.cia.gov/resources/csi/static/Article-FBI-Project-Solo.pdf.

24 Daniel Rosenberg, "From Crisis to Split: The Communist Party USA, 1989–1991," *American Communist History* 18, nos. 1–2 (2019): 22–23, https://doi.org/10.1080/14743892.2019.1599627.

25 "Remarks of William J Casey, Director of Central Intelligence Before the Dallas Council of World Affairs," September 18, 1985, 19, CIA Reading room, accessed January 9, 2024, https://www.cia.gov/readingroom/docs/CIA-RDP88B00443R001804350023-9.pdf.

26 "Reagan Backs FBI over Surveillance," *New York Times*, February 4, 1988.

27 Committee on the Judiciary, House of Representatives, *CISPES and FBI Counterterrorism*, Subcommittee on Civil and Constitutional Rights (U.S. Government Printing Office), 114.

28 ADIC [Assistant Director in Charge] New York to Director, FBI, September 23, 1990, FBI CPUSA file, 1990–1992, 171.

29 SAC Chicago REDACTED to Director, FBI, "Subject Communist Party USA (CPUSA), Illinois District, Chicago Division," July 31, 1990. FBI CPUSA file, 1990–1992, 33.

30 Rosenberg, "From Crisis to Split," 51.

Conclusion

Epigraph: George H. W. Bush, "Remarks to the National Guard Association," Salt Lake City, Utah, September 15, 1992, https://www.govinfo.gov/content/pkg/PPP-1992-book2/html/PPP-1992-book2-doc-pg1561.htm.

1 "Secretary of State Dean G. Acheson's Speech, Crisis in Asia—an Examination of U.S. Policy," National Press Club, New York, January 12, 1950, Department of State Bulletin 22, no. 551 (January 23, 1950), 111–118, World of Japan Database, accessed January 27, 2025, https://worldjpn.net/documents/texts/docs/19500112.S1E.html.

2 Gitlow v. People of New York, 268 U.S. 652 (1925), Justia U.S. Supreme Court, accessed January 27, 2025, https://supreme.justia.com/cases/federal/us/268/652/.

Selected Bibliography

Barron, John. *Operation SOLO: The FBI's Man in the Kremlin*. Regnery Publishing, 1996.

Belknap, Michael R. *Cold War Political Justice: The Smith Act, the Communist Party, and American Civil Liberties*. Greenwood Press, 1977.

Blake, George. *The Ideological Struggle Against White Chauvinism*. New York State Communist Party, Education Department, 1950.

Budenz, Louis. *Men Without Faces: The Communist Conspiracy in the U.S.* Harpers, 1950.

Budenz, Louis. *This Is My Story*. Whittlesey House, McGraw Hill, 1947.

Calomiris, Angela. *Red Masquerade: Undercover for the FBI*. Lippincott Press, 1950.

Caute, David. *The Great Fear: The Anti-Communist Purge Under Truman and Eisenhower*. Simon and Schuster, 1978.

Chambers, Whitaker. *Witness*. Random House, 1952. Reprint ed. Regnery, 2014.

Cherny, Robert W. *San Francisco Reds: Communists in the Bay Area 1919–1958*. University of Illinois Press, 2024.

Counterattack. *Red Channels*. Counterattack: The Newsletter of Facts to Combat Communism, 1950. Reprint, Create Space Independent Publishing, 2017.

Davis, Lisa E. *Undercover Girl: The Lesbian Informant Who Helped the FBI Bring Down the Communist Party*. Imagine, 2017.

Deery, Phillip. *Red Apple: Communism and McCarthyism in Cold War New York*. Fordham University Press, 2012.

Dennis, Peggy. *The Autobiography of an American Communist: A Personal View of a Political Life 1925–1975*. Lawrence Hill, 1977.

Donner, Frank. *Protectors of Privilege: Red Squads and Police Repression in Urban America*. University of California Press, 1990.

Dowell, Eldridge Foster. *A History of Criminal Syndicalism Legislation in the United States*. Johns Hopkins Press, 1939.

Draper, Theodore. *The Roots of American Communism*. Viking, 1957.

Elwood, Ralph Carter. *Roman Malinovsky: A Life Without a Cause*. Oriental Research Partners, 1977.

Fast, Howard. *Being Red: A Memoir*. Houghton-Mifflin 1990.

Fast, Howard. *The Naked God: The Writer and the Communist Party*. Fredrick A. Praeger, 1957.
Fast, Howard. *Peekskill, USA: Inside the Infamous 1949 Riots*. Civil Rights Congress, 1951. Reprint, Open Road Media, 2011.
Foster, William Z. *History of the Communist Party of the United States*. International Publishers, 1952.
Fried, Richard. *Nightmare in Red: The McCarthy Era in Perspective*. Oxford University Press, 1990.
Gage, Beverly. *The Day Wall Street Exploded: A Story of America in Its First Age of Terror*. Oxford University Press, 2010.
Gage, Beverly. *G-Man: J. Edgar Hoover and the Making of the American Century*. Viking, 2022.
Garrow, David J. *The FBI and Martin Luther King, Jr.: From "SOLO" to Memphis*. W. W. Norton, 1981.
Gates, John. *The Story of an American Communist*. Thomas Nelson and Sons, 1958.
Gentry, Curt. *J. Edgar Hoover: The Man and His Secrets*. W. W. Norton, 1991.
Gilbert, Ronnie. *Ronnie Gilbert: Radical Life in Song*. University of California Press, 2015.
Gitlow, Benjamin. *I Confess: The Truth About American Communism*. E. P. Dutton, 1939.
Goldstein, Robert Justin. *Little "Red Scares": Anti-Communism and Political Repression in the United States, 1921–1946*. Routledge, 2016.
Green, Gil. *Cold War Fugitive: A Personal Story of the McCarthy Years*. International Publishers, 1984.
Haynes, John Earl, and Harvey Klehr. *Venona: Decoding Soviet Espionage in America*. Yale University Press, 2000.
Healey, Dorothy Ray, and Maurice Isserman. *California Red: A Life in the American Communist Party*. University of Illinois Press, 1993.
Hoover, J. Edgar. *Masters of Deceit: The Story of Communism in America and How to Fight It*. Henry Holt, 1958.
Hoover, J. Edgar. *On Communism*. Random House, 1969.
Horne, Gerald. *Black Liberation / Red Scare: Ben Davis and the Communist Party*. International Publishers, 2016.
Hoyt, Edwin P. *The Palmer Raids 1919–1920: An Attempt to Suppress Dissent*. Seabury Press, 1969.
Isserman, Maurice. *Reds: The Tragedy of American Communism*. Basic Books, 2024.
Isserman, Maurice. *Which Side Were You On?: The American Communist Party During the Second World War*. Wesleyan University Press, 1982.
Johanningsmeier, Edward P. *Forging American Communism: The Life of William Z. Foster*. Princeton University Press, 1994.
Josephson, Barney, with Terry Trilling-Josephson. *Café Society: The Wrong Place for the Right People*. University of Illinois Press, 2009.
Kahn, Albert E. *The Game of Death: Effects of the Cold War on Children*. Cameron and Kahn, 1953.
Klehr, Harvey, John Earl Haynes, and Fridrikh Igorevich Firsov. *The Secret World of American Communism*. Yale University Press, 1996.
Kling, Jack. *Where the Action Is: Memoirs of a U.S. Communist*. New Outlook, 1985.
Lendler, Mark. *Gitlow v. New York: Every Idea an Incitement*. University Press of Kansas, 2012.
Leonard, Aaron J. *The Folk Singers and the Bureau: The FBI, the Folk Artists and the Suppression of the Communist Party, USA, 1939–1956*. Repeater Books, 2020.

Leonard, Aaron J., and Conor Gallagher. *Heavy Radicals: The FBI's Secret War on America's Maoists: The Revolutionary Union / Revolutionary Communist Party 1968–1980*. Zero Books, 2015.

Leonard, Aaron J., and Conor Gallagher. *A Threat of the First Magnitude: FBI Counterintelligence & Infiltration from the Communist Party to the Revolutionary Union—1962–1974*. Zero Books, 2015.

Lichtman, Robert M., and Ronald D. Cohen. *Deadly Farce: Harvey Matusow and the Informer System in the McCarthy Era*. University of Illinois Press, 2008.

MacMahon, Robert L. *The Cold War: A Very Short Introduction*. Oxford University Press, 2003.

Martelle, Scott. *The Fear Within: Spies, Commies, and American Democracy on Trial*. Rutgers University Press, 2011.

Medsger, Betty. *The Burglary: The Discovery of J. Edgar Hoover's Secret FBI*. Knopf, 2014.

Megargee, Geoffrey P. *War of Annihilation: Combat and Genocide on the Eastern Front, 1941*. Rowman & Littlefield, 2007.

Morros, Boris, as told to Charles Samuels. *My Ten Years as a Counterspy*. Viking, 1959.

Murray, Robert. *Red Scare: A Study in National Hysteria, 1918–1920*. McGraw Hill, 1964.

Murrell, Gary. *The Most Dangerous Communist in the United States: A Biography of Herbert Aptheker*. University of Massachusetts Press, 2015.

Naison, Mark. *Communists in Harlem During the Great Depression*. University of Illinois Press, 1985.

Navasky, Victor. *Naming Names*. Viking, 1980.

Oshinsky, David M. *A Conspiracy So Immense: The World of Joe McCarthy*. Free Press, 1985.

Ottanelli, Fraser. *The Communist Party of the United States: From the Depression to World War II*. Rutgers University Press, 1989.

Peraino, Kevin. *A Force So Swift: Mao, Truman and the Birth of Modern China*, 1949. Reprint, Crown, 2017.

Philbrick, Herbert. *I Led Three Lives: Citizen, "Communist," Counterspy*. McGraw Hill, 1952.

Poverda, Tony. *The FBI: A Comprehensive Reference Guide*. Greenwood Press, 1998.

Prial, Dunstan. *The Producer: John Hammond and the Soul of American Music*. Macmillan, 2006.

Rosenberg, Daniel. *Underground Communists in the McCarthy Period: A Family Memoir*. Edward Mellen Press, 2008.

Ryan, James G. *Earl Browder: The Failure of American Communism*. University of Alabama Press, 1997.

Sakmyster, Thomas. *Red Conspirator: J. Peters and the American Communist Underground*. University of Illinois Press, 2011.

Sbardellati, John. *J. Edgar Hoover Goes to the Movies: The FBI and the Origins of Hollywood's Cold War*. Cornell University Press, 2012.

Schmidt, Regin. *Red Scare: The FBI and the Origins of Anticommunism in the United States*. University of Copenhagen Press, 2000.

Schrecker, Ellen. *Many Are the Crimes: McCarthyism in America*. Little, Brown, 1998.

Shannon, David A. *The Decline of American Communism: A History of the Communist Party of the United States Since 1945*. Harcourt Brace, 1959.

Snyder, Timothy. *Bloodlands: Europe Between Hitler and Stalin*. Basic Books, 2016.

Starobin, Joseph R. *American Communism in Crisis, 1943–1957*. Harvard University Press, 1972.

Steinberg, Peter. *The Great Red Menace: US Prosecution of American Communists, 1947–1952*. Greenwood Press, 1984.

Storrs, Landon R. Y. *The Second Red Scare and the Unmaking of the New Deal Left*. Princeton University Press, 2012.

Tanenhaus, Sam. *Whitaker Chambers: A Biography*. Modern Library, 1998.

Taylor, Greg S. *The Life and Lies of Paul Crouch: Communist, Opportunist, Cold War Snitch*. University of Florida Press, 2014.

Wiegand, Shirley A. *Books on Trial: Red Scare in the Heartland*. University of Oklahoma Press, 2007.

Index

Page numbers in italics refer to figures.

About the Author

AARON J. LEONARD is the author of *Heavy Radicals: The FBI's Secret War on America's Maoists*; *The Folk Singers and the Bureau: The FBI, the Folk Artists and the Suppression of the Communist Party, USA, 1939–1956*; and *Meltdown Expected: Crisis, Disorder, and Upheaval at the End of the 1970s*, among other works. He lives in Los Angeles.